D0657840

THE IMPERIAL WAR MUSEUM BOOK OF
THE FIRST WORLD WAR

THE IMPERIAL WAR MUSEUM BOOK OF
The First World War

A Great Conflict Recalled in Previously Unpublished Letters, Diaries, Documents and Memoirs

MALCOLM BROWN

SIDGWICK & JACKSON
LONDON

Published in Association with The Imperial War Museum

Author's Acknowledgements

The first acknowledgement must be to the people on whose experiences and whose talent in recording them, whether in letters or diaries at the time or in reminiscences later, this book is largely based. Their names will be found in the Index of Contributors on page 286, together with the names of those who have graciously allowed material in which they are copyright holders to be here published. With them I must link the photographers and artists to whose work I have turned to provide the bulk of the illustrations; they have left a rich legacy from which it has been a privilege to draw.

Next I must express my gratitude to my publisher, William Armstrong, whose idea it was that a book of this nature might be made out of the resources of the Imperial War Museum, and to those senior members of the Museum staff who put my name forward as author. I refer here to Dr Christopher Dowling, Keeper of the Department of Museum Services, and Roderick Suddaby, Keeper of the Department of Documents, who have supported and encouraged this venture from first concept to finished product.

I should also like to offer my warm thanks to those other Keepers to whom I have turned for help and guidance: Jane Carmichael, Department of Photographs; Angela Weight, Department of Art (and here I must bracket the name of Michael Moody); Dr Gwyn Bayliss, Department of Printed Books; Margaret Brooks, Department of Sound Records; David Penn, Department of Exhibits and Firearms; and Anne Fleming and, later, Roger Smither, Department of Film. Not only have they been generous with advice and knowledge, they have also encouraged me to consult the numerous experts and enthusiasts in whom their departments abound. This I have done gladly, with the result that the book has gained as much from conversations on stairways and corridors or over coffee as it has from more formal encounters. Unfortunately, lack of space restricts the naming of names, but I am confident that those whose assistance I have found stimulating and valuable know who they are and how deeply grateful I am to them. One person I must mention, however, is my friend of many years, Michael Willis, of the Department of Photographs; I have availed myself too often of his talent for finding answers to obscure enquiries for his name to be omitted here.

Other vital roles in the making of the book have been played by Peter Shellard as agent-cum-editor and by Paul Watkins as designer. I am very much in their debt.

Finally, I must add that I have been conscious throughout of the strong interest and support of the Director General of the Museum, Dr Alan Borg FSA, and of the Deputy Director General, Robert Crawford. I am especially grateful to Dr Borg for contributing a Foreword.

Frontispiece: Men of the 4th Battalion Worcestershire Regiment resting on the way to the trenches, Somme front, 28 June 1916 (Q 718)

First published in Great Britain in 1991 by Sidgwick & Jackson Limited

This paperback edition published 1993 by Sidgwick & Jackson Limited

1 3 5 7 9 8 6 4 2

Copyright © 1991 The Imperial War Museum and Malcolm Brown

Designed by Paul Watkins

All rights reserved. No part of this book may be reproduced or transmitted in any form or by any means, electronic or mechanical, including information storage and retrieval system, without permission in writing from the Publisher

ISBN 0 283 06152 9

Typeset by Spectrum Typesetting Ltd, London
Printed by Butler & Tanner Ltd
Frome, Somerset

Contents

Foreword

EVERYONE knows that there is more to a museum than its public galleries. Behind the showcase displays are reserve collections which, in the case of Britain's national museums, form vast archives for study and research. We had long wanted to find a way of conveying to all some impression of the riches to be found in the Imperial War Museum collections, but it was difficult to see how this could be done. A book seemed an obvious solution, although it was clear that this could not be a conventional 'Treasures of the Museum' volume. This is not because we are short of treasures – there are plenty, with many illustrated in these pages – but because the Museum's subject is essentially that intangible but infinitely varied thing, human experience. Moreover, it is concerned with the extremes of that experience which are the result of modern war.

Once we had defined our purpose, it was clear that we would need to restrict our focus, hence the decision to begin with the First World War. It was also going to be difficult to find the right author. We needed someone who already knew something of the collections and was prepared to find out more, but who could stand back to take in the overall picture and then present it with imagination. He had to be able to deal with documents, photographs, film and sound recordings as well as the more traditional types of museum objects. It was our particular good fortune that Malcolm Brown was prepared to take on the task and I think everyone who reads these pages will agree that he has more than met the requirements we set.

This book does not attempt to give anything more than a glimpse into the vast collections held by the Museum. It cannot really touch the true nature of film nor can it convey the immediacy of our oral history holdings. It can reproduce original photographs and, through modern photography, can reveal much about inanimate museum exhibits. What really comes to life, however, are the words of the men and women who, finding themselves caught up in the greatest war the world had known, also found time to set down something of their individual experience on paper. The stories they tell form an essential part of our own history, for, in a very real sense, the life of everyone alive today has been shaped by that experience. I hope that this book will attract many new visitors, both to our public galleries and to our archives, for it shows above all that the Museum is a primary source for the study of all those topics which are central to our understanding of humanity as a whole.

Alan Borg
Director General
Imperial War Museum

Introduction

DESPITE its somewhat formidable exterior – a portico and dome impressive enough for a cathedral, fronted by two 15-inch naval gun barrels which jut towards the approaching visitor like a gigantic Churchillian salute – the Imperial War Museum is a benign and welcoming place. Its principal clientèle, of course, is the general public, but it has also been over the years open house to countless authors and researchers, encouraging them to make use of its almost inexhaustible reserves of pictures, posters, postcards, photographs, films, pamphlets, books, diaries, letters and documents. It has been, as it were, a kind of military Harrods, offering its wares and its professional services for the improvement and adornment of the books, articles, dramas and documentaries in which such customers have been engaged.

In making this book the tables have been turned: in a sense the 'author' is the Imperial War Museum itself. The idea behind it is that, among the many books still being produced on the First World War, there is space for a substantial, fully illustrated volume which is the Museum's own, and which incorporates the specific intention of using material not hitherto published and drawing on the resources of as many as possible of the Museum's departments. A corollary of this is that, though this book deals with many aspects of the 1914-18 war, it is not a comprehensive history of that conflict nor is it meant to be. It inevitably leans towards those areas in which the Museum is strongest, and if there is nothing or little in the archives on a certain subject it is ignored. Thus, for example, the Eastern Front features little, while in the case of the Western Front the available material is unlimited and, therefore, although allocated only one specific section in the table of contents, will appear in various ways in other sections as well.

While the Imperial War Museum is the 'author' of this book, it has handed its writing and compilation to an outsider who has been given the freedom, while drawing on the advice of the Museum's many experts, to make his own selection. If I am an alien I can, however, claim to be a benevolent one, having been a regular user of the Museum's resources for over a quarter of a century, first as a television documentary maker for the BBC and later as the author and co-author of several books on First World War subjects. This long acquaintance has one disadvantage: it has made me aware of how much material there is that cries out for use and how little in the end one can cram into a single book. One thinks of those publicity stunts when a person is allowed, say, two minutes to see how much merchandise he or she can pile into a supermarket trolley; the spoils may be considerable but there is still so much that is highly desirable left on the shelves.

There are many ways in which this volume might have been compiled. While not forgetting that this was an intensely political and a highly technological war I have chosen to put a strong emphasis on the particular and the personal. The essence of the book is, therefore, the experience of the men and women who are featured in it. It is not basically a book about war, but about people caught up in war. It is about you and me as we might have been in a crisis which even as this book is published is within vivid living memory. The war is still near enough for one to realize, say, when reading the letter or the diary of a soldier who lost his life on the Somme or in the Ypres Salient, that but for the unhappy chance of the shell or the bullet that did for him he might still be alive or, at any rate, not many years dead. I am reminded of a former territorial of the London Rifle Brigade whom I first met through the Museum, who became a personal friend and who died only a year or two ago; on Christmas Eve 1914 a soldier in his company, a popular young man well known for his excellent singing voice, was shot through the head by a sniper. Private Bassingham has lain these seventy years and more in a military cemetery at Ploegsteert, Belgium ('Plugstreet' to the Tommies); Graham Williams lived a full life until the late 1980s. The First World War is as close as that.

This personal approach has dictated to a substantial extent the style of presentation I have adopted. There are narrative sections on various subjects, and there are 'features' in which a range of other subjects are dealt with pictorially, but there are also numerous profiles of individuals – servicemen and servicewomen, civilians, even conscientious objectors – who largely speak for themselves through their letters or diaries or their spoken or written accounts; in some cases the range of experience was such that they appear in several parts of the book. If there is one such profile worth singling out as a keynote example it is the one based on a small file held in the Department of Documents which caught my imagination shortly after I began work on the book: the papers of the late Private Jack Mudd, who was posted as missing in the final stage of the battle popularly known as Passchendaele, whose body was never found and who is commemorated on the memorial walls of the largest British military cemetery in the world, Tyne Cot, near Ypres. Four days before he disappeared he wrote an eloquent and loving letter to his wife Lizzie, on rough lined paper in a clumsy halting hand, now permanently held in the Museum together with photographs of the thirty-one-year-old soldier himself and of his young wife. That letter and those photographs appear on pages 70-71. A member of the Museum's staff to whom I showed this material, plainly affected by it, said: 'That says it all.' There is much else here, I believe, which also says it, convincingly and well, and in many and various ways.

Shortly after the Armistice of November 1918 Frederick Arthur Robinson, a civilian over-age for soldiering who had kept a detailed diary throughout the war – running to well over 3000 pages, subsequently bound in four large volumes and now preserved in the Museum – wrote as virtually his final entry:

This horrid ghastly thing that we have lived with for four long years and more is past and done. There are to be no more brave lads butchered by the Huns or poisoned with their gas, or to die of disease in the trenches: no more long casualty lists for dreading relations or friends to eagerly scan every morning. No more atrocities on land or sea. No more passenger ships to be torpedoed; no more air raids, all done with and gone now and for ever. It is at present unbelievable; it is too good to be true, we shall wake up to find it is only a dream, a trick of the imagination. Yet it is not so, and we know it is not so.

Sadly it all happened again a generation later and has continued in endless variations since. The new Imperial War Museum guidebook highlights the grim fact that during this century more than 100,000,000 people have died as a result of war. This book is offered in the same way as the Museum offers itself to the public interest, not to revel in the 'horrid ghastly thing' – to use F.A. Robinson's words – which was the First World War, but that we might look afresh at it, assimilate knowledge about it in as precise and objective a way as possible, and, perhaps, be enriched by the experience.

Malcolm Brown

Format The book begins in 1914 and ends in 1918 but its material is not arranged chronologically but by theme, each theme being dealt with – though there are some inevitable overlaps – in a separate part under its own title. Each part has its own brief introduction, in which the scope and range of the matter following are explained; and each introduction is accompanied by a list of relevant dates. Thus, for example, Part VII, The Civilians' War, contains dates relating to air raids and food rationing but the dates of the first use of gas or of the Battle of the Somme will only be found under Part II, The Western Front. Because of this there is no general chronology, but since in a work like this place should be found for some sort of overall statement about the war, a short year-by-year account of it has been included, which follows next.

Quotations The text includes many direct quotations, from written documentary material and interview tapes. These are reproduced verbatim whenever possible, but obvious errors have been corrected and minor confusions have been clarified. It has not been thought necessary to indicate where quotations have been abridged.

A Brief History of the First World War

1914 'Few of us,' wrote H.G. Wells after the war was over, 'realized in the earlier half of 1914 how near the crash was to us.' The assassination of an Austrian archduke in the Balkans in June of that year led to much international sabre-rattling throughout July and war became virtually inevitable by August, arriving at the height of a summer in which, for the British, there had been greater fears of a conflict in Ireland than in Europe, although thoughts of a European showdown between hostile alliances – an 'Armageddon' – had been in the air for years. Mobilization evoked a mood of high-spirited patriotism in most of the belligerent nations (Germany and Austria-Hungary being the key powers on one side; France, Russia and Britain the principals on the other), which made them all believe they had a good and noble cause. In the east the so-called 'Russian steamroller' (the phrase implied the virtually bottomless well of manpower on which Russia could draw) lumbered towards Germany but was stopped decisively at Tannenberg. In the west France launched her armies with much *élan* and dash at her former territories of Alsace-Lorraine, only to be thrown back with huge losses.

While other participants rallied conscript forces, Britain called for volunteers to reinforce an army (or more strictly an Expeditionary Force) which was swiftly despatched to the nearest appropriate scene of action: Belgium (whose neutrality had been violated by the Germans) and northern France. There, after some months in which the armies marched and counter-marched with a speed reminiscent of the wars of Napoleon, and after a number of high-casualty encounters of which the last and most bloody was the First Battle of Ypres in October-November, a stalemate ensued which was to continue for almost four years. The power of twentieth-century artillery (a world away from the cannon of Waterloo or the Crimea) forced the armies to dig in; the

'The Battalion Going Up Into the Line'
Drawing by Private Alfred Thomas, Oxford and Bucks Light Infantry

9

machine-gun and the rifle made 'over-the-top' attacks highly costly; the efficiency with which reinforcements could be rushed to stem any breakthrough caused even the most promising offensives to fail. For Britain, France and (later) America the 'Western Front' – as it soon came to be known – was to be, as it were, the central stage of the war. Britain, being the world's maritime superpower, had expected that the Navy would play a decisive role, and indeed it did so up to a point but not in the manner expected, in that the battleship was to prove less important than the submarine and blockade was to prove a more effective weapon than the broadside.

1914 also saw the immediate rallying to the flag of troops from the British Empire. Indians were in action (in France) that autumn; Canadians, Australians, New Zealanders, South Africans, Newfoundlanders and others would soon follow suit. The year ended with a Christmas truce along much of the Western Front – a remarkable display of camaraderie between enemies that would never occur on such a scale again.

1915 was a year of frustration. In the west, hopes of breaking the trench deadlock faded as a series of relatively minor frontal attacks resulted in few gains and many casualties. Air raids started, in which civilians – their traditional spectator role gone for ever – found themselves potential victims. Zeppelins (military airships) were the first purveyors of destruction from the sky; aircraft (bombers) would appear later. In April poison gas was used by the Germans during the Second Battle of Ypres, a weapon which seemed basically evil and to break all the chivalrous rules; it was soon adopted by the Allies. In May a famous transatlantic liner, the *Lusitania*, was sunk with much loss of life – producing strong anti-German feeling in Britain, and, more significantly, in America.

The year also saw a number of attempts to influence the outcome of the war through 'sideshows', ie initiatives away from the main areas of confrontation. With a view to relieving pressure on Russia by challenging Turkey, Germany's principal eastern ally, British and French naval forces were despatched to break through the Dardanelles into the Sea of Marmara – the ultimate target, if fortune favoured, being Constantinople itself. When this purely seaborne effort failed, Allied land forces kept up the pressure on Turkey by invading the Gallipoli peninsula; a bitterly fought campaign ensued which the Allies ultimately had to abandon. Meanwhile, another sideshow opened at Salonika in northern Greece, basically to resist enemy moves in the Balkans – though following the Allied failure to prevent the swift conquest of Serbia, this front settled into a condition of uneasy stalemate which continued until well into 1918. Further east in Mesopotamia (present-day Iraq) a British Indian Army, engaged in yet another sideshow, failed in its attempt to seize Baghdad. Italy, which had come in on the Allied side, seemed to offer a theatre closer to the centre of action where the sideshow philosophy might be invoked, the idea being to knock out Austria. The year saw four battles on the Isonzo front which cost Italy a quarter of a million casualties with only minor gains to compensate; there would be seven more Isonzo battles before the war ended.

1915 was notable for a growing acceptance that the original bright hopes of a swift return to peace would not be easily realized. Among its numerous significant events in Britain the formation of a Ministry of Munitions was a potent symbol of the kind of war now being fought; the main source for the workers in the new munitions factories was the nation's womanhood. Women would play many roles in the conflict, short of actual fighting.

1916 was a year of killing. The Germans mounted a massive attack against the garrison city of Verdun in north-eastern France and the French fought back ferociously; it was a battle that would not only claim hundreds of thousands of lives but would permanently scar the French psyche. To this day one can visit the site of ghost villages uninhabited since, but still cherished like shrines. The British, not to be outdone, suffered their own Verdun that year – on the Somme, a name that will always ring in the memory of the people of the British Isles; including Ireland, where the achievements and sacrifice of such as 36th (Ulster) Division are still remembered as though July 1916 were only months ago. Thousands of the eager volunteers of 1914 died on the chalk downlands of Picardy, and with them went not only their lives given for King and Country but much of the spirit of patriotic optimism which had inspired them to enlist in the first place. Significantly, the idea of 'Pals' battalions – locally raised units with a deliberate emphasis on recruitment of men 'in bodies' (members of sports clubs, workmates etc) – was not heard of again. Indeed, conscription had already come into force in Britain in March, removing the traditional volunteer principle for the foreseeable future.

On the Eastern Front, a Russian general, Brusilov, launched a major and, to begin with, successful offensive; ultimately the Germans forced him back, but not before he had broken the spirit of the Austro-Hungarian army. Two empires emerged crucially weakened from this episode and, though there were other contributory reasons, would ultimately collapse: the Habsburgs (the ruling family of Austria-Hungary), and the Romanovs (the family of the Russian Tsars). At sea on 31 May there was at last a meeting of British and German battle fleets in the North Sea, with the disadvantage that there was no clear victory; the fact that the German surface fleet would hardly ever seek combat again could not be known until the war ended more than two years later. The argument over this ambiguous encounter, famous as the Battle of Jutland, has never been quite resolved. Meanwhile in the Middle Eastern theatre, the army that had failed to reach Baghdad was forced to surrender after several months of siege at Kut, and June saw the opening of the Arab Revolt against the Turks – a first milestone on what was to prove a very long and tortuous political road.

1917 was a year of pessimism and confusion, though not without its hints of better things to come. Blockade threatened to debilitate Britain fatally, revolution actually did take her eastern ally Russia right out of the war, and with the Bolshevik *putsch* in Petrograd in November (October according to the Eastern calendar) Marxism-Leninism arrived on the world scene. On the Western Front the failure of an over-optimistic French initiative (known as the Nivelle offensive after its plausible but ineffective commander) led to widespread mutinies in the French army; thereafter the British contribution would take on an ever-increasing importance. In late July another major 'push' was launched by the British, this time in Flanders. Officially the Third Battle of Ypres, this three-and-a-half-month marathon is now generally named after its final objective, Passchendaele. The offensive slowed up in the mud of the Ypres front much as the previous attempt had done in the mud of the Somme. Its relative failure produced despondency, but it hit the Germans hard as well as the British, not least because in terms of the logic of attrition, the Allies, even without Russia, were ultimately bound to win. The reason for this confidence lay in the fact that 1917 saw the Americans coming in on the Allied side. It would, however, be many months before 'Uncle Sam' could become anything more than a token participant.

There were other positive aspects to the year. Baghdad fell to the Allies in March. Though the French had failed in April, the British and Canadians, attacking near Arras, performed effectively, seizing that famous vantage point, Vimy Ridge. In June the Battle of Messines, memorable for the explosion of nineteen huge mines under the German lines, proved a Western Front triumph. In October the French achieved a small but notable success under Pétain on the Aisne, and though in the same month the Austrians and Germans launched a devastating onslaught on the Italian front at Caporetto, the Italians, forced to reel back in retreat, nevertheless held their new line on the River Piave. In November British tanks won a spectacular, if unexploited, success at Cambrai; the ground gained was soon retaken but not before church bells had been rung in London, a portent of ultimate if not immediate hope. December gave the Allies a modest but much heralded Christmas gift – the capture of Jerusalem from Turkey as the Allied campaign in Palestine at last began to make headway.

1918 was the year of disarray, and of sudden, almost unexpected victory. Vigorous implementation of the convoy system, already adopted in 1917, solved much of Britain's blockade problem; attempts by the Royal Navy to sink blockships at Zeebrugge and Ostend – to prevent German U-boats going to sea – were less successful, though they were good for national, and naval, morale. However, starting in March, massive German attacks on the Western Front destroyed the idea that trenches could not be overrun, and Britain and France, with America only just beginning to deploy, seemed almost to be facing defeat. In a famous phrase of the British Commander-in-Chief, Field Marshal Sir Douglas Haig, they had their 'backs to the wall'. But then the German thrusts petered out in exhaustion and it was the Allies' turn to break through and march. Among other achievements they forced their way through the well-defended Hindenburg Line with astonishing speed, gaining a victory whose brilliance and importance have never been fully acknowledged. They were still marching – though they had not put one foot on German soil – when Kaiser Wilhelm II abdicated, leaving it to politicians who had had little say in the war to take on the humiliating task of suing for peace.

Meanwhile, there were notable successes elsewhere: in Italy, where the Italians advanced across the Piave, taking vast numbers of prisoners; in Macedonia, where Allied forces based on Salonika were at last able to show their fighting spirit; and the Middle East, where the Palestine Campaign was brought to a victorious conclusion, most memorably with the seizure of Damascus. Air power, growing through the war, never quite reached its apogee (though Britain acknowledged its significance by constituting a separate arm, the Royal Air Force, in 1918); a scheme for bombing the German capital, Berlin, in progress as the political negotiations began, was necessarily aborted. Such concepts, thus put on the shelf largely untried, would be dusted off for use a generation later. By way of a curious footnote to the cessation of hostilities, two days after the guns fell silent in Europe, a resourceful German commander in East Africa, Lettow-Vorbeck, who had teased the Allies for years, captured a small town in Northern Rhodesia; informed of the Armistice he decided he had no option but honourably to lay down his arms.

With hindsight it can be seen that the war's somewhat untidy conclusion (Hitler and others would later argue that Germany had not been militarily defeated but betrayed by weakling democrats), compounded by the vindictive peace settlement which followed, made it almost certain that within not too many years the armies would march again. There are those, indeed, who see the period 1914 to 1945 as virtually one long civil war of the Europeans. But that is another story: for the purposes of this book the war began in the summer of 1914 and ended at eleven o'clock on the eleventh day of the eleventh month of 1918.

*   *   *   *

In 1917 it was decided that there should be a National War Museum to commemorate and record the great crisis through which the country was passing. Subsequently the other nations of the Empire demurred at a merely national concept and so the name Imperial War Museum was devised. It began collecting material relating to the war almost at once and it was established by Act of Parliament in 1920. Now in the 1990s its function and future are more firmly established than ever, with an increasing emphasis on the social as opposed to the military aspects of war. This book can perhaps be seen as a token of its continuing, indeed increasing, self-confidence and awareness as this century of conflict moves towards its close.

PART I
The March to War

THIS first part explores a number of aspects of the transition from an uneasy peace to full-scale war. The reaction of civilians is set against the response of men who would have to do the fighting, and there is a section on people who faced a special dilemma when hostilities began, that of how to get home to Britain from a Europe where passports had suddenly become necessary and frontiers were now dangerous. There are early instances of action, including a heroic encounter during the Retreat from Mons which became instantly famous and produced some of the war's first VCs, and a successful naval attack which raised the morale of a nation which confidently believed in Britain's supremacy at sea. There is a section on the senior NCO of a territorial battalion which would be much engaged on the Western Front over the next four years, while the view from the other side is also represented, in a German's account of his experience in the First Battle of Ypres. Both these men will appear later in the book. There is a pictorial sequence on the early experience of the 2nd Battalion, Scots Guards, who took their own unofficial photographer with them when they crossed to the continent in October 1914. Finally there is a section on the Kitchener volunteers (so called after the newly appointed war minister, the redoubtable Earl Kitchener of Khartoum), who responded in their tens of thousands to the call of King and Country in the early months of the war.

A long line of troops on the march (Q 69587)

15

The March to War | Important Dates

1914

June 28 Assassination of Archduke Franz Ferdinand at Sarajevo

July 23 Austrian ultimatum to Serbia
25 Serbian reply rejected
28 Austria-Hungary declares war on Serbia
31 General mobilization in Austria and Russia
German ultimatum to Russia

August 1 Germany orders general mobilization
Germany declares war on Russia
France mobilizes
2 German ultimatum to Belgium
German troops move into Luxembourg
3 Germany declares war on France
4 Germany invades Belgium
British ultimatum to Germany
Britain declares war on Germany
Sir John Jellicoe assumes command of the British Grand Fleet
Sir John French appointed to command British Expeditionary Force
5 Lord Kitchener appointed Secretary of State for War
6 Austria-Hungary declares war on Russia
7 British Expeditionary Force lands in France
12 Britain and France declare war on Austria-Hungary
13 Austro-Hungarian forces invade Serbia
14 Battle of the Frontiers between French and German forces
20 German occupation of Brussels
23 Battle of Mons
Japan declares war on Germany
26 Battle of Le Cateau
Battle of Tannenberg begins
28 Heligoland Bight naval action

September 6 Battle of the Marne begins
13 Battle of the Aisne begins

October 9 Fall of Antwerp
14 First Canadian soldiers arrive in Britain
October 19-November 22 First Battle of Ypres

1914: From Peace to War

'The Great War' – most wars are named by historians after they have happened or when they are well under way, but the name by which the conflict of 1914-18 was generally known, until a second major confrontation a generation later, was already in people's minds in August 1914. 'We have been in a state of great excitement', wrote schoolmaster Robert Saunders to his eldest son, who was living in Canada, 'as the reservists are being called up, all the railways are guarded, wire entanglements, trench guns, etc, have been hurriedly put round Portsmouth and even our post office has had orders to keep open night and day. Everything points to the Great War, so long expected, being upon us, so you can picture the restless excitement among all classes.' This was on 2 August, at a time of crisis and mobilization across Europe but two days before Britain took the irrevocable step of proclaiming a state of war with Germany.

Saunders was writing in the little village of Fletching in Sussex. Not far away in the Isle of Wight, Winifred Tower, who had gone to Cowes for the annual yachting festival, described the fateful day itself in the diary she kept throughout most of that summer and autumn. She was equally convinced of the inevitability of war, if perhaps surprised by the suddenness of its arrival:

August 4th. Isolde and I went to a Red Cross meeting in the evening and when we came out, 6 p.m., the Territorials had just received orders to mobilize. War was declared at midnight. It was really almost a relief to hear this definitely announced. Every day seemed like weeks, everything was unsettled, and we were wishing one minute for peace at any price, and the next were furious at the idea that we might back out of our treaty obligations. But it was impossible to believe that 'the Day' had really come. We had talked about it, argued about its possibilities, volumes had been written about it, it had been a sort of nightmare always hanging over us, and yet I don't suppose many of us ever thought that it would become a reality in our time, and that we were destined to live in the most stirring days of our history. But now it was on us, and so suddenly that it seemed like a bad dream that we should soon wake from to find our world unchanged.

The last days before Europe slid into war were dramatic ones in the British House of Commons. Holcombe Ingleby, a Conservative Member of Parliament, writing on 4 August, described the mood at Westminster in a letter to his son – an officer who would soon be involved in the fighting:

The house was great yesterday and would have been greater, had it been shorn of the dirty crowd of little Englanders. The Liberal Government did well – for them: up to Saturday they were intending to stand neutral, then the combination of Winston [Churchill] and circumstances was too strong for them and they decided to do their duty in a half-hearted sort of way. However, the infringe-

ment of Belgium will drive them into definite action, and we must then go the whole hog. In fact we are in for the biggest thing in wars that the world has ever seen. We may even get to know the respective value of the Battleship and the Submarine.

'The biggest thing in wars that the world has ever seen': Holcombe Ingleby was right in foreseeing that. He was also right in suggesting that the struggle to come would sort out the pecking order of those two great instruments of naval war, the much vaunted capital ship and that sly new undersea weapon, the submarine. The battleship would play a relatively minor role in the conflict to come; the submarine – in its German manifestation the U-boat – would almost bring Britain to her knees. Where Ingleby was less than prescient was in his implicit assumption that the major theatre of war would be the sea. Britain had long been principally a maritime power; it was largely Germany's challenge to Britain's supremacy at sea that had made a clash between these two great nations seem, in the end, inevitable. But it would be as a land power that Britain, allied with the French and the Americans, would force Germany to an armistice four years and three months later.

The thought of the conflict about to begin inevitably stirred traditional feelings in the citizens of a nation conscious and proud of its martial past – among those of an age to be involved, and, perhaps more easily, of an age not to be involved. In the second month of the war Ingleby wrote to his son: 'How I wish I were 30 years younger! It is curious that, though a modern battle is a perfect inferno, one asks for nothing better than to be in it.'

Britain's prime weapon of war – as it was thought in 1914: capital ships of the world's largest navy (Q 63695)
All four battleships of the Orion class, *Orion*, *Thunderer*, *Monarch* and *Conqueror*, in line ahead. All completed in 1912. Principal statistics: length 584 ft, beam 85 ft; displacement 22,500-25,000 tons; speed 21-2 knots; guns 10×13.5-inch, 16×4-inch; torpedo tubes 3 (later 2) 21-inch; complement 800-900 men. All four present at the Battle of Jutland; all four survived

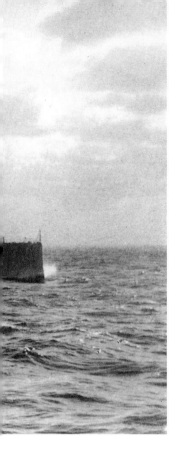

Commander-in-Chief of the British Grand Fleet, Sir John Jellicoe, photographed on the deck of his flagship, HMS *Iron Duke* (Q 62697)

Ingleby was plainly distressed to find himself – in terms of Shakespeare's *Henry V* – among the 'gentlemen in England now abed', unable to be present on St Crispin's Day, but for those whose duty it would be to risk life and limb the prospect concentrated the mind significantly. On 9 August 1914 Surgeon Duncan Lorimer, an officer of the Royal Naval Volunteer Reserve recalled on the day war was declared, scrambled by rope-ladder aboard the cruiser HMS *Bacchante* just as she was about to sail from the Nore. As flagship of the Cruiser Force 'C' *Bacchante* was to join the Second Fleet in the English Channel whose task was to safeguard transports of the expeditionary force *en route* for France. Late that night he wrote in his diary:

There was a magnificent sunset and the black forms of the other cruisers were only just visible, not a light showing amongst us all. The silence, the feeling that this was real, that it was war with all its possibilities, could not but make one think. The Padre held service just outside the wardroom, holding Communion just before. There was a good attendance.

Another naval officer, Lieutenant Ronald Trevor RN, a submariner, wrote the following to his sister in November 1914, echoing the view which Wilfred Owen would later deride as 'the old lie', that it was 'dulce et decorum pro patria mori' (ie 'sweet and fitting to die for one's country'), his thoughts perhaps influenced by the fact that his submarine was on the sea-bed and close to enemy waters at the time:

Sometimes I wonder if I will spend the remainder of all time on the bottom for although we never talk of death and very seldom think much about it, it is when everyone is asleep and only you are awake that sometimes you look into the future and wonder. We must all die sometime and what finer death could a man die and what finer tomb than one of H. M. ships could he have?

Captain Oscar Greig of the Royal Flying Corps flew to France early in 1915. He wrote to his 'Dearest Dad and Mother':

I have written to almost everyone to say I am going across. I don't know that there is much more to say. I think that we are all sure of meeting again some-where. I expect and feel that I shall come through this war, but one never knows.

Whatever happens it is better that I should be doing my share than to be amongst the crowd who are doing nothing.

If there was ardour on the British side, it was paralleled on the German, but the future contestants were also at one in their innocence, and in their ignorance of what was to come. F.L. Cassel, later to fight at Ypres and on the Somme, was a 25-year-old reservist in 1914. In his post-war account of his military career he commented:

We had no idea what horrors, what suffering was ahead of us. There was *Enthusiasmus*, and conviction of victory, in spite of the fact that we had no vision of war, of the adversaries, their weapons. Nobody had heard grenades burst or bullets whistle. There were no casualty lists.*

Meanwhile the very young – or some of them – were as eager to be involved as the elderly. The Reverend Victor Tanner, later to have a distinguished career as an army chaplain in France (see page 247), was chaplain of a Dorset public school, Weymouth College, in the first year of the war. He preserved the text of a sermon delivered on Sunday 31 January 1915, preached, as he put it, 'when the war fever was at its height and when boys in the upper part of the school were experiencing a feeling of frustration because they were at the moment under the age required for military service.' These stirring sentences enshrine the es-sence of his message:

War has broken out in Europe and Britain's manhood have responded in their thousands to the call for service in the fighting line. Others perforce have to stay at home and amongst them you – and I – at present find ourselves. We think with pride of those who have already gone from here into the battle, and we are confident that they will bring honour and credit to their country and their school and we only wish we could be at their side. Indeed I know that there are many of you in the upper part of the school who are already beginning to feel unsettled. Every day you hear of great deeds being done and of young lives cheerfully sacrificed in the cause of righteousness and freedom. You know that their places have to be filled and you are beginning to think 'Aren't I wasting my time here? Oughtn't I to offer for the front?' Well, it is not for me to decide for you. Each must take his own particular circumstances into account, though certainly if you are physically fit and when you are old enough, there can be little doubt where the path of duty lies. What I want to impress on you, however, at this moment is that to be here at school is no waste of time. You must look on your school routine in the light of a preparation for the time when your country will need you. England needs men who are big enough to subordinate their own interests to the interests of the whole; men who are imbued with the spirit of self-sacrifice and who have a high sense of duty; men who will inspire those whom they are called upon to lead. Look at your school work here and your life

*Cassel wrote his memoir in German in 1924, then translated it into English himself thirty years later for his family, having moved to England in the 1930s because of Nazi persecution.

The Young Men of August
Above: In London, British recruits wait for their pay in the churchyard of St Martin-in-the-Fields, Trafalgar Square, August 1914 (Q 53234)
Left: In Berlin, a German officer reads out the Kaiser's order for mobilization, 1 August 1914 (Q 81775)

Mobilization in Europe, 1914

Right: Enthusiastic send-off for German soldiers leaving for one of the fronts (Q 81779)

Far right: Austrian soldiers in a troop train responding to the mood of the times (Q 81808)

Below: Massed French reservists leaving the Gare du Nord, Paris, on the way to their depots (Q 81852)

together here in that light and there will be no need to offer your services when the time and opportunity come your way. Above all, make Christ your example and the Captain of your soul and with him at your side fight tooth and nail against anything that would degrade your character and make you less than the best. If you regard your time spent here at school in the light that I suggest, then when the time comes for you to be 'weighed in the balance' you will not be found wanting.

But war brought many humbler forms of sacrifice, not all accepted happily by those called upon to make them. In another letter to his son, written in August 1914, Robert Saunders commented:

Poor Mr Fenner was awfully cut up yesterday as they came round and commandeered his black horse Kitty. They have been round taking everybody's horses that were suitable and at Uckfield they took horses out of the carriages and carts. As you will see from the papers Kitchener is at the war office and is making his influence felt. I am sorry for Mr Fenner as he was so keen on Kitchener coming to the war office and taking charge of things and it seemed rather rough on him, one of the first results was the loss of his horse of which he was so proud.

In September Saunders reported an equally unenthusiastic response, this time to the activities of a local billeting officer:

One old maid in Lewes who lives in a large house, objected on the plea that she hadn't had a man in the house for ten years. The unfeeling officer merely remarked 'It's quite time you did' and chalked 8 on the door and 8 very soon arrived.

If the countryside was feeling the effect of the change from peace to war, the capital was doing so to an even greater degree. After paying a visit to London in September 1914 Saunders commented:

You can't live in London at the present without feeling an atmosphere of restless excitement that tells on the nerves and leaves you tired and more or less irritable and used up. Everywhere you go you see flags flying, appeals to enlist, men in khaki, special constables with their badges, photographs and war telegrams in shop windows and recruiting stations.

This was also a time of high animosity against all things German. Many shops bearing German-sounding names were ransacked; anyone with a hint of German in name or background was open to victimization. This bitterness against 'aliens' (which would eventually cause even the British Royal Family to change its name) was not confined to Britain. F.L. Cassel was living in Berlin in the summer of 1914 and later described the city's excitable mood:

The streets began to fill with excited people, who were inclined to become the victim of any rumour. I experienced the sensation of a beginning of a war psychosis, the chase of suspected spies, after a declaration of imminent war had been issued. Coffee houses were destroyed, e.g. the English café at the Wittenberg Platz, ostensibly because it was alleged that enemy hymns had been played by foreign musicians.

In such a volatile situation Britons in German or Austrian territory could find themselves in considerable difficulties. The unfortunate ones were interned like the aliens described above; the fortunate were able to make their escape.

Escape from Europe, Summer 1914

When war came in August 1914 many British people living or holidaying on the continent found themselves facing the alarming prospect of being caught in Europe for the duration of hostilities. Rigby Wason was on holiday in Marienbad, Austria, with his father, a well-known Liberal MP, and their situation was such that on 22 August he sent a postcard to his mother with the telegram-style message:

> BOTH SAFE AND WELL AT MARIENBAD BUT MAY NOT LEAVE CITY LIMITS
> – INTERNED IS WORD. RETURN MOST DOUBTFUL – PROBABLY NOT TILL PEACE.

In fact they were able to make their way to England via Switzerland in September, but only after Rigby, who was forty-three and in less than perfect health (which was why he had been taking the cure at Marienbad), had formally agreed to take no active part in the war. The undertaking not to bear arms was signed on his behalf by a Mr Walter Behrens, Chevalier of the Legion of Honour and President of the Chamber of Commerce in Paris, fortunately also a visitor to the spa, and was endorsed by Rigby's father. The British War Office honoured this undertaking when Rigby Wason became liable for conscription.

Nevertheless, as he stated in notes of his experiences dictated in 1918, he felt that it was a 'monstrous proceeding' that he should have been kept in Austria when he wished to return, for shortly before the outbreak of war the Governor of Marienbad, 'in fear of having the season spoilt, had issued a proclamation saying that there was no danger and that if anybody would stay in Marienbad not one hair of their head would be injured.' As for the reason why in the early days of August he and his father failed to make a 'bolt for home', his answer was that 'the Military were then mobilizing and there was no train, except the one post train a day, which had Third Class only, and travelled at the rate of some ten miles an hour.' It would have taken the best part of a week to reach Switzerland.

For many other people the only option was the 'bolt for home', often to be accompanied by memorable and at times frightening experiences. Margaret Foote, aged fourteen, in Germany with her mother for a Rhine cruise, recorded what she called her 'little adventures' in a vivid day-by-day diary which spanned four school exercise books. Daisy Williams, aged sixteen, who had planned to spend a year in Dresden with her mother, learning the language and studying music, described what she called her 'Great Adventure' in a 180-page pencilled account written nine years later, her original diary having been lost in the confusion of her prolonged journey home. Rosie Neal, a member of a Norfolk-based five-girl troupe of vocalists, banjoists and dancers known as the Royal Brewsters – who had arrived in Hamburg by boat on 27 July with a view to beginning a continental concert tour on 1 August – described their ordeal in a letter which became so long and included so many twists of fortune that she was finally driven to muse: 'now I don't know whether to call it my letter or my story.'

The Royal Brewsters had heard hints of possible conflict between England and Germany soon after their arrival but their reaction had been to make light of the prospect:

At last the 1st Aug arrived, we were all excitement, we were going to work tonight. When night came round we set off extra light hearted to work, but alas there we sat and waited; presently one man came in, who inquired if there wasn't going to be a show, the manager had to tell him he didn't think so, as he was the only audience that had made an appearance and it was then ten o'clock; so there we sat far into the night talking of the war. We returned home very down hearted as the war was the cause of no audience and no show.

There was one other immediate consequence of the crisis. Rosie and one other 'artiste' had been with one landlady, her elder sister Kitty and the two remaining 'artistes' had been with another. Now Rosie's landlady told them that her nephew was coming to stay and that she would require their room forthwith:

I tell you we were jolly sorry to leave, but it is only now [she was writing eight days later] that we know that she was a wicked old bounder, she had heard rumours of the war and wouldn't have us in our house as we were English. Anyway Kit's landlady took us in.

They still had hopes that their show would go on despite the crisis, but it was not to be:

Well, we went to work Sunday evening only to find the theatre was closed. Now we began to get really worried, the best thing to do would be to go to the British Consul first thing in the morning. This we decided to do.

By this time Margaret Foote and her mother had cruised far into the Rhineland on their Dutch-crewed steamer the *Hollandia*. On Saturday 1 August they had been stopped by a boat full of German soldiers, but, after their papers had been checked, they were allowed to proceed: 'when going away we all waved our hands and handkerchiefs and the soldiers waved back at us.' However, when a police boat stopped them and asked if there were any French or Russians aboard – there weren't – a second attempt at fraternization failed: 'the men in the boat positively refused to smile.' The Foote ladies disembarked at Mannheim and together with some friendly Americans went by taxi to the station and took a train to Heidelberg. 'A lot of soldiers got in, singing as they came', the young diarist noted. 'The roads were simply crowded with people and soldiers.'

They stayed in Heidelberg overnight. The next day the situation began to deteriorate. Mrs Foote wished to write to her husband but was told that 'no letters could be sent out of Germany unless *written in German and left open*'. Expressing a wish to change plans and head for Strasbourg she was informed that that was out of the question. Even tourist photography was forbidden: a policeman told them that two ladies had been put in prison on Friday for photographing Heidelberg's historic old bridge. Like the concert troupe in Hamburg, they decided

The British passport
issued to Mrs Amy Nora
Foote and her daughter
Margaret by the American
Consul in Stuttgart on 6
August 1914 and endorsed
by the British Consul in
Lucerne on 19 August
(HU 57190)

their next port of call should be the British Consul, but he was away for the weekend.

On Monday 3rd they travelled to Stuttgart, the home of Fraülein Heigel, the governess who had recently had charge of Margaret's education in England. Happily, mother and daughter encountered little animosity. Their luggage was carried to their train by two very polite and friendly Germans: 'one was interested in English politics and wanted mother to tell him all about Ulster and Women's Suffrage!' When they reached Stuttgart, one of these gentlemen even accompanied them to their hotel: 'he refused to leave us until we had arrived safely there'.

On the following day, Tuesday 4 August, they were able to meet the British Consul in Stuttgart, who informed them that they would be quite safe 'until England declared war'. (As she recorded this statement in her diary Margaret had no idea that this was to be the fateful date of Britain's entry into the now burgeoning conflict.) Comforted by the Consul's assurance, they went to see their former governess's family, who in the circumstances gave them a most friendly welcome. The family's two sons had just hurried home from Berlin, preparatory to joining their regiments. One of them was already in his military uniform, the significance of which was not lost on the young English girl: 'He looked such a nice young fellow, it seems so awful to think of all these fine young men having to go to the war, and so many of them, alas, will never come back.'

'War is declared with England', wrote Margaret Foote in her diary on Wednesday 5 August: they had heard the news at breakfast. Now the mood of tolerant friendliness began to change: 'The manager of the hotel came in, and said that of all the mean, unchristian countries, England was the worst! At these words the old gentleman behind us and the two girls who were with him clapped vigorously.'

For Daisy Williams, living with a German family in Dresden, the first signs of hostility had come earlier. One night, not long after the assassination of Archduke Franz Ferdinand, as the subsequent shock waves began to ripple across Europe, Daisy noted a strange gleam in the eyes of the daughter of the house, her friend Kattie – it was as if 'something had darted between them like lightning':

I said goodnight and turned away with something clutching at my heart that then I could not fathom, but I know *now*; it was the grim shadow of war flashing between us *just for an instant*, a blind dropping swiftly upon the Germany we thought we had known and the Germany we were to know.

Yet Kattie in Dresden, like Margaret Foote in Stuttgart, was moved to pity at the thought of the consequences that war would inevitably bring. Daisy noted that Kattie was very upset at Germany's declaration of war on Russia, which took place on 1 August, saying 'how awful it was to think of the young men who would be killed'.

For Mrs Williams and her daughter, as for their compatriots elsewhere, the next step was to contact the local British Consul. 'We found we should have to get a passport,' wrote Daisy, thus bringing out a fact rarely realized, that before the First World War such documents were not required: a British citizen could travel freely without passport or permission just as a foreigner could spend his life in Britain without

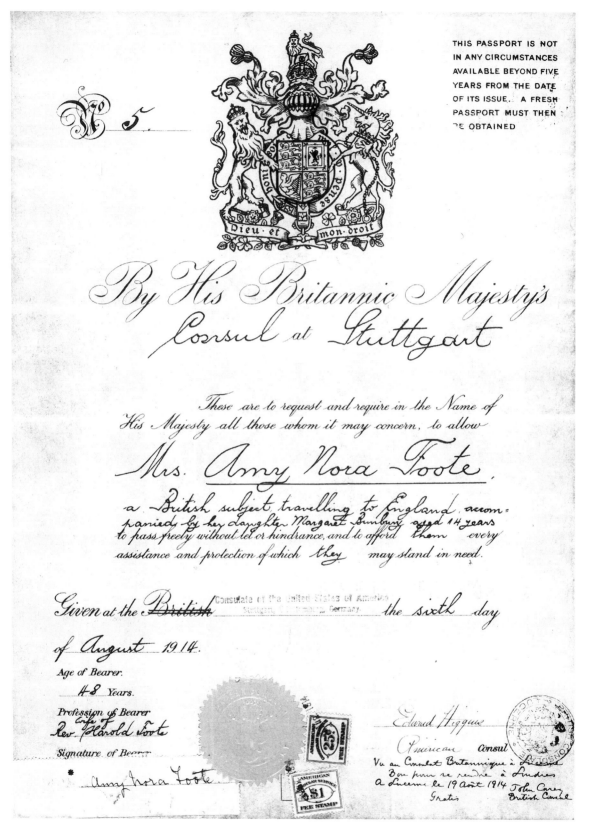

№ 5.

THIS PASSPORT IS NOT
IN ANY CIRCUMSTANCES
AVAILABLE BEYOND FIVE
YEARS FROM THE DATE
OF ITS ISSUE. A FRESH
PASSPORT MUST THEN
BE OBTAINED

By His Britannic Majesty's
Consul at Stuttgart

These are to request and require in the Name of
His Majesty all those whom it may concern, to allow

Mrs. Amy Nora Foote,

a British subject travelling to England accompanied by her daughter Margaret Bunbury aged 14 years
to pass freely without let or hindrance, and to afford them every
assistance and protection of which they may stand in need.

Given at the ~~British~~ Consulate of the United States of America
Stuttgart Kingdom Germany the sixth day

of August 1914.

Age of Bearer.
48 Years.

Profession of Bearer
Wife of
Rev. Harold Foote

Signature of Bearer

Amy Nora Foote

Edward Higgins
American Consul

Vu au Consulat Britannique à Lucerne
Bon pour se rendre à Londres
à Lucerne le 19 Août 1914 John Carey
Gratis British Consul

permit and without informing the police. Overnight that simple ancient dispensation disappeared, as people queued and clamoured for documentation, since without that vital piece of paper they were little better than stateless refugees.

The British Consul in Dresden proved to be a German: 'He did his best to dissuade us from leaving', wrote Daisy, 'he said that in a few weeks Germany would have conquered Russia.' But they insisted and together with several other British nationals, mainly ladies, they began a slow and tortuous railway journey to the frontier. At Leipzig another English traveller joined their carriage – 'a strange figure clad in tennis clothes, he had white duck trousers, a straw hat and blazer! He had been at Bayreuth for the Wagner festival and hearing that the last train to England was leaving that day in ½ hour, had flown to the station as he was.' At Magdeburg they had to change trains, and Daisy was helped by a friendly porter, who sympathized with their lot. 'I have never forgotten his face,' she commented; 'later when I read of German brutality I used to think of that man's face.'

Eventually they reached Hanover, where the station was so crowded with soldiers that the 'significance of the vast mobilization dawned upon us with tremendous force'. They went for refreshment to a nearby café, but the atmosphere was scarcely conducive to relaxation:

The air was thick with smoke, heat and the odour of beer, an orchestra played patriotic airs and everyone bawled the refrain; it was our first experience of *Deutschland, Deutschland, über alles* and *Die Wacht am Rhein*, enthusiasm rose to fever pitch, the soldiers beat time, the lids of mugs were clicked, officers slapped their boots with their whips and whenever there was a pause it would be filled up with shouts of '*Hoch! Hoch! Hurra! Hurra!*' The culminating point was the German National Anthem, which was the same tune as ours*; everyone bellowed, the noise was ear-splitting; oh the heat and those stolid men with red perspiring faces – never did we think so acutely as at that moment that we were aliens in a strange land.

Shortly after they left Hanover, their journey took on elements of farce – though potentially dangerous farce, as Daisy enthusiastically recalled:

No sooner did the train draw up at Bielefeld than the bulls of Basham fell upon us with much bellowing and purple countenances – two or three officials headed by the station master burst into our carriage and a soldier popped up at either window – and to our great astonishment we heard ourselves accused of being Russian spies, and that we were to leave the train instantly under arrest. We were all marched off surrounded by a cordon of soldiers with fixed bayonets while the charming people in the train jeered and called out 'Russian spies, Russian dogs' at our retreating backs. We were taken to a little room and told to wait there for the head of the police in Bielefeld to inspect us. Soldiers were put outside the door and the window and an official sat in the room – this last then proceeded to bully us in a way which I trust and believe is peculiarly German – told us, our first information, that England had declared war – of course knowing full well we *were* really English – how that Germany would sink our fleet and beat us to our knees – and similar gibes, all more or less trash but galling. At nine o'clock there was a clanking of swords and spurs and the head of the police came in, very pompous and resplendent. He asked various questions and examined our passports – then he conferred in low tones with the nasty fellow who was the bully and Miss Heyham heard him say very quickly and low that our arrest was a *dumme sache*.

Heil Dir im Siegeskranz: 'Hail to him with the victor's crown'. *Deutschland, Deutschland, über alles* did not become Germany's national anthem until 1922.

A *dumme sache* – a stupid thing, a silly mistake – their arrest might be, but the chief of police would not let them proceed with their journey. Eventually they were to be sent back to Dresden and had to begin their attempt to return to England all over again.

Similar boasts of easy victories over Britain and her allies were noted by Margaret Foote in the course of her journey home. She and her mother had been unable to get their travel documents from the British Consul in Stuttgart since he had packed and gone the moment that Britain declared war. His departing advice had been to try his American counterpart, which they duly did, eventually being given – on 6 August – a British passport issued by the American Consulate and clearly stamped to that effect. This document was their lifeline and with it they set about making their exit from Germany. A special carriage for English people was put on a train heading for Friedrichshafen on Lake Constance, and after a slow crawl across the country with many stops on the way – at stations crowded with civilians cheering the numerous troop trains which came through – they reached neutral Switzerland. It was during their long wait there that one evening in late August she and her mother, at supper in their hotel in Lucerne, talked with a young German lieutenant:

He had been sent by the German government to take back all the Germans in a certain part of France and Switzerland. He had been in the Battle of Mül-hausen, he said, and had quite a wound from it even though the battle was on August 13. He said the plan of the Germans was, *first*, to destroy the French army and overrun France, and make it promise never to have any army again, *secondly*, to do the same with Russia, and *thirdly*, to destroy the British fleet entirely ('which will be quite easy', he said) and *fourthly* to make peace! Quite a simple programme, isn't it?

For the Royal Brewsters trapped in Hamburg the solution to their long struggle to leave Germany was also provided by the Americans. The British Consulate being closed and attempts to get a sea passage having failed, they had become 'nothing more or less than prisoners'. They were allowed to walk about the streets but, wrote Rosie Neal, 'we are not allowed to speak, unless we speak German, and as we can't do that we have to say nothing, and people look at us as though we have done something terrible'. But then there came the breakthrough: 'One fine morning we became Americans. Yes, it is quite true, we paid 5/4d for a sheet of paper with a big red seal, we were Americans, and nobody could say otherwise but I never knew until then that one could change one's nationality so quickly.'

Several days later they were on their way by train, but the most dangerous obstacle was yet to be faced – the crossing of the frontier. Rosie's elder sister Kit, senior member of the party, took charge of the precious document:

We got into the customs house and had our hand baggage well looked into; when the custom house officers found no ammunition we were politely handed over to the policeman to whom we had to show our passport. Here we tried our best to hold our tongues, and only speak when absolutely necessary in the best American accent we could muster which was very bad. Kit produced her passport and handed it over; one man glanced at it and the soldiers with the bayonets were ordered to lock all doors. Here the trembling and cross question-

The concert troupe 'The Royal Brewsters'. Rosie Neal is second from left, her sister Kit is far right. Their local newspaper, the *Norwich Mercury*, wrote of their 'thrilling experiences' and their 'dramatic escape from the enemy', adding that once they reached Holland they were 'treated with the greatest kindness and courtesy by the dear Dutch people' and that 'they arrived in London after eleven days on a journey that could normally be completed in one.'
(Doc 157)

ing began, we lived in holy dread of being sent back, or even worse than that, to prison, where we should be made to dig the ground and eat that terrible black bread. Now they wanted to know how five people could travel on one passport, so Kit told them that in America young girls didn't need passports and another thing, she was a teacher with her four pupils and if he didn't let her through she would inform President Wilson on her return to America. At this the poor man began to quiver and handed her back the passport telling her everything was quite all right. We all wanted to shout 'Bravo, Kit' but knew we dare not.

For Daisy Williams and her party their second journey west from Dresden was 'not without many alarms and excursions. We changed innumerable times: I believe *eleven* times.' But they had set off at a time of high euphoria in Germany, with Paris apparently within the grasp of her armies – it was just before their advance was held at the Battle of the Marne – so, as she put it, 'we slipped through on a tide of enthusiasm.' Margaret Foote saw this crucial period from the French side as she and her compatriots at last made their way across France, being told that the 'great German army was only 70 kilometres (46 miles) from Paris' and noting that 'in almost every station the waiting-rooms were made into places for the wounded.'

A few days earlier another trainload of returning English tourists had made its way through France from Switzerland, among them a redoubtable twenty-nine-year-old English lady from Hampstead, London, named Winnifred Adair-Roberts, who was to rally to her nation's call immediately on return (see page 191). With her young friend Winnie Pollock she had been in the Swiss resort of Grindelwald when the war began and had fretted and chafed to get home. 'It gave me a vivid feeling of exile', she stated in a long account of their adventures written immediately on their return, 'to know that most of the world is taking part in a war that defeats human imagination, that one's own country is involved, and maybe one's friends and people in danger – possibly dead – and yet to be able to get absolutely no news.' Dangerous outings across remote glaciers or impromptu concerts to keep up the spirits of fellow-tourists were not enough and it was with enormous relief that she and her colleagues settled into their homebound train, even though it was a very old fashioned train of second-class carriages – 'some even without corridors or lavatory accommodation'. The arrangements she had made for her return showed all the organizational skills that she would soon be using to good effect as an officer of the Women's Legion:

I had menus written for each meal and also a complete list of provisions brought which included roast chicken, tinned tongue, tipsy cake (very) and tinned peaches, hard-boiled eggs and fresh lettuces, lemons, prunes, muscatelles, butter and marmalade. When I produced marmalade for breakfast it was the last straw to the other passengers' endurance.

The most striking occasion of their journey to the Channel coast was their half-hour at Lyons Central, where they received 'a perfect ovation':

That huge station was flooded with people – well over 1000 had come to welcome *Les Anglaises*. A terrific cheer rose up, enough to make the train leave the metals. The crush and the excitement were so great that we were obliged to stop in the train for some time while the French cheered us and we cheered them. And then we sang *God Save the King* and they sang the *Marseillaise*, and then *they* sang *God Save the King* and we sang the *Marseillaise*. Then we all shook hands with exquisite officers, dirty porters, refugees, any and everybody. When it was time to go, all the officials were practically stripped of buttons, badges, ribbons, etc, as mementos, and the passengers gave in exchange little Union Jacks. Then of course there was more cheering, more '*Vive la France*', '*Vive l'Angleterre*', *God Save the King* and the *Marseillaise*, and we steamed out of Lyons Central Station, with a wonderful memory picture of the cordiality, sympathy and fraternity that the people of France had given the people of England, in a never to be forgotten welcome.

Miss Adair-Roberts was 'devoutly thankful' when nothing prevented their boarding the cross-Channel steamer at Dieppe. For Margaret Foote her journey was exciting to the last; even the brief voyage to Folkestone was not without drama:

The sea was calm enough at first, but as we got further out it became rougher and we rolled about beautifully. The wind, too, was so strong that one could hardly stand, which made it all the more fun.

The Royal Brewsters on return immediately secured an engagement at Wisbech 'where we spent a most enjoyable week, in fact I might tell you we made up for lost time'. But Daisy Williams probably spoke for all with the comment with which she drew her account to its end:

Such a relief to hear nice English voices. Blessed cliffs, heavenly food, heavenly baths, heavenly clean, cool sheets; oh bed! how good after 49 hours continuous travelling.
England: yes, there is no place like HOME!!!

The Néry Gun

'Well, war has been declared as you see and we are very busy mobilizing', wrote Lieutenant John Campbell to his 'dearest Mama' in early August 1914. 'I do not know when they propose that we should cross over. I suppose they will keep it fairly quiet. I am afraid I shall not be able to see you all before we go and possibly it is better so for us. Goodbyes are very harrowing so do not try and come and see me. You will understand what I mean. You must all keep cheerful for my sake and it will not be very long before I am back again, at least the general opinion is that it will not be a long show.'

The writer was a regular officer aged thirty, son of Mr and Mrs J.D. Campbell of Tiverton, Devon. He had been in the Army since 1901. When war broke out he was attached to L Battery, Royal Horse Artillery, stationed at Aldershot. On Sunday 16 August the battery left for the continent:

Here we are at sea. My dear I do not think I have ever spent three such awful hours getting the horses on board and in their places. The heat was intense, however everything got on board eventually and here we are. It is beautifully calm thank goodness and the horses are behaving very well and not kicking themselves to death. I have not the vaguest idea whereabouts our destination is when we go up to the Front and of course could not tell you if I did know. We are all in the best of spirits and very cheery and all hoping for the best.

The Campbells were to receive only two more communications from their son. One was a plain postcard for which – the writer having no stamp available – they were charged one penny (postage due). The kernel of his message was: 'We are having a good time as it is gloriously fine. No rain at all so far. Everyone is most kind and gives us all sorts of food and smokes.' His final message, signed 'Jack' as were all his letters home, was a 'Field Service Post Card' postmarked 13 September. He had in fact sent

it on 30 August and two days after doing so – almost a fortnight before it was datestamped – Campbell was dead. He had fallen in one of the earliest 'glorious' actions of the war, at Néry, near Compiègne.

It took place during the so-called 'Retreat from Mons' – though to those who survived that necessary but exhausting movement of forces they did not 'retreat' they 'fell back', and by 1 September they had been falling back through Belgium and northern France for six days. L Battery was part of the rearguard, its function being to keep the advancing Germans at bay at all costs, so that the bulk of the British Expeditionary Force should continue its march unimpeded. On 31 August the battery had halted overnight at the tiny village of Néry with the rest of the 1st Cavalry Brigade. However at 4 am on 1 September the German 4th Cavalry Division appeared out of the dawn and mounted a surprise attack. The British artillerymen managed to get three of the battery's six guns into action, but two were hit almost at once. The remaining gun continued to fire until only the Battery Sergeant Major and one wounded Sergeant were left to serve it and the ammunition was used up. Nevertheless three German guns were disabled and the timely arrival of reinforcements forced the Germans to withdraw.

The cost was high; twenty-three of the officers and men of L Battery were killed and thirty-one wounded. Subsequently three Victoria Crosses were awarded, one *Légion d'Honneur* and two *Médailles Militaires*. Lieutenant Campbell was not among those so honoured. His family had to be content with the information, which they formally received in November 1915, that their son had been mentioned in despatches by the British Commander-in-Chief, Sir John French, and with such glowing newspaper reports as the following, faithfully preserved: 'Lieutenant John Campbell passed to and fro through the sheet of bullets carrying shell after shell to feed the gun. He did all the work he could possibly do, for this brave man was killed just as he handed the last shell to the gunner.' One other report stated: 'The officers played the part of true British gentlemen and worked their guns themselves unto the last.'

The gun which he and his comrades served (pictured above) is now part of the Imperial War Museum's permanent collection. With his letters – also held by the Museum – are a handful of faded photographs sent to the family soon after the action which show the scene of the encounter and the graves of the three officers of the battery who lost their lives. Each grave has a wooden cross finely inscribed with the name and rank of the officer and is draped with both the Union Jack and the French tricolour.

Postcard from
Cyril Bower's papers
celebrating
HMS *Laforey*'s
successes in 1914-15;
she did not survive
the war, however,
being sunk by a mine
in the English
Channel in 1917
(HU 59424)

Laforey
was a three-funnel
version of the L class
destroyer.
Basic statistics:
displacement 1000 tons;
top speed 29-31 knots;
armament three
4-inch guns, one
2-pounder and
four torpedo tubes;
complement 77

A First Strike at Sea

'Re my personal feelings, I must say that on Thursday night the anticipation of the morning made me feel a bit nervous, but while under fire I felt perfectly quiet and happy, one's only idea being to hit the enemy, which I can assure you we did with much success.'

Sub-Lieutenant Cyril Bower RN was among the earliest to face the prospect of being in combat in the Great War. He took part in the action known as the Battle of the Heligoland Bight on Friday 28 August 1914 and wrote the above in the long account he sent to his mother immediately afterwards. The battle came about because the enemy had shown no signs of challenging Jellicoe's Grand Fleet as it swept up and down the North Sea, so the Admiralty had despatched a force under Vice-Admiral Sir David Beatty to attack the light naval forces which regularly patrolled near the island of Heligoland off the German North Sea coast. It was an action in which audacity and decisiveness compensated for inexperience and it badly shook the German Navy, whose surface ships thereafter followed a policy of avoiding rather than inviting a contest. Bower was in the torpedo boat destroyer *Laforey*, which, with her sister ships *Laurel*, *Liberty* and *Laertes*, was heavily involved; the last two had casualties while everyone was wiped out on *Laurel*'s bridge. But British losses were light in comparison with the enemy's; the Germans lost three light cruisers and a destroyer and three other cruisers were badly damaged. No British ship was sunk and British casualties were as few as thirty-five killed and forty wounded. The action began at 7.30 am. *Laforey* and her sister ships went for the German destroyers and almost immediately opened fire:

Shells then started to drop around us. Soon we sighted two of their cruisers, and later on we were within range of the Heligoland Forts, so you can just imagine the state of affairs then. It is an absolute mystery to me why we weren't hit, for there was shrapnel bursting in the air and enormous white splashes all round us. As a matter of fact a big splinter from a shell went through an iron ventilator about four feet from where I was standing. I sunk one German torpedo boat with my own gun. The poor little boat (she was only about 300 tons) was making a desperate attempt to reach Heligoland, but we got three or four shells right into her, one blew the entire bridge off, the other got the boilers. Having practically finished the two cruisers, the destroyers hauled off and I thought that was the end of it, not a bit of it though, back we went and soon saw a large three-funnelled cruiser the *Mainz*, who put up a magnificent fight. Her shells were dropping, some of them just twenty yards short and others twenty yards over us, in fact I got drenched by the spray from one of them. Heaps of times we heard the buzzing of a shell just above our heads. It was most marvellous! I'm afraid she hit three of our boats and the *Arethusa*, a brand new ship, was very nearly disabled.

We were finally out of action at about 12.45 p.m., having been under a very heavy fire for nearly five hours. I was on deck from midnight Thursday till 3.0 p.m. on Saturday and only got two small sandwiches to eat the whole of Friday.

It was so glorious to get into harbour and talk it all over with the other 'subs' etc. We went round the other ships and examined the shell holes and bits of shells etc. There was great enthusiasm.

But the battle had its sombre side, too, as he duly reported: 'The *Lurcher* went alongside the *Mainz* just before she sank and took off 240 men many of whom were terribly wounded. Isn't it awful, civilised nations fighting with this appalling carnage? I wonder how long Germany is going to stick it.' However, there was no denying that the outcome was a cause for celebration, and for gratitude: 'We have been congratulated from all branches of the service, and I think it is a case for offering great thanks to Almighty God for the great victory.'

Members of the Liverpool Scottish
who are prepared
to go Anywhere, or do Anything
the War Office may ask.

R. A. Scott Macfie: Veteran Territorial

The Liverpool Scottish, September 1914. Top: The Battalion and (bottom) 'E' Company (HU 57196, HU 57197)

Robert Scott Macfie, aged forty-six, former Colour-Quartermaster-Sergeant of the 10th Battalion King's Liverpool Regiment – generally known as the Liverpool Scottish – rejoined his old unit on the first day of mobilization in August 1914. An ex-public schoolboy (Oundle), an MA of Cambridge and a BSc of Edinburgh, he was the Chairman of Macfie and Sons Ltd (which he proudly claimed as 'probably the oldest sugar-refining firm in the world'), and he was also an expert on gypsy lore and the author of several small books. Yet throughout the war he resolutely refused to apply for a commission, preferring to remain in the ranks where he felt he could play a more effective role in supporting and steadying his men. He felt no servility in 'sirring' his nominal superiors, and in his letters he was ready where necessary to criticize anyone in authority up to and including his divisional general (see page 61).

Since the Liverpool Scottish was a territorial battalion its prime obligation was home defence, but in the circumstances of the time, with the Germans marching through Belgium and the British Expeditionary Force despatched to help confront them, it was obvious that Britain needed men ready to fight wherever the need arose. To begin with Macfie found a 'miserable response' (as he put it in a letter home) to the request for volunteers for overseas service, but as time went by more men came forward until the necessary number was achieved. Despondency could now give way to the kind of satisfaction that produced the proud caption on the first of the two photographs shown here, and the cheerful resolution of the men in the second – soldiers of Macfie's 'E' Company, to which he was now attached with his former rank restored.

Macfie had no illusions as to the nature of what lay ahead. 'It is horrible,' he wrote, 'to think of all the suffering which may follow our mobilization: I suppose the less one thinks of it the better – but at 46 one can't quite forget these things.' Yet he knew where his duty lay, and in a letter of 1 September he wrote warmly of one recruit who had come forward as though he were rejoicing over a repentant sinner:

I have one member who did not intend to volunteer for foreign service, but when appealed to agreed to go. He was an only son, and his parents heard from somebody else that he had volunteered and sent a long telegram forbidding him to go abroad. He came to me almost crying and withdrew his name. Then he wrote to his parents and said he felt like a coward and that he hoped they would not write to him for a long time. Last night we had another telegram from his mother. 'It is we who are the cowards, you must go' – so he came to me again, almost crying and said that it was the best news he had ever heard in his life. This is the sort of fellows we have in E Company and I'm very proud of them.

Preparing for war was not easy, however, and when the news came through that they were to be posted overseas Macfie was frank about the battalion's shortcomings. He wrote on 27 October:

Today we have been instructed to hold ourselves in readiness to go abroad on Friday, Oct 30. Not being anywhere near ready the message is rather sarcastic: we have damaged rifles, many men are short of clothing and equipment. Head Quarters is in confusion, lots of us are recruits, and the rest are imperfectly trained. I never saw so incompetent a set of officers or such a pathetic waste of good material.

Macfie was not impressed by the conditions on board ship when at last, two days behind their original schedule, they sailed for France. The boat was 'most comfortably fitted for horses,' but without any provisions for men' so that his soldiers found themselves 'packed tighter than proverbial sardines'. Twelve hours after leaving England they were still 'slowly describing circles outside Havre.' The train journey that followed 'in so-called cattle trucks' (normal loading eight horses or forty men) was equally long drawn out, but 'amusing':

At the stations the inhabitants assembled to chat and distribute tea, coffee, apples, candles, cigarettes, picture-postcards etc, and occasionally we made dashes into small towns to get drinks or omelettes, being received everywhere with absurd enthusiasm.

The war was near, but not too near, and the battalion was rapidly making up for wasted time:

We are at last beginning the training we should have begun three months ago, and it is profoundly interesting. But we are so comfortable and happy that it is more like a picnic than work, and even the boom of the distant guns scarcely reminds us that anything unpleasant is going on.

After their first experience of digging practice trenches, he wrote (15 November): 'They are not at all what I imagined them and in hot weather must be most uncomfortable. I expect the scientific Germans will put in hot water radiators before the cold weather comes.'

For Macfie and the Liverpool Scottish, however, the light-hearted early days of active service were soon over. On 16 November he wrote that they had moved to 'a little village where are the remnants of several regiments which have been almost wiped out'. The weather had now broken and the farm where they were billeted was 'a sea of mud, ankle deep, and the roads are like rivers with yellow soup'. They were not in France but in Belgium, in fact – though he could not tell his family precisely because of the rules of military censorship – in the neighbourhood of Ypres. 'Tomorrow', he wrote, 'we go to the trenches.'

A Camera Goes to War: The 2nd Scots Guards

FROM THE CAMERA OF CHRISTOPHER PILKINGTON

In July 1930 Christopher Pilkington, Fellow of the Royal Geographical Society, a distinguished Far Eastern traveller and a popular lecturer (under such stirring titles as 'From Fleet Street to the Far East', 'Cycling in the Tropics' or 'Chippings from China'), responded to a letter to *The Times* by the then Director of the Imperial War Museum appealing for photographic or other material relating to the Great War. 'I have a considerable number of snapshots taken in the neighbourhood of Ypres, etc,' he wrote. 'I was attached by invitation to the 2nd Scots Guards and spent nearly six months with them in the 7th Division. I don't know whether any would be of interest to you but I shall be pleased to let you "look see".'

As a result of that reply the Museum acquired one of its most notable private collections and one which graphically illuminates the important period in which the campaign of movement with which the war began mutated into the battle of the trenches which was to continue for most of the following four years. Pilkington, a professional photographer at the time, was officially a Sergeant of the Artists' Rifles in 1914 but he was released at the request of the 2nd Scots Guards and he chronicled their progress almost daily as they completed their training in England, crossed to Belgium, landing at Zeebrugge on 7 October, dug their first trenches near Ghent and then were drawn into the series of fierce attacks and counter-attacks which were to become known as the First Battle of Ypres. Finally he was with them as they settled into more permanent trenches in the area between Armentières and La Bassée where they spent the winter of 1914-15.

From the diary which he wrote throughout his months at the front (also deposited in the Museum) it is clear that he worked hard and enthusiastically and was prepared to take considerable risks to carry out his assignment. But he was rarely near enough to give any clear impression of the reality of action. However, by relating his diary notes and the captions provided in the Museum's albums to his pictures, it is frequently possible to read into what he modestly called his 'snapshots' more than is conveyed by their mere surface image. In effect, the following photographs (apart from the first, chosen as a rare picture of men under fire) present a storyboard of the 'blooding' of a top battalion.

Left: First Battle of Ypres. Men of the Oxford and Bucks Light Infantry sheltering from shrapnel behind the Headquarters of the 20th Brigade, 7th Division, near Ypres, October 1914 (Q 57205)

From Pilkington's diary:

'On Sunday Oct 4 a sudden order came to move for an unknown destination and the same evening about nine with half the battalion I marched out of the camp for a nine mile journey to Southampton and embarked on the transport *Lake Michigan*. Monday Oct 5. The noise and crowding on the transport was awful. Wednesday Oct 7. Woke up to find ourselves at the quay at Zeebrugge.'

Below: Men of the 2nd Scots Guards and 2nd Royal Scots Fusiliers in SS *Lake Michigan* 6 October 1914 (Q 57123). **Right: Joke played by fellow-officers on the Quartermaster who was caught asleep on board the SS *Lake Michigan* whilst crossing the Channel, 6 October 1914** (Q 57128).

Above left: 2nd Scots Guards entrenching near Ghent, 9 October (Q 57170)

'Sat Oct 10. Spent the day going round the trenches and gave what assistance I could cutting barbed wire etc. for entanglements. An attack was expected at any moment. We did hear once a few shots on our right and heavy guns booming in the extreme distance.'

Above right: The 2nd Scots Guards nearing Ypres after marching from Roulers, 14 October 1914 (Q 57189)

'Left Roulers about 8 a.m. It was fine at first but very soon down came the rain again even worse than yesterday. It ceased before arriving at our destination in the afternoon in the environs of Ypres. The transport turned off before entering the town and we billeted in the grounds of a large chateau.'

Below: First Battle of Ypres, 1914. 2nd Scots Guards leading the reconnaissance in force towards Gheluvelt, 20 October 1914 (Q 57222)

'Tuesday Oct 20. A recce in force took place this day towards Menin. I went on and joined our fellows who were the advanced line and stayed until this was over and the order to retire was given. When returning I came across the body of Drummer Steer.'

Above: First Battle of Ypres, 1914. Roll call of the 2nd Scots Guards on the Ypres-Menin Road, 27 October 1914. Twelve officers and 460 men answered (Q 57240)

'Tuesday Oct 27. I found I was wanted to take if possible Major Fraser's grave [killed 26 October, when, states Pilkington, 'the battalion had again been badly hit']. On my way I came upon a muster of all that was supposed to be left of the Battalion. I could not get into Gheluvelt as the shells were uncomfortably near. I was here informed that it would be quite impossible to reach Major Fraser's grave. As a rule I do not take "impossible" without being absolutely sure.'

Below: Funeral of a private of the 2nd Scots Guards (Q 57393)

There are no diary notes relating to this photograph, but its caption indicates that the dead soldier was being taken to the cemetery at Estaires in December 1914; ie the battalion was now in its entrenched position in the British line between Armentières and La Bassée which it would occupy on and off for many months to come. Pilkington would leave it there when he returned to England in January 1915.

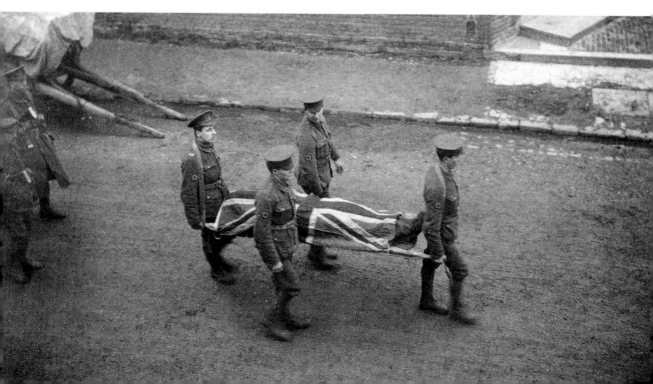

The First Campaigns:
A German View

F.L. Cassel, who had witnessed the mood of the Berlin crowds as Germany went to war (see page 20), knew what his next step had to be. He belonged to the 2nd Reserve and he was under orders to report to Darmstadt – his home town – on the seventh day of mobilization. In fact he set off much earlier:

I arrived in Darmstadt and had now still a few days to prepare myself for the life of a recruit, as I had not served in the Army before. On the seventh day I arrived, notorious carton box under my arm for returning civilian clothes, 'with clean body, washed', only to be dismissed with the request to return next day. This repeated itself several times. Then came the introduction – a medical examination at the Alexandertstrasse Barracks. 'Are you healthy?' 'Yes.' 'Able-bodied! Infantry!' That was the medical examination.

After four weeks we had to make room in the barracks for the next levy. At the beginning of September we left Darmstadt for further training as 1st Reserve Battalion Infantry Regiment 116 in Rheinhessen. Bouquet on top of the rifle, we left the barracks with the band playing. We came into a small village, Sprendlingen, and were quartered with farmers who looked very well after us with food and drink. Our new training consisted mainly in marching and rifle service. We were not really soldiers enough to be more than cannon fodder.

They moved to Strasbourg where they were transformed into the Reserve Battalion to Infantry Regiment 143. Then in October there was a further reorganization: 'we were pulled apart and allocated to various units according to the losses they had suffered'.

The Kaiser had boasted that his armies would be back before the falling of the leaves. 'But the leaves were already wilting. No talk of going home!'

No talk of rest either! For days we marched, first westwards towards St. Quentin, then Ham, then northwards uncertain where to. Day and night, often ten and fifteen hours. Not we alone. On all roads bodies of troops of all arms rolled on. A whole army was regrouped and thrown towards the right wing, where in those days the notorious running match towards the sea had begun and the fight for Ypern.

'Ypern' was Ypres, where the Scots Guards had had their first encounter with the enemy. Cassel's unit arrived in November, as the Germans continued their desperate attempts, begun on 17 October, to fight through to the Channel coast and the British and French as desperately fought to stop them. On the seventh day of their march Cassel and his comrades paraded in front of the Corps Commander, General von Deimling, in Douai. Next night they camped in a village which had just been taken and was completely destroyed. On the following night they found themselves for the first time under fire:

We were moved over dark meadows in zigzag, partly in open formation, then across bridges and through hedges, without seeing more than the man in front of you. We heard overhead the buzzing and whizzing of shells and shrapnel and nearby the hissing and whizzing of rifle projectiles and far behind the explosion of grenades. There was uninterrupted rifle and machine-gun fire, a few star shells already – later the regular accompaniment of trench warfare. One comrade from Darmstadt disappeared that night and was not sighted again. Another got shrapnel in his buttocks and saw Darmstadt again very soon. Eventually we stopped behind a hedge and were ordered to dig in.

German infantry on the march, 1914 (Q 56791)

But Cassel had not yet been sent into action:

My platoon was reserve so we were not required for several days, until came that notorious day, the 11th of November*, the day of the 'young regiments', announced by an Order of the Corps, which ordered the breakthrough and the conquest of Ypern. We had already heard during the morning that our Company C.O. had fallen. In the afternoon we were ordered to attack. Roaring din of artillery fire, smoke, stink in the air. We advanced in zig-zag through trenches hardly a foot deep, past English soldiers who were lying terribly mutilated amongst our own comrades, with bayonets fixed. Out of the trenches, across meadows towards a hill with a little forest – the notorious 'Hill 60' – without looking back, without seeing anything, without thinking anything but 'Forwards'. I cannot remember to have had any feeling of fear, once we had started to move.

Eventually I found myself in a little wood, at an alley crossing it, in front of me a clearing with some barns, from which machine gun fire came. I threw myself on the ground and started firing my rifle in the direction of the machine guns. Then I felt a strike on my hand, blood runs hot down from it, the rifle falls down. Wounded, but the thumb is there! I dress myself with an emergency dressing and think of retreat. Around me some have become silent, others cry and ask for help. I reach the alley and push myself creeping across it. There are shots sideways through the alley. I see people running, they appear to be French soldiers, who advance again. While crossing the alley I feel another strike, this time in my thigh. Got again! I manage to reach the thicket, I feel my leg, it runs hot down it, no pain, the bone is healthy. I let fall everything, knapsack, coat, breadsack, to get away quicker. I have reached the edge of the wood, 100 metres further is a German line. As if the grenades and machine guns could not do any harm to me, I ran right up to it.

Cassel recovered from his wounds and was later to find himself in Picardy in 1916 during the Battle of the Somme.

*Cassel wrote '12 November', but the day when the Germans attacked Hill 60 was the previous day, 11 November: 'a date of prophetic symbolism', Liddell Hart subsequently called it, since it represented the final turning-point of the 1st Battle of Ypres and was the date of the Armistice in 1918.

**Enlistment: Volunteers
with a recruiting sergeant
(Q 30072)**

Kitchener's Men

On 10 September 1914 the British Prime Minister, H.H. Asquith, reported to Parliament: 'We have been recruiting during the last ten days every day substantially the same number of recruits as in past years have been recruited every year'. The total figure he quoted in his speech was 'practically 439,900'; eventually a further 2,500,000 would follow this first wave of volunteers in offering to bear arms for King and Country. Some of these men would find themselves at the front sooner than they expected as replacements in Regular or Territorial units which had suffered heavily in action. The vast majority, however, became members of the so-called 'new armies', which were also often known collectively as 'Kitchener's Army'; in other words, they were 'Kitchener's men'.

These photographs show volunteers going through the process of transformation from civilian to soldier. The first is notable for the social mix of the recruits. In a group of half a dozen can be seen at least three classes, each identified by appropriate head-gear; the cloth-cap of the working-man, the straw-boater of the 'gent' or 'toff', the trilby of the man of business or professional man. (See page 241 for a similar mix in the propagandist film cartoon *Britain's Effort*.) There is also a typical range of ages. The original requirement in August had been for men between nineteen and thirty; on 11 September 1914 the age limit was raised to thirty-five. The youth at the front appears to be very near the lower limit, the (?) business man in the trilby near if not past the higher one, but then the age-limit was frequently breached through the patriotic complicity of enthusiastic applicants and 'blind-eyed' recruiting sergeants.

The second photograph shows men putting on soldiers' khaki. Many recruits, however, trained at first in their own clothes or in any uniforms that could be found; one new battalion of the Devonshire Regiment even briefly used the traditional redcoats of the British Army of Wellington and the Crimea.

Enlistment: Recruits putting on uniform
(Q 30061)

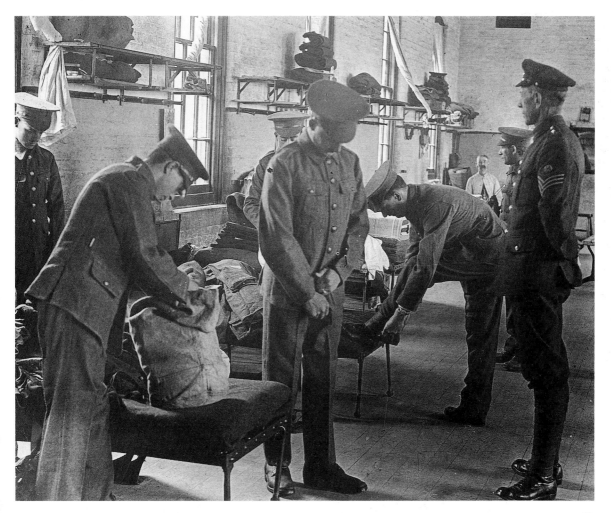

Bernard Britland from Marple, Cheshire, was an enthusiastic Kitchener volunteer, typical of many thousands who answered the nation's call in 1914. Cheerful, optimistic, always making light of difficulties, he joined the colours as S7532 Rifleman Britland, C Company, 8th Service Battalion, the Rifle Brigade. Short but athletic, he was an outstanding cross-country runner, winning numerous medals during his period of training. Proving an excellent shot with the rifle, he was picked out as a likely sniper, tempering his pride in being chosen for that key role with assurances that he would be in no greater danger when he reached the front than any other of his comrades. The following extract from a letter written to his family in January 1915 from his camp at Hindhead, Surrey, not only shows a soldier fully contented with his new life but gives a lively and detailed description of its daily routines:

We are doing champion here. We get up at 6.30 then we have to roll our beds up, fold our blankets neatly, then fold our greatcoats up. We are sleeping on a soft mattress on the floor and we have three good blankets so we are quite comfortable and warm. We roll the mattress up and then tie it up with a piece of rope. We have to put our kitbags on the back of the bed and we haven't to leave anything lying about. It looks quite neat I can tell you when we have straightened up.

At 7.15 we have the first parade but before that we have a cup of tea and two biscuits. At 8.0 we have breakfast. On the first parade it is mostly marching about the field and doubling to keep us warm. After breakfast we have to shave and tidy ourselves up for the next parade at 9.0. From then until 12.30 we are kept hard at it. Company drill first, then Swedish drill, then company drill again. We have a short interval between each so it is not so bad. We have dinner about 1.0 and then on parade about 2.0 till 4.30, tea at 4.45 and then a lecture at 5.30 till 6.30. After that we are free for the night. We have to be in by 8.30, lights out at 9.15, so you can see we are fully occupied.

The Sergeant Major was so set up with the progress we made that he served twenty-five rifles out to the smartest of us. I was one of the twenty-five so you can bet I didn't half feel proud of myself. The draft that was here before us were two or three weeks before they got their rifles and we had them in three days so that is something to be proud of isn't it? I was drilling with the rifle yesterday, it made it a lot more interesting.

Today (Sat) I was orderly man for our room so I did not have to do any parades. I was busy helping to serve breakfast, then we had to wash all the pots up, scrub the tables, sweep all the rooms and tidy up generally. This morning we were inoculated for enteric fever. My arm has become stiff and swollen since and just before dinner I felt a bit seedy but after I had had my dinner I felt a lot better but my arm is still sore. Some of the fellows have been ill with it, couldn't hold up but I haven't been like that.

We are being well fed here. This morning we had a tin of sardines each for breakfast and we have half a pound of bread for breakfast and the same amount for tea. For dinner we generally have potatoes, haricot beans, roast meat, stewed meat, cabbage and green peas so there is plenty of variety. Will you please send me one pair of running knickers, two pairs of slips and if you can a small mirror? If you have any old toothbrushes send one or two as they come in very handy for cleaning our rifles.

Like the majority of his fellow-volunteers, Britland was eager to go to France to take on the enemy – that, after all, had been their purpose in enlisting. Typically when the time came he wrote, in a letter to his sister Pollie: 'Above all things don't worry about me but trust to providence.'

Rifleman Bernard Britland to his mother, 14 February 1915:

I had my Photo taken yesterday (Sat) and I am sending three of them home. I only had 6 taken as I did not know how they would turn out. I was taken at 5.0 and they were ready by 7.45 so you can see it was sharp work. They only cost 1/- for the half dozen. In the photo my face looks white but that is with the glow of the electric light. At the present my face is very brown. You will notice we haven't got brass buttons, the Rifle Brigade doesn't wear them. Our buttons are brown with a horn or a crown on them. They look smart I can tell you, on the khaki. You must let me know how you like me in my uniform. We have not got belts yet so the tunics look something short. You will see from Pollie's letter that we have had it a bit rough this week but it has done me no harm. It is surprising what we can stand. (HU 59425)

PART II
The Western Front

'WHATEVER happens we are far better off than the unfortunate fellows in the trenches who must be having a hell of a time.' This comment, by a submariner, Lieutenant Ronald Trevor RN, was written in only the fourth month of the war – on 9 November 1914. It shows how early it was that people elsewhere took notice that there was something particularly grim and inhuman about the pattern of warfare developing just across the Channel in France and Belgium. The concept of 'the trenches' was indeed to become firmly fixed on the general imagination, where it would remain indefinitely as the standard image and symbol of the Great War. And, it might be added, it has found a useful application in other conflicts since; 'trench warfare' and 'entrenched positions' have become cliché phrases brought out to define any dispute not easy to resolve, from a personal impasse to major controversies of national or international politics.

The reality behind those phrases is the subject of this second part of the book. From the end of the First Battle of Ypres in November 1914 until the break-out in the summer of 1918 the Western Front (as it soon came to be known) was a vast military log-jam extending from the Belgian coast to the Swiss border. The trench-lines moved from time to time as efforts of varying intensity were made to gain territorial advantage, but basically the Front was constant for most of four years. Such advances as there were rarely altered the trench maps by anything more than a matter of a few miles at most. Almost every action resulted in huge casualties.

Space voyagers who have observed the Great Wall of China, and (a more transient phenomenon than was once thought) the Berlin Wall, would undoubtedly have been able to spot the Western Front, though they might also have been surprised by its narrowness. Soldiers withdrawing a mere matter of ten miles or so from it would find themselves in a world where, to all intents and purposes, the war had never been. Inside the trench-zone, however, the kind of experience on hand could mark a man for life if it did not actually kill or maim him.

The accepted wisdom after decades of argument is that this was probably the only theatre of war in which a result could be achieved. Certainly it was here that in the end the conflict *was* won. The fear that there might be a return to the Western Front style of warfare dominated attitudes in the years that followed and was a central element in the determination of strategy – on both sides – in the Second World War.

This part of the book therefore contains sections on such subjects as life in the trenches, on No Man's Land (the inevitable consequence of trench warfare – and a phrase promoted to similar general use by the Western Front), the power of artillery, the impact of gas, and the role of that remarkable military newcomer, the tank. There is also a section on the experience of action, though not on any one of the famous set-piece battles which took place here – too large in sheer scale to be included in a general book of this nature. As elsewhere there are personal stories, about some who survived and some who did not – among the former a talented soldier-artist whose work also appears in the colour section. Finally there is a short pictorial feature on the American involvement on the Western Front in 1918.

Lancashire Fusiliers in a front-line trench opposite Messines, January 1917 (Q 4650)

The Western Front **Important Dates**

1915	(1914 dates in Part I, 1918 dates in Part VIII)
March 10-13	Battle of Neuve Chapelle
April 22-May 5	Second Battle of Ypres; first use of poison gas by Germans
9	Allied offensive in Artois; Battle of Aubers Ridge
14	Battle of Festubert
September 25	Allied offensive in Artois and Champagne; first use of poison gas by British at the Battle of Loos
December 19	Sir Douglas Haig replaces Sir John French as Commander-in-Chief of the British Expeditionary Force
1916	
February 21-August 31	Battle of Verdun
July 1-November 18	Battle of the Somme
September 15	First use of tanks at Flers-Courcelette, Somme front
1917	
April 9-May 4	Battle of Arras
April 6	Opening of disastrous Nivelle offensive on the Aisne
May	French Army mutinies
June 7	Battle of Messines begins
25	First Americans in France
July 31-November 10	Third Battle of Ypres (Passchendaele)
November 6	Canadians capture Passchendaele
November 20-7 December	Battle of Cambrai

Trench World

At times the great bombardments of the Western Front were audible in southern England. Nearer at hand they were not only audible but visible, like vast firework displays towards which those bound for the trenches were compulsively drawn. At night searchlights, Very lights (flares fired from pistols, named after their nineteenth-century inventor, Edward W. Very) and streams of tracer bullets added to the multi-coloured flashes from the artillery. Such displays were not constant. There were many quiet times when the trenches were masked in impenetrable darkness; there were other occasions which evoked the standard description, quoted verbally or in letters home, that it was a case of 'all hell let loose'.

Private Alfred Thomas, B Company, 2/4th Battalion, Oxfordshire and Buckinghamshire Light Infantry, illustrated his neat handwritten account of his months in France in 1918 with a whole range of precise documentary drawings, among them – even though his medium was pen and ink with no colour – images which capture aspects of the front at night in a manner scarcely available to the camera.

Thomas captioned the drawing opposite: 'The fatigue party at the artillery dugouts at Laventie. A Very light sailing.' It conveys the impact of the front as seen from just behind the lines. In the drawing on page 9 Thomas records the experience which would eventually bring the infantryman to within, literally, shooting distance of his enemy: 'The battalion going up into the line. Here the men march in single file, with eyes and ears straining in the intense gloom of the night, for a sudden burst of machine gun fire or the whining of an approaching shell and the tension is only relieved by the arrival into the line.'

The photographs cover various other aspects of trench life. Inevitably official photographers were rarely present at moments of danger, but when they convey a sense of doldrum, of wearisome and frustrated hanging about (eg see page 46), they are doing invaluable work – if not for the propaganda purposes they were meant to serve, at least for history. For the trench experience was by common consent roughly nine-tenths boredom and only one-tenth action. Yet tension is present nevertheless. The photograph on page 51 was taken in a lull during the battle popularly known as Passchendaele. The picture on page 52, showing British troops observing from a trench near Thiepval, becomes much more interesting when one realizes that it dates from a long-awaited moment in the Battle of the Somme when the British at last captured the village of Thiepval, which had been a target for the first morning's attack on 1 July 1916. Similarly the Canadian photograph, if its caption is accurate, shows men steeling themselves for a bombing raid on the enemy lines – an operation which traditionally produced many casualties in the attacking force.

Conditions in the trenches and the routines and risks of trench life were much discussed in soldiers' letters and diaries at the time and have been a rich source of reminiscence, and of heroic or anti-heroic polemic, ever since. The following extracts have been chosen because they have the virtue of immediacy and vividness and are concerned only with factual description.

The first was written by Captain J. I. Cohen, 1st Battalion, East Lancashire Regiment, soon after arriving in the line, to a friend who would shortly be following in his footsteps; it is in effect a brief introductory guide to trenches and trench techniques, 1915-style. 'I am afraid it is terrible shop,' Cohen apologized to his fellow-officer (writing on 9 March that year), adding however: 'In the possible case of your finding this useful, well and good.'*

My regiment is just east of Ploegsteert, which is in the southernmost corner of Belgium – in fact France is on three sides of us as we look around.

Instead of having an area divided between ourselves and another regiment, and going in and out of the trenches as a unit, we have a line of trenches belonging to ourselves only, and we have two companies at one time for three days in, the others spending their three days in support (half a mile behind) and in billets (four or five miles behind) respectively. Thus each company in turn does three days in, three days in support, three days in, and three days rest.

Our trouble of course is drainage. This horrible country is made of mud, water and dead Germans. Whenever water is left in a trench it drags the earth down on either side and forms a fearful sticky viscous matter that lets you sink gently down and grips you like a vice when you're there. The chief business is revetting and draining, and improving parapets and traverses. We use no loopholes in the ordinary sense, or overhead cover; there is not enough material, and loopholes are death traps if not properly masked. But at intervals snipers' loopholes with iron plates properly concealed and masked are put up. Cover is got by building 'bugwarms' or 'tamboos' i.e. dug-outs, behind the trench. Two walls of sandbags with a sheet of corrugated iron on top and an oil-sheet under it to make the whole waterproof.

The parapet to be bullet-proof should have two sandbags with brick between. The sides of the trench must be revetted with sandbags etc, if possible supported by stakes which are driven in the ground inside the trench and wired over on to pegs outside the trench. A sheet of iron or pieces of timber between the stakes and the sandbags is useful as a support. Sandbags must be evenly filled with solid earth – liquid mud is useless; and when put in position hammered well down and squared with a shovel or some flat instrument.

In front of the trench, wire; there is plenty of wire to be had. Make two tripods of wooden stakes roughly, and place another stake over the top of them, then wire heavily from end to end, up and down etc. This instrument can then be lifted properly into position or easily replaced if a shell knocks your wire about. Trip wires weighed down with sandbags are also used.

The bottom of the trench has planks running along it, otherwise progress is impossible. At intervals, 'sump-holes' the size of a coal scuttle are dug to receive the water which collects: thus baling is much easier. Finally every section of trench has a latrine dug out of the back of it.

The parapet should be a couple of feet higher than a man standing in a trench. A plank stand i.e. planks laid along sandbags, is put at the bottom inside the parapet, sufficiently high for a man to fire standing. One man in four or six goes on sentry at a time. He looks over the parapet occasionally to see how things are progressing and is rarely hit in that way. When his first relief comes in he does any baling that is necessary.

*Certain techniques would change in later years but basically Cohen's 'guide' would hold for most of the war. It should also be noted – re the photographs in this section – that steel helmets did not appear until late 1915 and were not standard until 1916.

Above left: Front-line
trenches were regularly
used by Artillery Forward
Observation Officers
whose function was to
identify likely targets and
convey the necessary
information back to their
battery. Here a Royal Field
Artillery officer is
observing from a trench
firestep; his linesman
stands by his side ready to
communicate his officer's
findings by field telephone.
Near Croisilles, south of
Arras, January 1918
(Q 10610)

Above: British troops
observing from a trench
near Thiepval, Somme
front, September 1916
(Q 1069)

Left: Troops of the 8th
Winnipeg Battalion
receiving bombing
instructions, June 1916
(CO 149)

Working parties are formed most of the night and in the day where possible to repair or rebuild damaged parts or make improvements. A party goes after dark to fetch rations, or a small party before light for the rum. It is also necessary to send parties out for ammunition material etc. in the dark. We 'stand to' directly it begins to be light and at such times when heavy firing and cheering etc make it probable that an attack is in progress somewhere.

We get our sleep not so much according to our inclination as when we are off work! It is impossible to do much work by day. The platoon commander carries out the company commander's general directions as to scheme of repairs etc in the trench: after that it depends on the platoon sgt if the work is properly done. He must be able to get every ounce of work out of his men. This is very important.

Second Lieutenant Cuthbert Aston, 1st Battalion, Bedfordshire Regiment, spent some weeks on the Western Front in 1915 before serving in Gallipoli and later in Mesopotamia. The following are extracts from a long letter he wrote to his mother:

We are now back at B---- at rest for eight days. I spent Sunday and Monday in the fire trenches, going in Saturday evening about seven. I was very lucky – in the whole six days in trenches I only lost one man and he wasn't badly hit.

It was fortunate that on Saturday night I had built up my trench and made the parapet very strong as on Monday afternoon and evening their snipers gave us no peace, but not a single bullet came through the parapet.

One goes up to trench and out of it above ground but there isn't much risk though the first time one's heart jumps a bit whenever bullets whiz by. The people who relieved me on Monday night had two men hit on the way up but I got my men down all serene. I was a bit nervous particularly as I rather wanted not having lost any so far to bring them all down intact so I was rather braced. One is under fire for about one mile back from the trenches.

The shells are really Hell there's no other word for it when they do hit men but only one out of twelve finds its billet but bullets one simply ignores. On Saturday night we were working the whole night – beautiful moonlight – outside and some in front of the trench but no one hit. I don't think more than two or three bullets came along.

The men are on the whole very good and some of the poor beggars coming home here on Monday night were perfect heroes the way they stuck it and kept up with the Company, their feet giving them Hell all the time and nine miles over beastly cobbles pretty well weighted with a pack etc is no mean walk. One poor beggar was staggering as he had been concussed that day by a shell which wounded three in a trench on my left.

Rifleman Bernard Britland (see page 44) first went to the trenches in June 1915. His letters home (until his capture two months later) are full of breezy down-to-earth accounts of aspects of his life as an ordinary infantryman.

First, after an early spell at the front (in the Ypres Salient):

We have had ten days in the trenches this time and it has been a very lively experience I can tell you. I am very thankful to be able to say that I am still safe and sound and without a scratch upon me. I am also in very good health. I am beginning to think I have no nerves at all for it never seems to bother me however near a shell bursts. I have gone through experiences this last ten days that before the war I should have been afraid to think about. We were in support trenches and there were an average between two and three hundred shells bursting within three hundred yards radius of our trenches every day. You can tell how little it worried me when I tell you I used to sleep nearly all day.

53

Second, an account of his experiences in a ration-carrying party:

One night we were pretty close together and a shell came so quick we had no time to get into the ditch, we simply dropped flat in the road. My pals and I were straight under it and as we looked up we could see the flash in the air as it exploded. It seemed to me it must have been the safest place we could have been in as there wasn't a piece dropped anywhere near us. It was shrapnel and they seem to spread more than anything else when they explode.

One night we had to go almost bent double, carrying biscuits in large tin boxes. You talk about sweating, it simply poured off us. The Germans had spotted us where the parapet was low and turned rapid fire on us. They simply wasted a lot of lead without hurting anybody.

Third, an episode when he was acting as a battalion runner, after important telephone wires had been put out of action by enemy shell-fire:

Our Colonel could not get messages through to Brigade Headquarters, so he sent urgent messages through to our officer to be sent down at once. The Headquarters was down in the town which I have mentioned in other letters [Ypres]. Our officer came and wakened me and told me to take the messages. I had to go across a cornfield as I left our trench, and whilst crossing this field I had to drop four times in about fifty yards whilst shells bursted. I got there safely and when I was coming back I got to a certain point on the road about one and a half miles from our trench when I could not get any further up the road, as the Germans were dropping shrapnel shells just over the road about every two seconds. I did not know what to do for about two or three minutes as I had a message to take back for our Colonel, so I got down in the ditch whilst the shells were bursting. At length I decided to go across the fields and I got back safe without another shell dropping anywhere near me.

I have written these experiences to let you see what the life is like out here, but for goodness sake don't let it worry you or else I shall be sorry I have written them. You will see from what I have written that I am learning how to take care of myself. I hope you are all improving in health, it sounds funny to hear of so many of you ailing. We are living under conditions which twelve months ago would have killed me and I never felt better in my life.

Second Lieutenant Norton Hughes-Hallett, 7th Battalion, King's Shropshire Light Infantry, served in France from September 1915 until July 1916, when he was badly wounded during the Battle of the Somme. The following are extracts from the long account of his experiences written while recuperating in St Thomas's Hospital, London. First, a note on trench noises:

Reports are continually stating that sounds of mining can be heard under such and such a bay. Well, if one lies flat and listens with an ear to the ground, every movement sounds like the tap-tap of picks below. But get a couple of experienced miners, elderly for preference, leave them there, and they'll soon tell you if there's anything. Tunnelling officers are frequently called up to the line to investigate noises; and the causes of those noises are sometimes rather curious. Rats burrowing is the commonest; flies in a pool of water; and all manner of weird and unexpected things. Of course, should one have any real doubt, the trench is cleared for fifty yards on either side, only leaving sentries. To test for mines (I mean the miners themselves, not the instruments used by the tunnelling companies) they stick a bayonet in the ground and grip it with their teeth. It is supposed to help the hearing. It certainly has the effect of making you imagine the whole German Army is digging under you!

Cold, like rain, mud and ice, was a particular enemy in the trenches. Troops coming out of a communication trench near Arras after a snowfall, February 1917 (Q 4695)

Second, a note on those invaluable, unsung heroes of the trenches, the sanitary men:

There is one of these men to each platoon. He must of course empty all latrines at night, which he does into shell-holes, and then fills the hole in; he spends most of the rest of his time walking round with a sprayer of creosol and chloride of lime, and sprinkles the trenches thoroughly and the surrounding ground, as much as possible. The actual vicinity is filthily foul, of course. These men are invaluable, and are usually elderly, dependable men, as they are excused most parades in camp, doing their own work by themselves.

After heavy fighting and particularly if that fighting coincided with bad weather, trench conditions could become virtually intolerable; sometimes, indeed, the word 'trench' was virtually a misnomer. Perhaps the most extreme case was the situation in late 1917 in the final Passchendaele stage of the Third Battle of Ypres. Weeks of attacks and counter-attacks in a period of exceptional rainfall had turned the battle ground into a morass. The following is from a recorded interview with Captain Ulick Burke MC, 2nd Battalion, Devonshire Regiment, who served as an infantry officer on the Western Front from 1914 until his capture during the German offensive of 1918.

There were no trenches at all at Passchendaele: only a series of shell holes which had been reinforced with sandbags so that you could hide your body.

If you wanted to do your daily job of urinating and otherwise there was an empty bully beef tin, and you had to do that in front of all your men, and then chuck the contents, but not the bully beef tin, out over the back.

Now you can imagine a man being in those trenches for a week, where he couldn't wash. He got a petrol tin of tea given him. Now those tins were baked, boiled, everything was done to them; but when you put a hot substance in you got petrol oozing from the tin. And that of course gave the men violent diarrhoea. But they had to drink it because it was the only hot drink they had.

The conditions were terrible. You can imagine the agony of a fellow standing for twenty four hours sometimes to his waist in mud, trying with a couple of bully beef tins to get the water out of a shell hole that had been converted to a trench with a few sandbags. And he had to stay there all day and all night for about six days. That was his existence.

Many men got trench feet and trench fever. With trench fever a fellow had a very high temperature, you could see he had. It wasn't dysentery but he had constant diarrhoea, it left him weak and listless. Trench feet was owing to the wet sogging through your boots. In many cases your toes nearly rotted off in your boots. We lost more that way than we did from wounds. Then again it was difficult getting them back through all this muck and sludge.

My job was to go round the sector once a night with the sergeant-major. When you left one trench you had to ask which way to go because you didn't know where the next one was. One night the people on our left were going to do a night attack and we were to give them heavy covering fire. It was to start at ten o'clock. About half past nine the order came through the attack was off. So I and my sergeant-major had to go round twenty-four front-line posts, in the dark and quickly, in case they started firing when there was nothing to fire at – and to put them in the picture because they would think the men had gone, disappeared, on the left. It was awful, awful. You didn't know whether you were going towards the enemy. At one time my sergeant-major was within about ten yards of the enemy when a Very light went up behind him. Because of the kind of Very light he knew damn well he was out in front. So he doubled back and suddenly found the post he was looking for.

Drawing by Private Alfred Thomas, Oxford and Bucks Light Infantry. His caption for it reads: 'No Man's Land. Between the lines in front of Nieppe Forest. The German line is dimly shown by the dark smudge of barbed wire [see artist's own asterisk extreme right]. A farm stands in No Man's Land. Shrapnel bursting over enemy line.'

Trenches and No Man's Land as seen from the air. Reconnaissance photograph of the trench system between Loos and Halluch, taken at 7.15 pm on 22 July 1917. The British lines are to the left, the German to the right; being a British photograph the German trenches are the prime subject. No Man's Land is the river-like black strip centre left. The trenches leading off the picture top right and centre right are communication trenches, which linked the firing and support lines with the safe area behind. The vertical line left presumably marks the course of an unused road or track which is incorporated into the British trench system at the top of the picture and goes straight through No Man's Land to the German trenches lower down. The whole area shown is pock-marked with shell craters (Q 45786)

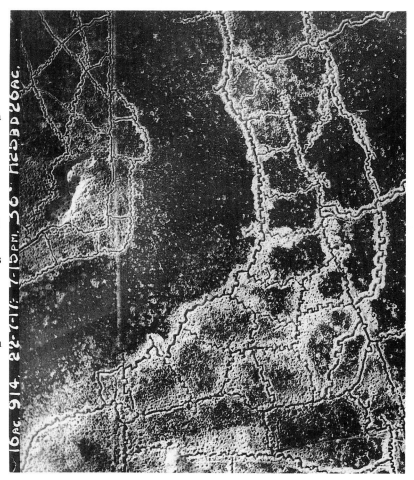

No Man's Land

The space between the trench lines on the Western Front – and in all theatres where the same situation applied – was given a memorable and chilling name: No Man's Land. In the Middle Ages, as 'nonesmannes-lond', the term defined disputed territory – an area over which there were legal disagreements. Later it was the specific name of a plot of ground lying outside the north wall of the city of London assigned as a place of execution. In the days of sail it was an area of deck containing blocks, ropes, tackle and other equipment that might be required on the forecastle. Towards the end of the nineteenth century it began to appear in a military context – sometimes in the variant of No Man's Territory. By the beginning of the 1914-18 war it had acquired the meaning which now dominates all others: the terrain between the front lines of opposing armies. From the beginning of entrenchment onwards it was in constant currency – usually, though not always, spelt with initial capital letters as though it were a precise location on a map, which in a sense it was, for most of four years.

Its width on the Western Front varied enormously; there could be half a mile between the trenches, or there could be as little as twenty yards, though these extremes were rare. Sometimes, particularly by day, it could be a place of stillness and silence; at night by contrast it was often an area of intense clandestine activity, as wiring parties worked to improve defences, patrols crawled out to reconnoitre, or, occasionally, raiding parties crept across to the enemy lines to launch their sudden vicious attacks. The object of these raids was to kill as many opponents as possible and – this was standard practice – to seize prisoners for interrogation and identification. It was considered of prime importance to know who your enemy was (a trench raid was almost mandatory when a new unit arrived in the opposing lines) and what were his likely intentions.

Inevitably No Man's Land fascinated people. The new arrival was curious to peer into it, photographers photographed it when the conditions were appropriate, artists made pictures or sculptures* about it, it was frequently described or referred to in letters or accounts.

On the British side, it should be added, No Man's Land did not officially exist. The doctrine of the offensive dictated that any ground short of the enemy's line should be considered to be British; in other words, the German wire was the British front line. Not all those who manned the trenches took so possessive a view – in fact there were many who saw this policy as pointless sabre rattling leading to unnecessary losses. A thoughtful and humane commanding officer, Lieutenant-Colonel A.P.B. Irwin, 8th Battalion, East Surrey Regiment, expressed his opinion on this contentious subject in a recorded interview in 1972:

*See colour section p.141: *No Man's Land*, by Charles Sargeant Jagger.

I think we were doing the right thing in dominating No Man's Land, which we set out to do always, and we were usually successful, but whether it achieved any good or not I don't know. We didn't lose many casualties – every day in the trenches somebody was killed by shell fire or machine gun fire; in proportion to that I don't think we increased those losses at all, but we did dominate No Man's Land, we had patrols out every night, and I think it gave the troops some confidence to be on top of the land instead of down in the trench.

Whatever the rights and wrongs of this nocturnal activity, it went on throughout the war – and on many occasions for sound military reasons, as is clear from the following description, from a letter to his family by Major D.C. Stephenson, Royal Field Artillery, written on 18 July 1916, during the Battle of the Somme:

I had a nasty experience yesterday. Another gunner officer and I, with one of my signallers, were reconnoitring to see a very difficult new trench the Germans have dug. We got a good long way out in what was then No Man's Land (of course the lines are altering all the time, according to our attacks) and suddenly got severely sniped at. The other officer got back safely, and my signaller and I started to crawl back. All of a sudden he got up for some reason and ran. He hadn't gone two steps before he spun round and fell, just in front of me. I plugged up his wound as well as I could, and then a very gallant infantryman came out, on his own, to help me dress him. This man raised his head for a moment while bandaging, and then fell, shot through head and helmet, on top

Official British photograph of an area of front and No Man's Land taken for intelligence purposes, one of many so-called 'Western Front Panoramas'. Taken from Molenaarschthock, direction Dadizeele Church to Jericho Pill Box, Ypres area. Undated, but probably late 1917 (Q 27030B)

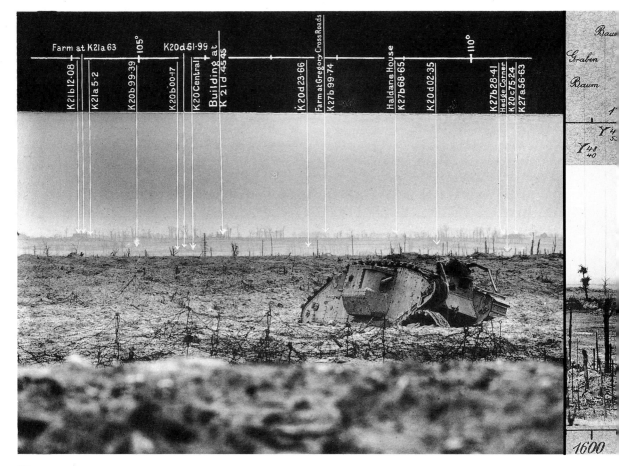

Official German intelligence photograph, showing German trenches (*Graben*) and 'enemy' trenches (*Feindliche Graben*). Ypres area, August 1915 (Q 47750)

of me. I knew he was dead, because his brains were out on my sleeve, but he didn't seem quite so. So there I had the two of them. I shouted to the other fellows to try and scratch a small trench out to us, but we got hold of a telephone wire and I tied it on to my poor signaller's legs, and they pulled him in, I supporting his head and keeping the pad on the wound. Then the wire broke, and these other two gunner officers crawled out and pulled him in by the ankles. He was plucky, 'cos it must have been awful for him. The poor infantryman who had come out to help was quite dead when I got back to him. The ground that had to be traversed like that was about 25 or 30 yards. You couldn't raise your head more than a very little. All that was done had to be done lying flat. I was very lucky. It was a real tight place. I am sorry to say the signaller died on the way to the dressing station.

No Man's Land was almost always a place of horror and desolation. The following is an extract from the diary of Father J.B. Marshall, Roman Catholic Chaplain to an infantry brigade in the 21st Division, written in July 1916, immediately after the opening of the Somme offensive:

I was told there were fellows out in No Man's land – in the old 'No Man's Land' before the attack of the morning had converted it into our land. There was one man who they did not propose to bring in because he was practically dead. So I determined to get over the parapet to see him. It was a terrible scene of devastation I looked at in the twilight – a ground churned up with shell holes, littered with broken wire, and a piteous array of dead bodies. He proved not to be a Catholic, but I spoke acts of love and contrition into his ear and then hurried back into the trench with undue precipitation and jumped upon a bayonet, which luckily only made a great rent in my breeches.

When the trench-lock was finally broken in 1918 and the armies moved eastwards, swathes of former No Man's Land were left behind in which, as it were, the archaeology of Western Front warfare could be studied. On 10 October 1918 Major P.H. Pilditch, Royal Field Artillery, bicycled with a fellow-officer to find the grave of a close friend who had been killed in October 1914. He noted in his diary:

On the way back we spent some time in the old No Man's Land of four years' duration, round about Fauquissart and Aubers. It was a morbid but intensely interesting occupation tracing the various battles among the hundreds of skulls, bones and remains scattered thickly about. The progress of our successive attacks could be clearly seen from the types of equipment on the skeletons, soft caps denoting the 1914 and early 1915, then respirators, then steel helmets marking attacks in 1916. Also Australian slouch hats, used in the costly and abortive attack in 1916. There were many of these poor remains all along the German wire.

However, even No Man's Land could have its less grim aspects. Private G.W. Durham, of the 3rd Canadian Division Cyclists, wrote in his diary in November 1916:

Many little things amuse us – such as the musical machine-gunner (Hun of course) who played tunes on his gun. He tried to play the *Maple Leaf* on his gun one night, we had tolerated him till then as a comedian but this was too much. We organized a raid and took his gun from him, and lest he should be blamed for neglect of duty, brought him with us. Then there is the trench cat, a strict neutral, we call him 'Wilson'* because we found him asleep on a haversack with a rat rifling the contents! 'Too proud to fight.' He walks across No Man's Land at will and knows the meal times on both sides.

*After the American President, Woodrow Wilson; the United States at this stage was still maintaining her attitude of benevolent neutrality.

R.A. Scott Macfie: The Realities of War

R. A. Scott Macfie (HU 57195)

Colour-Quartermaster-Sergeant Robert Scott Macfie (see page 35) was to see his Liverpool Scottish fight bravely but suffer heavily on the Western Front. Their first experience in late 1914 had been arduous. After it he wrote, 'Having been in the firing line (the front line) once my curiosity is satisfied and I don't think I ever want to go there again.' Observing troops coming out of the trenches after a bad mauling he described them as 'a pitiable sight, trudging mechanically back home in a disorderly mob, bent double with fatigue and looking longingly at the side of the road scarcely able to refrain from lying down.' He soon came to realize that war combined grimness with a singular lack of excitement:

I do not think anyone can understand the horrors of war without seeing devastated country such as this, nor the wearisome monotony of fighting unless he has spent a night in the trenches. It is deadly dull, and the dullness, far more than the discomfort, is what strikes me. Today I am covered in mud, having fallen in the dark into a veritable slough and wallowed in it when trying to get out.

With the unclouded eye of a mature and intelligent man – never anybody's fool – he allowed no patriotic ardour to disguise the reality of what was happening around him. After describing an attack made in December 1914 which had virtually no chance of success, he added this chilling detail: 'The order was given that any man who fell out or turned back was to be shot or bayonetted; and one man was actually killed for this reason.'

The Liverpool Scottish took part in a major action at Hooge near Ypres on 16 June 1915, in which they lost many men. Macfie's Y Company marched off to take part in their attack and he busied himself at the transport lines making ready to welcome their return:

We set to work to prepare a good reception for our troops. Cyril had sent me about thirty-five boxes of delightful biscuits – I put them in the tents, a box for every five men. We set out the letters and parcels, candles, food and prepared tea and pea soup in the cookers. Of my own company a hundred and thirty had gone to the trenches: I was ready to feast them when they came back.

At last we heard the distant sound of pipes and after a while there passed through the gate a handful of men in tattered uniforms, their faces blackened and unshaven, their clothes stained red with blood or yellow with the fumes of lyddite. I shouted for Y Company – *one man* came forward! It was heart-breaking.

Gradually others tottered in, some wounded, all in the last stages of exhaustion, and when at last I went to lie down at about 5-30 a.m., there were in camp only 25 of my 130 men who had gone out six hours before. Since then the number has risen to a little over 40, and I know of 11 killed and 68 wounded but 25 are 'missing'. Some will doubtless turn up in hospitals; others may now be prisoners in Germany, but most, I fear, will be among the unidentified dead. Two officers survive, one belonging to my company who had to go to the headquarters sick at an early stage of the battle. All my sergeants are gone, eight of them, and at the present moment I have for NCOs only two corporals and one lance-corporal. It is terrible: the regiment is practically wiped out.

Despite all this he could not but be amazed at the curious resilience of the survivors:

They are queer chaps: you will imagine our camp plunged in gloom. Not a bit of it! After a good sleep and a good meal the men at once recovered their spirits, and are peacocking about in German helmets taken with their own hands, and proudly showing their souvenirs, and the rents in their clothing, and recounting how they bayonetted Huns, or how they had narrow escapes.

A year later the battalion was on the Somme and in August was involved in an action that was as ill-devised as it was costly. Writing to his father on 15 August Macfie did not mince his words:

Our attack, in the early hours of Aug 9, was directed against a certain village which had been attacked before and has been attacked several times since, always without success. Our performance was no exception to the rule: of my company 177 went up – 20 were killed, 42 wounded, and about eight are missing (i.e. in all probability dead). The want of preparation, the vague orders, the ignorance of the objective and geography, the absurd haste, and in general the horrid bungling were scandalous. After two years of war it seems that our higher commanders are still without common sense. In any well regulated organization a divisional commander would be shot for incompetence – here another regiment is ordered to attempt the same task in the same muddling way. It is worse than Hooge, much worse – and it is still going on.

A rare photograph of a battle in progress – the Liverpool Scottish during the action at Hooge referred to in Macfie's letter (opposite), taken by a member of the battalion, F.A. Fyfe (Q 49750). Its caption reads:
'First attack on Bellewaerde, 16 June 1915. 'Y' Wood, Hooge, at 6 am. The flag on the right was one of those put up to show that the German trench had been captured, and that the troops were going on. Men of the King's Liverpool (Liverpool Scottish) are taking cover under the parapet of the captured German front line. The Officer standing with cap on is the F.O.O. [Forward Observation Officer], 3rd Division.'

Zero Hour and After:
The Experience of Battle

'It is utterly impossible', wrote Thomas Hudson in his account of his career as a private in the Lancashire Fusiliers, 'to describe one's feelings during the hours of waiting for "zero" – the mind is full of wild thoughts and fancies etc which are utterly beyond control. Recollections of friends and dear ones, places we have seen and known and different phases of life all seem to pass in review before one's eyes and one is recalled to the bitter realities of the moment by the officer's voice: "fifteen minutes to go, boys, get ready". Immediately there is a great stir and excitement, a final setting of equipment etc and examination of arms and then a handshake with one or two dear comrades. 6.45 am, "Over you go, boys", and we are away on that strange journey across "No Man's Land".'

Thousands of men from many nations and on many fronts made that 'strange journey across "No Man's Land"' during the war, some many times, some just once as in Private Hudson's case (he was in a group that was taken prisoner), others getting no more than a yard or two beyond their wire before being wounded or killed. Going 'over the top' to do battle with the enemy was the experience which virtually every front-line soldier knew he would have to face sooner or later. Losses were inevitable except in the rarest of cases; everybody was aware that some, perhaps most, of their number would be down or out in the next few minutes. There are – understandably in the absence of the lightweight cameras of today – few genuine photographs of this climactic kind of warfare, and while scenes of action (usually wildly implausible) were popular in the illustrated magazines the official war artists tended to avoid painting what they could not see. Many survivors have tried to describe the experience, however, as the following accounts show.

Sergeant Charles Quinnell, 9th Battalion, Royal Fusiliers, was in an attack launched towards the German-held village of Ovillers on 7 July 1916, the seventh day of the Battle of the Somme. Zero hour was 8.15 am; the preliminary artillery bombardment began at 4.15. Quinnell's account is from an interview:

As soon as the bombardment started the Germans' retaliation came and for four hours we had to sit there and take four hours of everything he slung at us. We lost twenty-five per cent of our men before we went over. I was in the second wave. My platoon officer was in the first wave, he took two sections over and I followed with the other two sections.

As soon as the first wave had gone I gave the order 'advance – up the ladders – over the top'. The first wave, when I got through our wire, were down, two machine guns played on them and they were all absolutely wiped out. Everybody was either killed or wounded. We went through, we got half way across and then the two machine guns found us and they traversed – they played on us like spraying with a hose. At the finish I was the only man standing but I'm not one of those heroes who want to take on the German Army on my own and so I went to earth, I got down behind the lip of a big shell-hole.

I kept looking to see where those machine guns were. I couldn't see them but there was a German in the trench about a hundred yards away and he was standing up on his parapet and flinging bombs, so I shot him. The machine gun crew spotted me and they opened up on me. I ducked my head down and I was just behind the lip of this shell-hole and the dirt was just spraying down the back of my neck. 'You bastard!' I said. Then he thought he'd got me and he played his machine gun somewhere else.

I put my head up again, he spotted me and back came the machine gun, and down I had to go and I stopped there for about a quarter of an hour. By this time the machine guns had stopped and I took one convulsive leap over into the shell-hole and there were seven wounded men there. Well, we bound one another up and there we stopped all day, and at night-time when it was dusk I brought them back to our own line.

Second Lieutenant Norton Hughes-Hallett, 7th Battalion, King's Shropshire Light Infantry, was in another Somme attack near Montauban just a week later, this time the largely – though far from entirely – successful one made after an exceptionally brief bombardment and under cover of darkness early on 14 July. He wrote his account in hospital (page 54), when recovering from wounds received during the attack:

Everything was perfect. Not a sound was made and the Bosche showed no sign of having seen us, even when we were 100 yards or so from his line. We had to wait some time there. At 3.20 am our barrage was going to be put on to their first line, and was to last exactly till 3.25; watches were synchronized when the officers went to Battalion Headquarters. Then the barrage was to lift to their second line and behind it. At that moment, as the barrage lifted, we were to go forward, the first waves crossing the front line, leaving it to the bombers, and going forward to the second and last Bosche line. We had aeroplane photos, correct to July 13th showing that he had no line beyond his second. The barrage was to allow us two minutes for this, for, at 3.27, it was to lift behind their second line.

3.25, zero time, came and the line suddenly rose from the grass and went forward in dead silence: silence as far as *we* were concerned, I mean! Immediately rifles and machine guns started spitting fire at us from the Bosche trench, though I don't think we got any shells from them; but behind, the Royal Scots, supporting us, did, and I believe got a lot of our own too, while lying out. We reached the wire, but found it absolutely uncut and far too thick ever to get through. For about two minutes we hacked at it, the men falling by scores the while; then I am told the remnant retired as best they could to the sunken road, though without me.

I saw Sergeant Davies killed, and Sergeant O'Leary hit. These two were within a couple of feet away from me, and then I got it, and tipped head first into a big shell-hole in the wire. I remember Ainsworth, late company storeman, and sacked for getting drunk, cutting off my equipment and propping me right end upwards and putting a body under my knee. I was found about twelve hours later by the 'C' Company stretcher-bearers. When collected I was the only one living of nine in that hole, and when they got me to the dressing-station, I was at first put among the pile of dead. In the end I had to be stretchered back through Montauban to Carnoy, and was then driven to Corbie in an ambulance.

In the attack eight officers and 200 men were killed in Hughes-Hallett's battalion. His own company suffered badly, with thirty-eight killed and seventy-four wounded out of a total of 140.

If battle was traumatic for the attacker it was equally so for the attacked. F.L. Cassel was a German infantry officer at Thiepval on the first day of the Somme battle, 1 July. If the Germans were to repel the mass advance of the British, it was vital that they should react instantly when the massive pre-battle bombardment sustained throughout the previous week came to an end:

How long could this last? For a week we had lived with the deafening noise of the battle, and we knew that this went on not only in our sector but northwards almost as far as Arras and southwards as far as Peronne. Dull and apathetic we were lying in our dug-outs, secluded from life but prepared to defend ourselves whatever the cost.

On 1 July, at 7.30 am, the shout of our sentry 'They are coming!' tore me out of the apathy. Helmet, belt, rifle and up the steps. On the steps something white and bloody, in the trench a headless body. The sentry had lost his life by a last shell, before the fire was directed to the rear, and had paid for his vigilance with his life. We rushed to the ramparts, there they come, the khaki-yellows, they are not more than twenty metres in front of our trench. They advance fully equipped slowly to march across our bodies into the open country. Machine gun fire tears holes in their rows. They discover our presence, throw themselves on the ground, now a mass of craters, welcomed by hand-grenades and gun fire, and have now to sell their lives themselves.

With my rifle firing, I felt my right hand hit by a heavy stroke, a bullet from a distance of twenty yards, the gun fell out of my hand, blood is running. I see how a British rifleman tries to throw himself out of reach of a hand grenade thrown by Kühnel. In vain, it explodes, and will probably have finished him. I have my wound dressed by an orderly and take over again the leading of the platoon. Another half hour, and it becomes clear that the attack has been repelled, at least in our section. Only a few men who had reached the second trench are left over. Volunteers, amongst them Kühnel, begin to drive the intruders out proceeding from breastwork to breastwork throwing hand grenades and slowly succeed. Badly wounded Tommies fall into our hands.

The weapon that cut down so many on the first day on the Somme: the German G8 machine gun, with rate of fire of 300-450 rounds per minute (Q35445)

Getting Out the Wounded

In late September 1917 the 2nd Battalion, Worcestershire Regiment was involved in heavy fighting in the Ypres Salient in the early stages of the battle for the Passchendaele Ridge. The Reverend Victor Tanner, Chaplain to the battalion (see page 247), was in a forward aid post – established in a captured German pill-box during much of the action. He was to win a Military Cross for his conduct in sustaining the men in the post under fire and also in helping to carry out the wounded – the latter task being necessary because of the non-arrival of stretcher-bearers of the Royal Army Medical Corps. The following description of a casualty evacuation at the height of the battle is from the letter he wrote to his family on 13 November:

Had we had to go down singly, we would have gone down long before, shells or no shells. But for four men to walk over 1½ miles of that desolate shell-pitted country, in the midst of such a tornado, and carrying another man on their shoulders, was by no means the same thing; and further, when once we had started off we should have to go right on – there was no chance of sheltering afterwards. However, the congestion in the Aid Post was acute, and was getting worse every minute. It was so bad that after a time even stretcher cases had to remain outside, exposed to the shower of earth and splinters, so at last I decided that we must go; and we went.

That journey I shall never forget. The stretcher seemed like lead. It was the continual going up and down into shell holes which made it seem heavier than it was; and then to make matters worse we lost our direction, there being no landmark to guide us. Still we kept steadily on. Every time we stopped to change ends the poor chap on the stretcher would say 'Oh don't bury me here. Do go on. We shall all be killed', and so on. I cannot describe the variety of feelings which I had during that journey, but somehow or other I did not feel a bit frightened. I suppose it was that I felt that it rested with me to keep up the spirits of the other three. I knew too that we were in the path of duty, and therefore under God's immediate care. Well, at last we reached our destination, and I shall never forget the gratitude which the poor chap showed as we handed him over to the relay bearers. He wrung my hand and burst into tears. 'I shall never forget you, sir; you have saved my life.'

After we had had a drink of water and a rest, I found the Doctor in charge of the Dressing Station, and told him that at all costs we must have stretcher parties. He said that they had gone up to every other battalion, but that they had made three attempts to get through to the Worcesters, but had had to go back each time owing to the terrific fire. However I said we must have them; I would take them back with me; so he gave me two parties, eight men, which were all that he could spare. He promised to send more later. The men – they were little more than boys – did not want to come at all, and I felt sorry for them; but I knew what the need was, and insisted on them going. The Sergeant amused me by saying 'Well, if the padre can go up, you can go.' We started and had only got half way when a fearful fire opened on the track just in front of us. It caught a

Medical Corps men on their way to a first-aid post with wounded men (Q 88580)

party of Highlanders, and lots of them fell, either wounded or killed. So we stopped where we were for a quarter of an hour or so, and then went on again, but had to leave the track and cut across country owing to the shelling. As we had no stretcher case to carry, we were able to run, and we took full advantage of the opportunity, I can assure you, until to our relief the Aid Post once more appeared in sight. Our Doctor was greatly relieved to see me again, and the Sergeant soon set about making some hot tea with our primus stove, and we were glad enough of it. A few hours later when things became quieter, twelve more squads came up from the Dressing Station and we were able to get rid of quite a lot of the worst cases.

If able to do so, casualties often made their own way to the aid posts or dressing stations. Second Lieutenant Blake O'Sullivan, 6th Battalion Connaught Rangers, became one of the 'walking wounded', as they were called, after a successful attack on the village of Guillemont during the Battle of the Somme in September 1916. In an account written shortly afterwards in a hospital in Chelsea (his wound was, in soldiers' parlance, a 'Blighty', ie severe enough for him to be sent for treatment to Britain) he described what happened during his slow progress from the front. The fighting had been very fierce and this was to be a grim journey:

Near the edge of the village a groaning and agonized German, with half his thigh blown off, feebly beckoned to me; and before going on I made some futile efforts to staunch his bleeding. Then, heading for the main east-west street still vaguely indicated through the pulverised rubble, I stumbled over a weeping and terribly mauled little man whose head cringed away from an expected bullet, and instead of the bullet put the water bottle to his lips. He grabbed it with both hands and tried to drain it. As the bottle was firmly attached to my equipment I finally had to drag it away from the poor creature in order to free myself.

Once well into Guillemont the masses of bestrewn dead simply staggered me. They lay in every imaginable attitude and in all directions. A rest soon became imperative and, after spotting two stretcher bearers coming towards me, I sat down in the midst of the sprawling corpses. The first-aid men unhitched most of the clinging equipment, dressed the wound and insisted on putting a sling for my left arm, before going quickly ahead again.

Dodging and zig-zagging through the enemy barrage which still battered away on Trones Wood was a nerve-racking ordeal – with the crashing explosions causing panic-stricken tangles between the in-coming carrying parties and hospital-bound stretchers and walking wounded.

I was soaked with sweat and ready to drop long before reaching the first Dressing Station, where the presiding orderly gave me a drink of water so petrol tainted that it was promptly vomited out again. Pushing on, and feeling as if a hundred-pound load were perched on my shoulder I gradually made my way up the hill to Montauban. There was no transport in sight, filth and dead horses littered the ground; but a rest had become absolutely imperative – and choosing the least putrescent of the horses I flopped down nearby.

Sergeant Casey passing on an old horse ambulance woke me up and helped me on board for a ride to the Casualty Clearing Station – which was already chock-full of Rangers. I lined up with the others and got a massive anti-tetanus shot – which promptly developed a plum-sized blob on my chest. Motor ambulances then took us to the hospital at Dernancourt. At midnight they shipped me to Heilly and thence by train to Rouen hospital.

At Rouen the X-ray located a Luger pistol bullet. It had stabbed in under the left arm, chipped a spinal vertebra and then lodged in my right shoulder. Two days after its excision I was sent by train to Le Havre and on, by Australian Red Cross ship, to arrive 4 am 9 September at Southampton.

Attitudes to War: Second Lieutenant Edward Chapman

Edward Frederick Chapman enlisted in 1915 after graduating at Magdalen College, Oxford, and sailed for France in 1916 shortly after the opening of the Battle of the Somme. He joined the 20th Royal Fusiliers as a replacement officer in a battalion which had suffered badly in the early attacks. He was determined to do well, but he had no blinkered view as to the nature of the challenges ahead of him. Throughout his ten months in France – he was severely wounded, losing an eye, in May 1917 – he monitored his own performance and described his experiences and his reactions in a series of remarkably frank and eloquent letters.

July 1916

I am enjoying life hugely. I love the army – and it is a great game. I haven't seen war yet really, but I know I shall hate it. But army life is grand, and I wouldn't be a civilian just yet for anything. But I shouldn't like the army in peace time.

August 1916

I hate all this business from the bottom of my soul. It has turned a beautiful country into a desolate waste. All this area is one vast cemetery. Dead bodies taint the air wherever you go. It has robbed thousands and thousands of men of life, and thousands more of the things that made life seem worth living. I have come to look on peace and quiet and home life as the summum bonum. I feel that all I want to do is to be able to live quietly, and tend a garden, and study a bit.

I am sorry to be writing such a dismal letter, but I cannot always look at the war from a Bairnsfather point of view*. Thank heaven so many people can.

September 1916

By the way don't swallow all that the papers say about the 'great push'. When you read of German battalions being decimated, don't forget that English battalions get wiped out too.

September 1916 (out of the line)

This is a jolly life, but it is not war. The three weeks in the Somme area pretty well knocked me out but I feel fit for anything again now – even the Somme if necessary.

I really hope something will happen before long, and this time I shall be able to bear the strain far better. Meanwhile I am gaining experience and when the great day comes I hope I shall not make a mess of anything.

February 1917

I think I must be about the happiest man in the whole B.E.F. The first few weeks out here nearly broke me. Instead of breaking me it *broke me in*. Since then I have been able to bear any strain that has been put on me.

You who remain at home and worry about us out here have far the worst of it. Don't worry about me, for there is no need.

As you say, life can never be the same again as it was before 1914. But I think it will be *better* after the war than it ever was before. We must have learned a wisdom that nothing else could have taught us. And when we get home again we shall have the happiness of men who have seen terrible things, who have been in hell, and have come back to a blessed haven of peace. Different from the old careless happiness, but more permanent.

February 1917

I think only those who have been in front line trenches can realise how delightful ordinary things are. What a blessed thing sleep is: the relief of *not* being shelled. And how nice it is to have clean hands and wrists. Periodic tours in trenches are necessary to keep one's appreciation of these things keen.

April 1917 (about the photograph opposite: Chapman was now an Acting Captain)

Isn't it good? We are all awfully pleased. We went in just as we were, with dirty boots and our old tunics on. It turned out a great success. We shall never be all together again. Soro is killed, and Morison and Clark are both in other companies at present. I have still got Bower, who is a most priceless fellow.

Chapman continued to serve despite his injury, though not at the front. After the war he qualified as a doctor. He died in 1969 at the age of 75, having had to retire a few years earlier from his country practice on account of increasing blindness in his remaining eye.

*A reference to Bruce Bairnsfather, infantry officer and cartoonist, whose drawings in *The Bystander* magazine became famous for portraying the humorous side of Western Front life.

BEAUVAL. APRIL 4th 1917.

W. Soro	Morison	F. W. Bower
killed April 16	wounded May 20	killed later
H. Clark MC	E. F. Chapman	P. J. Tompkinson
gassed	wounded May 20	

(HU 59103)

Private Mudd

Private Jack Mudd
(HU 57198)

Mrs Lizzie Mudd
(HU 57199)

John William (Jack) Mudd was a Cockney from Bow in the East End of London. In 1917 he was thirty-one and married with a family; his wife was Elizabeth Mudd, generally known as Lizzie.

On 26 October that year, as a Private of the 2/4th Battalion, London Regiment, Royal Fusiliers, Jack Mudd took part in a dawn attack in the Ypres Salient. This was during the latter stages of the Third Battle of Ypres, the battle often called after the ridge – and the village – which marked the high tide of the British advance, Passchendaele.

In the attack Mudd's battalion met determined opposition. In addition the ground conditions were very bad, with many men going in up to their knees in the slime. According to one report it was subsequently found impossible to bring in the dead and wounded. When the roll was called Private Mudd was not among the survivors. On 22 November 1917 a copy of Army Form B. 104-83 was sent to Lizzie Mudd informing her that her husband had been 'posted as "missing"'; on 4 December she was sent a copy of Army Form B. 104-82A stating that 'no further news having been received' the Army Council had been 'regretfully constrained to conclude' that her husband was dead. Private Mudd's body was never found. His name is one of 34,888 recorded on the Memorial to the Missing at Tyne Cot Cemetery, Belgium, a kilometre below the summit of the Passchendaele Ridge.

Four days before he was killed, he wrote a long letter to his wife in which he poured out his feelings about the present and his hopes for the future.

My darling Lizzie

At last I have the opportunity of writing to you a real letter. In the first place dearest I trust you and the children are quite well. I guess you have been worried with the air raids. You know dear it's hard to be out here fighting and yet your wife and children can't be safe. Still dearest don't worry, you have a 20,000 to 1 chance and God will watch over you as he has been with me ever since I have been out here. I have tried dearest to be as good as I can since I have been in France. I never close my eyes without praying for myself you and the children. He has answered them up till now and I hope and trust it will please Him to look after us until the end.

We are expecting to go up again in 2 or 3 days, so dearest pray hard for me and ask Marie for God will not refuse her prayers, she doesn't know the wickedness of this world. Dear Lizzie it's nearly six months now since I saw you, how I long for you and the children, God bless you all. I love you more than ever. I long to take you in my arms again, what a lot of love we have missed but please God it will make it all the sweeter when I see you. I often take your Photo out of my pocket and look at your dear face and think of the times we have had together, some lovely days eh love, and when I think again of some of the worry I have caused you it makes me only the more eager to get home to you to atone for all the worry and anxious moments you have had to put up with. You always stuck by me in all things dear God bless you for it. And my dear little children, I think of them, God bless them also. I hope dear you will always trust in me for I am always faithful your face is always before me and I couldn't deny you and as for you dearest I know you are faithful and no matter what happened you would always be true and keep your word.

Out here dear we're all pals, what one hasn't got the other has, we try to share each others troubles, get each other out of danger. You wouldn't believe the Humanity between men out here. Poor little Shorty, one of the fellows that came out with me, he used to tell me all about his young lady, his Hilda, that was his young lady's name, about his home he had already bought and when he got home he would get married and come over to see me and introduce her to you. He used to make me laugh with his talk, how he loved his Hilda but unfortunately he will never see her again poor fellow, he would give me half of everything he had. I often think of him yet poor fellow I don't think he even has a grave but lies somewhere in the open. Still dear I don't want to make you sad but it just shows you how we seem to stick together in trouble. It's a lovely thing is friendship out here.

Please God it won't be long before this war is over, we are pushing old Fritz back, I don't think he will stand the British boys much longer and then we will try and keep a nice home. I will know the value of one now.

Goodnight love God bless you and my children and may He soon send me back to those I love is the wish of Your Faithful Husband

xxxxxxxxx Jack

The Power of Artillery

It was not the machine-gun but the powerful weapons of the artillery that proved to be the main killing agent of the First World War; and it was artillery that produced the shattered towns and ravaged landscapes characteristic of the Western Front.

A 1916 British Bombardment, from the diary of Father J.B. Marshall, Chaplain to an infantry brigade in the 21st Division:

It was appalling. I could see the flashes from our guns from every side, far in the distance, behind me, every side of me, below me, before me. Every kind of gun was working its hardest and fastest – the great monsters behind sending their heavily roaring giant missiles, the smaller howitzers and the sixty-pounders belching forth their whirring shells, the busy 18-pounders with their sharp savage voice spitting out their swirling projectiles. And there before me was the awful view of the German line where all these thousands of explosives were bursting blood red, sending debris of the enemy trenches high into the air.

Description of Ypres in March 1917, from a letter by Colour-Quartermaster-Sergeant R.A. Scott Macfie, Liverpool Scottish:

At the present I am in the devastated city of which you have often heard, and living in a cellar below what was once a convent. I hate cellars but there is very little above ground that would give shelter from rain and wind, and absolutely nothing that would be the slightest protection against shells. This poor old city gets more dilapidated every time we return. The Germans still think it worth shelling, and nobody is allowed to walk through the Grande Place. Only one of the graceful pinnacles of the Cloth Hall is still standing, and there is very little left even of the Cathedral tower.

Below: Ypres, Belgium, 'capital' of the infamous Ypres Salient; held heroically in 1914, and thereafter the victim of constant bombardment over the next four years. Photograph shows: background centre, one of the towers of the Cloth Hall; background right, relics of the Cathedral. Official Australian photograph, 1917 (E(AUS)1226)

A Soldier-Artist at the Front

'Removing the Wounded, 60 Yards from the Enemy'

Harold Williamson tried to enlist in 1914 but was turned down on health grounds and it was not until January 1916 that he was finally accepted as a Rifleman in the King's Royal Rifle Corps. He remained in the ranks, eventually being promoted to Corporal. He had begun training as an artist before the war and was to resume his career afterwards, eventually becoming headmaster of the Chelsea School of Art. He produced a number of striking paintings during his service on the Western Front which eventually came to the notice of the Ministry of Information and he was about to be contracted as an official war-artist when the Armistice intervened.

What gives particular interest to the painting reproduced here and in the colour section is that the artist provided a precise account of the episodes on which they were based.

The first is described in a letter home of 7 January 1918. On Christmas Day 1917 his battalion, the 8th KRRC, had been in the front line in the Ypres Salient. His post had been nothing more than a 'shell hole converted into a bit of trench' on the edge of No Man's Land; nevertheless they had taken up their rations in valises, and had managed two reasonably festive meals. Williamson's letter continues:

I thought it was going to be quite decent on Xmas Day, but unfortunately a sad thing occurred: about 1 am Captain Brownsword [Williamson's Company commander] came round visiting. He bent down to drop in on my post. I said, 'Hurry up, get down quick!' but unfortunately he was not quick enough; there was a crack and I knew he was hit in the back, and he just toppled down and I caught him with my arms. Then the difficulty, imagine it, of looking after a man 6 foot 3, in a bit of trench half the width of your kitchen, and no longer; partly filled too with a fire step. I had to sit on the step, and hold him across my knees, while the stretcher bearer dressed him. Our stretcher was broken, and with difficulty we got another, one bearer being shot through the head bringing it. Ultimately we got the Captain on a stretcher on the fire step. Then there was nothing to be done but to wait for daylight, being too risky to get him out then, in view of the snow and the bright moonlight, the Germans being as near as 60 yards. It seemed a very big time till 7.30, and we could not keep him warm. I could feel that his arms were just as icy cold as his hands, and feared for his life. When daylight came we put out the Red Cross Flag (a mutual arrangement of that part of the front) and four men having been told off for the work, we hoisted the stretcher out of the hole and got him safely away. I heard afterwards that they carried him miles without incident, but only to have him die from exhaustion within sight of the dressing station.

The episode which produced the second painting (see pages 142-3) is described in a note Williamson produced as background to the picture when it was selected for showing in a Royal Academy exhibition late in 1918. One detail he omitted is that he himself is the wounded soldier on the far right clutching his arm. The wound was serious enough for him to be sent back to England and it was there after being released from hospital that he painted the picture. Williamson's note reads:

A recollection of a heavy local attack in the neighbourhood of Villers-Bretonneaux, during the great German offensive, Spring 1918. The Painter has tried to give the impressions of the tired soldiers. The remains of the 8th Battalion KRRC not a hundred strong, who had been on the retreat since March 21st, were hastily reorganized, and sent up in reserve the night before, to hold a sunken road, not a shot being heard from the Germans. Before dawn, an intensive bombardment of our lines opened up, and was maintained for a couple of hours. In the gloom and rain the storm troops then came over, and smashed through our two first lines. The picture shows them moving with exact discipline and just appearing to the few men in reserve. The shell holes in the foreground show the accuracy of the preceding bombardment. The British are hopelessly outnumbered, but training and discipline keep them going, without thought of retirement. Two men are firing a Lewis gun. The wounded man has a poor chance of getting away; he must cross much open country swept by enemy fire, and go through a heavy barrage. At the last the few left were surrounded, but fought their way out, some wounded, some being taken prisoner.

Western Front Soldiers

Below: 'Study of a
Canadian' by Augustus
John, 1918

Right above: 'A Famous
Raider of the Lancashire
Fusiliers' by Eric
Kennington, 1917

Right below: 'An Indian
VC' by William
Rothenstein, 1918

'Gassed':
Two Famous Pictures
Personalized

'The stream of men increased, those who could see led the way while the others formed a queue behind, each one placing his hands on the shoulders of his predecessor for guidance.'

Harold Clegg enlisted on 16 July 1915 just twelve days before his nineteenth birthday. He became Rifleman No 3684, 3/6th Battalion, Liverpool Regiment, better known as the Liverpool Rifles. He was gassed with mustard gas at Armentières on 28 July 1917. The above sentence from his vivid if bitter war-memoir could almost serve as caption to the painting opposite by the American artist John Singer Sargent, undoubtedly one of the most famous pictures produced during the war, and to the almost equally well-known official photograph below.

Sargent, who had been born in 1856, was a veteran artist of great distinction when in April 1918 he was approached by the British War Memorials Committee in these terms: 'In connection with a National scheme to commemorate the war by means of pictures, it is thought very strongly that you should be among the first painters to undertake a composition ... The subject the Committee have in mind is one that would suggest the fusion of British and American forces, but if you would like to name an alternative, I am sure that the Committee would hear your views.' The Committee's idea was that he should produce one of a number of large-scale pictures on the theme of Allied co-operation to be hung in the main gallery of a projected Hall of Remembrance (to be built on Richmond Hill) which would commemorate the war in art and sculpture. That this scheme was an important one is clear from the fact that shortly after Sargent arrived in London from the United States he received a personal letter of welcome from the Prime Minister himself, David Lloyd George, who expressed the hope that the 'great paintings' to be produced would be 'handed down to posterity as a series of immortal works.'

As it turned out the Hall of Remembrance was never built. Moreover when Sargent went to France he found no subject which effectively expressed British-American co-operation and instead chose to produce 'Gassed': a huge painting 9 feet by 20 feet based on what he had seen at the dressing station at Le Bac-du-Sud on the Arras-Doullens road. He worked up the painting in England from sketches and notes made at the time and it was finally purchased by the then National War Museum (ie the IWM) for £600 in March 1919. Arguably, though he did not do justice to the theme suggested to him by his sponsors, he produced a lasting 'document' of far greater significance and one that justified Lloyd George's best hopes.

'Gassed' by John Singer Sargent
Below: Men suffering from gas; advanced dressing station, Bethune, April 1918. Photograph by British official photographer Tom Aitken (Q 11586)

Sargent was accompanied for part of his time in France by Professor Henry Tonks, a surgeon and an artist (he had been Professor at the Slade School) who had himself had experience of war service – as a civilian doctor on the Marne and in Italy in 1915 and subsequently as an RAMC officer in Britain. Tonks was now commissioned to produce a large painting on a medical subject and in July 1918 he joined Sargent on the Somme. He was with Sargent in August when the latter came on the scene which inspired 'Gassed'; in 1920 in a letter to Alfred Yockney of the British War Memorials Committee he described what happened:

Sargent and I were staying at Arras at the time. I heard the night before a rumour that the Guards were intended to advance the next morning. After luncheon we started out in Sargent's car together along the road to Doullens, turning off to make enquiries at the Guards Head Quarters at Bailleaumont. We heard that General Fielding had moved his headquarters to Ransart, we did not go there as we thought he might not want to be disturbed but went towards Blaireville and stopped at a dressing station not very far from there. Sargent made a sketch but there were very few cases there. After tea we heard that on the Doullens Road at the Corps dressing station at Le Bac-du-Sud there were a good many gas cases so we went there. The dressing station was situated on the road and consisted of a number of huts and a few tents. Gassed cases kept coming in, led along in parties of about six just as Sargent had depicted them, by an orderly. They sat or lay down on the grass, there must have been several hundred, evidently suffering a great deal, chiefly from their eyes which were covered up by pieces of lint. The gas was mustard gas which causes temporary blindness from swelling of conjunctiva and lids. Sargent was very struck by the scene and immediately made a lot of notes. It was a very fine evening and the sun towards setting.

During the night of 27-8 July 1917 the Germans launched a massive artillery onslaught on Armentières. Harold Clegg's Liverpool Rifles were due to come out of the trenches which lay outside the town a mile or so to the east; Clegg himself was in reserve, waiting with two other men for the rest of their company to join them. He later wrote in his war-memoir, 'We three sat and watched the destruction of Armentières, yet we did not know that many of the shells used contained a new form of gas, for which the British Army was totally unprepared.' 3am came but there was still no sign of the rest of their company, so when the Colonel (ie Clegg's Commanding Officer) and his headquarters staff passed by on their way out from the line the Colonel instructed Clegg and his comrades to follow him. Clegg's account continues:

We picked up several stray men and followed a long route to avoid the shelling on the Houplines Road. The Colonel and his party were fresh and travelling light; we others were tired, fatigued and heavily laden and we were soon left behind. We caught the Colonel's party up as they were halted by the flames of the municipal gasworks. Word had passed down that the town was full of gas and that respirators were to be adjusted. This was complied with and we proceeded with difficulty, falling over stones and into holes and feeling generally fatigued and worn out. We ran into one dense cloud of gas, then out of it and into another until we reached the centre of the town. The H.Q. party left us for their billets in Rue Sadie Carnot, we made our way through the flaming streets to the Rue Nationale; we traversed several streets, only to find the ends blocked up with fire and debris but eventually arrived at the billet and reported to Second Lieutenant W.R. Collenge, the officer in charge, who ordered us to take shelter in the cellars. We expostulated that as gas was heavier than air, there would be more gas in the cellars than there would be elsewhere, also pointing out that the billet next door was burning merrily. He was under the influence of drink and threatened all sorts of punishment if we did not do as we were told.

Despite the respirators, we immediately fell into a dense and heavy sleep; the first for several days. Shortly after, the Company arrived, and Captain Eccles, pointing out the danger, took us to other billets in the Rue de Payee; stores had to be transported, so that it was daylight before we had time to look around. By this time a fresh wind had sprung up and all the gas had cleared away; we were permitted to remove our respirators, and in doing so it was noticed that parts of the rubber had perished, apertures were noticeable, and thus the whole respirator had been rendered useless.

The firing having died down and the burning property being confined to another part of the town, we lay down to rest at 6 a.m. Reveille was blown at 9 a.m. and having intense hunger we looked round for something to eat. The Sergeant Major had been rummaging around while we slept and found out that all available food had become tainted with gas and was therefore unfit for consumption. Some tea was eventually made and with this we tightened our belts and hoped that rations would not be long in coming.

Our eyes now began to feel irritated. The tea was instrumental in making all and sundry commence to vomit. After being violently sick I received instructions to prepare myself to join a party just about to proceed as guard for Brigade Headquarters; I began to scrape the accumulation of mud from my accoutrements.

While doing so I heard several men complain about the pain in their eyes, some even complained of going blind; one by one these fellows made their way to the First Aid Dressing Station, the battalion doctor and orderlies not being present. The stream of men increased, those who could see led the way while the others formed a queue behind, each one placing his hands on the shoulders of his predecessor for guidance.

After the vomiting I had not felt any ill effects, but after a short while my eyes became very painful, so I joined hands with my friend Lyon, and together we went to the Aid Station in Erquinghem Road.

Before leaving the billet, I noticed that it had been inhabited by civilians, but now the old couple were stretched out gasping for breath, while their young daughter was transfixed as if in a trance, staring at her dead child, which was only several days old.

A large school house served as a Dressing Station for the wounded. Outside this house were strewn all over the road a seething mass of humanity, civilians and military. Women and children wailing and groaning in their agony; everyone vomiting; some dead and many unconscious.

The hard worked doctors of the R.A.M.C. and several orderlies did what they could; drops were injected into the eyes of everyone in turn, after which attention they were passed along into a garden to await vehicles to convey them to the rear. The drops completely dimmed the eyesight and by 11 a.m. I was totally blind.

After time interminable, motor-lorries arrived, each was packed with groaning humanity in all positions. A very uncomfortable ride along the cobbled roads, and we arrived at Bac St. Maur at about 1 p.m. I managed to find my friend Lyon again and together we sat hand in hand on backless forms for over six hours. The orderlies placed more drops in our eyes and improvised shades to protect our eyes from the blazing sun. A high fever also set in.

Later in the evening, motor ambulances transported us to another dressing station at Estaires, where I stayed the night. Extreme fatigue, fever and pain overcame me and I slept throughout the night. Breakfast was served the next day, but my throat was now painful and I could not swallow.

At about 10 p.m., I was loaded into another motor ambulance in which I found three others of our 'C' Company, including Lyon, whom I had lost the previous night. After what seemed to be a long ride we arrived at the Casualty Clearing Station at Merville. I remember giving my name and home address to the Chaplain, hearing an English woman's voice and having more drops placed in my eyes. Thereafter I remember little; but there is a faint recollection of being in a hospital train.

On regaining consciousness I was in the 47th General Hospital at Le Tréport; the date was August 2nd. I was given a blanket bath; I had not had a hot bath since the previous May. I was loaded with vermin and I had not had my boots off for 15 or 16 days. My sympathies were with the nurses.

The symptoms were as follows:
Blindness
Deafness
Loss of voice
Inability to swallow
Weakness
High Fever
Burns on exposed and delicate parts of the anatomy
Choking cough
Difficult breathing

For the first few days, I spent my time sleeping and coughing. The marquee was full of gas cases, and there was a steady stream of shuffling feet which denoted stretchers being brought in and carried out; some of the latter to the mortuary.

On 7 August Clegg travelled by train to Le Havre, where he and his fellow casualties spent five hours on the quay until learning that no hospital ship would sail that day. They finally left for Southampton on the 8th. He was taken to the Military Hospital at Winchester from which he was eventually moved to Elswick Sanatorium, Kirkham, near Preston. He took no further part in the war and did not return home until May 1919. It was another five years before he was restored to normal health.

Humanity, and Hatred

A Scots Guardsman giving
a wounded German
prisoner a drink after an
attack, August 1918
(Q 6983)

'The ordinary soldier knew quite well in his heart that at bottom Fritz was much such another as himself.'

So wrote Canon E.C. Crosse DSO MC, who had served as a senior chaplain on the Western Front (see section on Chaplains in Part VIII).

The duty of soldiers of opposing armies was to kill each other, but it did not follow automatically that they must hate each other. There was inevitably much viciousness in combat, but once a man had been wounded or disabled, a different attitude took over. A wounded soldier was just another human being. The word 'enemy' was merely a label, and as such was instantly detachable if circumstances allowed.

The most notable illustration of the assertion of common humanity during the war was the Christmas Truce of 1914, a spontaneous upsurge of comradeship between enemies which in some areas continued for a number of days and in one or two sectors of the front lasted for several weeks.

Stemming from small episodes of fraternization shortly after the armies entrenched, a fellow-feeling developed between the lines which came to a head under the impact of the Christmas spirit. Usually beginning after nightfall on Christmas Eve, agreed ceasefires took place over two-thirds of the British line – in many cases followed on Christmas Day itself by meetings with the Germans in No Man's Land which went on for several hours and during which souvenirs were exchanged (bully beef and cigars being popular items of currency), a number of impromptu football games took place (more kickabouts than full-scale matches) and, in one bizarre instance, an English soldier from London had his hair cut by his pre-war German barber. More seriously, the opportunity was taken to bury both sides' dead; at one point there was a moving joint-burial service in No Man's Land. The British were not the only participants on the Allied side – there were similar if more scattered instances of camaraderie with the enemy on the French and the Belgian fronts. Officers, including even one or two battalion commanders, took part as well as ordinary soldiers (though inevitably there were others who strongly and forcefully disapproved). In a letter of early January 1915, Warwick Squire, a young private of the 1/13th Battalion, London Regiment (generally known as the Kensingtons) described what happened on his unit's sector:

We had a very cold but quite cheerful Christmas Day in the trenches and even a slice of plum pudding. And though you might not believe it, we had a truce for the day just along our bit of the line. Somehow or other we arranged with the Germans opposite to stop fighting till midnight on Christmas night; all Christmas Day we were walking about outside in front of our trenches. The Germans came out of theirs and we met halfway and talked and exchanged

souvenirs, our own bullets for theirs. They also gave some of our fellows cigars of which they said they had plenty and we gave them tins of bully beef as they said they had very little food. A great many of them spoke English and one said he had been a waiter in London. On Christmas Eve they were singing away as hard as they could go and they had lights all along their trench in front of us.

As the war ground on, such interludes of peace in No Man's Land became very rare, though they did occur. Second Lieutenant Leslie Hill, 1/6th Battalion, City of London Regiment, was drawn into one in the Vimy Ridge sector in March 1916, instigated (as had largely been the case at Christmas 1914) from the German side. Hill wrote to a friend at home:

The trenches we are going up to are simply a line of shell holes about 120 yards from the Boche and no wire between – but we are quite ready for them should they come over. However, there is quite a funny co-existence connected with it – the fellows opposite are Saxons who have been given sixty days field punishment by the Kaiser for refusing to go on a route march – we had this from one of their officers – so they have made a compact with us, that if we do not fire, they will not. I only wish their artillery would do the same and then we should have some holiday.

A private soldier in the same battalion, Rifleman Dick Harvey, wrote movingly of this episode in a letter to his mother – fully aware of the rarity of what had been taking place:

We have had a very peaceful time with the Germans. They used to walk about on top with our chaps, exchanging cigarettes, tobacco and shaking hands with us. It was a curious sight to see them strolling about in 'No Man's Land' as though war was the last thing they thought about. It has been a unique experience that I shan't forget for a long time to come.

A harsher attitude to the enemy – though not without a nostalgic backward glance to earlier days – emerges from a letter written on Boxing Day 1916 by Second Lieutenant Edward Beddington-Behrens, an officer of the Royal Field Artillery:

Above left: Whenever they could, men tried to shut out the horrors of war. Such attempts to make the best of things made good official photographs, such as this one, captioned 'Troops with derelict hansom cab found in Bazentin-le-Grand'. Evidence suggests it was taken in October 1916 and therefore represents a cheerful interlude in the Battle of the Somme, during which the tiny villages of Bazentin-le-Grand and Bazentin-le-Petit were seized from the Germans after fierce fighting (Q 4883)

Above: The enemy, too, enjoyed his moments of light relief. Here German artillerymen are shown with one of the massive railway guns which bombarded Paris in 1918 (Q 87406)

Off-duty pleasures on the Western Front: German soldiers (above) enjoying a row on a lake (Q 87452); and (below) officers of the 12th Battalion East Yorkshire Regiment, 92nd Brigade, 31st Division, relaxing in their mess dug-out thirty feet underground, Arleux sector, near Roclincourt, 9 January 1918 (Q 11546)

Everything was done to prevent any fraternizing between the two sides as the Boche would use the opportunity by getting useful information. Besides, things have got past the stage when one can fraternize with the enemy, there is too much hatred flying about, it would also induce bad discipline to our troops. However I must say going to talk to the Boche in No Man's Land like we did the first Xmas rather appeals to one's sporting instincts, don't you think so? Instead however, the artillery had a Christmas strafe at all hours of the day and night.

In the daily slog of bombardments and trench raids, with casualty lists increasing relentlessly even in the relatively quiet times, 'sporting instincts' and old-fashioned chivalrous attitudes lost their appeal. Fritz became not so much the other fellow in the ring, fellow-victim of the folly of war, as the vicious enemy who had killed or maimed one's friends, and was therefore fit only to be destroyed. A young officer of the 1st Surrey Rifles, Norman Taylor, wrote to his father in May 1916:

I am now beginning to realise the genuine hatred of Germans one gets after a year or so of this, which one cannot understand when one first comes out. You have no idea what a subtle thrill there is on a good moonlight night, a Hun working party perhaps faintly silhouetted and opening a sudden burst of fire with a gun on them.

Yet such hard-line attitudes could soften, even in the context of one of the war's greatest battles. Second Lieutenant E.F. Chapman, 20th Royal Fusiliers, wrote the following in November 1916 – during the last phase of the Battle of the Somme:

We were in some very rough trenches that had only just been dug. After we had been there about an hour, four Germans came over and gave themselves up. They may not have intended doing so – perhaps they had lost their way. Anyhow they didn't mind being taken prisoners. They were shaking all over with cold or fright. I tapped my revolver and said '*Sie verstehen?*' ['Do you understand?'] and they said '*Jawohl!*' ['Certainly'] I started telling them that I had been a student in Germany, and so enjoyed talking German again that I quite forgot that we were in trenches and very close to the Boche! War is so very strange and stupid when the people who do the fighting do not hate each other at all. War is the stupidest thing in the whole world.

Armoured Warfare:
The Tanks of Cambrai

On 16 September 1916 Major H.E. Trevor, Brigade Major, 37th Infantry Brigade, wrote to his parents from the Somme battlefield:

We have had great news this morning which I suppose you will see in tomorrow's papers. We seem to be doing splendidly and our new implement of war seems to have thoroughly frightened the Hun. I do hope we shall break through and am beginning to feel quite confident.

The 'new implement of war', many months in the devising, had been secretly transported from Britain under a cover-name to conceal its true purpose. The original term used to describe it – 'land ship' – would not survive this disguise; the innocent-sounding temporary name, chosen to suggest that these huge objects were being brought to the front merely to dispense water, would become permanent. Major Trevor used the name, with deliberate emphasis, when later on 16 September he resumed his letter home:

The news continues to be good, the *Tanks* seem to have done good work and fairly put the wind up the Hun who was seen to run like Hell in front of them

shouting 'This isn't war, it is murder'. For once in the war we come into the field with a new engine of war and not second-hand copied from the Hun.

In the event this first use of these so-called 'tanks' on the Somme front in 1916 was more a sensation than a success. There were not enough of them and too many of them broke down. Nor did they play a significant part in the principal battles of 1917, Arras and Third Ypres (Passchendaele). Their first crucial contribution came in November that year on the front of the British Third Army at Cambrai, where they carried out a mass attack on the Hindenburg Line over ground solid enough for them not to end up ingloriously stuck in the mud. A young Second Lieutenant of the 8th Battalion, Tank Corps, Gordon Hassell, commanded one of the 378 vehicles which took part in the Cambrai battle. Tanks – like ships – had official names; his, H7, was *Harrier*. The battle opened on 20 November; next day Hassell wrote a brief note to his family:

My precious people
Have come through yesterday's glorious success perfectly well and without hurt.
Have had good time. May be unable to write until things have settled down.
Self and crew all perfectly safe and fit.

A week later he was able to write at greater length about what had already been dubbed the 'glorious 20th'.

Really the whole show was absurdly simple – there being no sort of a fight in our particular sector. The Germans were only too ready to hold 'hands up' and came in almost without being invited.

Two tanks forcing their way through a wood near Elverdinghe, north-west of Ypres, September 1917 (Q 3241)

Mark V tank on display at the Museum: this is number 19, nicknamed 'Devil' which is believed to have served with 'B' Company, 4th Battalion, Royal Tank Corps. The Mark V tank was introduced in the spring of 1918; it was fitted with a new purpose-built Ricardo engine and had a new system of brakes and gears which allowed one driver to control it.

Statistics: length 26 ft 5 ins, width 13 ft 6 ins, height 8 ft 8 ins, weight 29 tons; maximum speed 4.6mph; armaments 2 × 6-pounder guns, 4 × .303-inch Hotchkiss machine guns; crew 8. This tank was first used in action at Le Hamel, Somme front, in July 1918. Gordon Hassell, then an Acting Captain, took part in this battle, which, he later wrote, 'was so successful as to be hardly believable. Sixty tanks, with no hint of preliminary bombardment, left their camp positions early on 4 July and, with Australian troops, captured a most valuable hill position overlooking the eastward Somme country. All our troops came out, the tank casualties could be counted on one hand.'

One could hardly realize that things were serious – the infantry coming with our Company had about five men wounded during the whole day during the advance of *about four miles*.

Many years later Hassell wrote a detailed account of Cambrai and of his two-year career as a tank officer, including a description of what it was like to be in one of these new mechanical monsters:

Terribly noisy, oily, hot, airless and bumpy! Without any sort of cushion, as we had no springs and had thirty tons' weight, any slight bump and crash was magnified and many a burn was caused by a jerk throwing the crew about. Instinctively one caught at a handhold, and got a burn on the hot engine. The crew had very little knowledge of where they were going, only by peeping through slits and weapon apertures could they see anything. In action if the tank was hit slivers of hot steel began to fly – bullets hitting the armoured plates caused melting and the splash, as in steel factories, was dangerous to the eyes. For protection we used to wear a small face mask.

The newly formed Tank Corps had a great deal at stake at Cambrai. This was its great opportunity to prove itself, so the attack was preceded by much realistic training and the most meticulous of preparations, including for one basic problem – encountering trenches too wide for a tank to cross – the provision of an ingenious special device:

We were given enormous 'fascines', consisting of 75 bundles of brushwood bound together with chains into a cylindrical mass. Each was 4½ feet high, 10 feet long and weighed about two tons. They were hoisted back onto the top of the tank, and when the tank was nosed up to the trench, a quick release gear allowed the fascine to drop straight into it, thus allowing the machine to be lowered gently down onto it, and the nose to grip the other side ... and away!

By the 19th [November] all final preparations had been made; I had filled up with 60 gallons of the finest aviation spirit, studied aero photos of my route, had

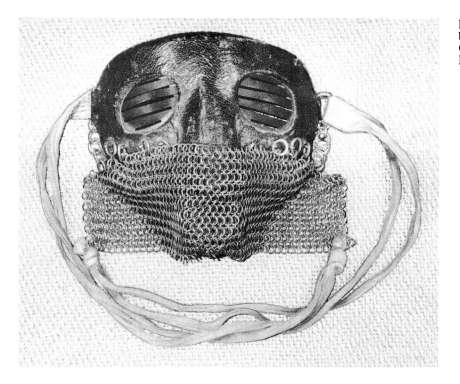

Protective face mask worn by Second Lieutenant Gordon Hassell in the Battle of Cambrai

maps and two pigeons supplied; had written my will and disposed of gear not required. Our morale was 100%. At 5 pm the whole battalion moved off on the long eight-hour approach march, in the dark, which our reconnaissance officers had previously taped at the final stretches, to enable each tank to get to its starting off position. By 1 am all tanks were on the starting line. Zero hour for the first wave was 6.10 am and *Harrier*, my tank, was in the second wave starting at 6.30 am.

Between 1 am and 4 am I saw that my crew got a cat-nap; I slept, so tired was I, with a blanket out in the open. At 4 am I decided that all eight of us could do with a hot drink, and took the risk of having cocoa brewed right in the tank, the crew surrounding the small pressure stove with all our fire extinguishers. No accident occurred, and, warmed up, we battened down and awaited the start. General Hugh Elles, the Commander of the Tank Corps, had meanwhile come up. In a famous order he told us that he would personally lead this first tank battle, and with his own flag he chose a tank near mine; *Hilda*, commanded by my friend, Lieutenant Leach.

At 6.30 am I gave the 'right away' and our engine purred with perfect tuning. As the mist cleared and the dawn got brighter I found it possible to recognize all the features shown on the air photos and maps, and the going was easy over the rolling grassy slopes. In the distance, where the Hindenburg system was heavily garrisoned, our shells were exploding. Return fire was not enough to be a real menace. Our infantry waved us on, one wounded soldier on the ground I particularly remember for his cheerful grin. The enemy fire withered, and it became abundantly clear that the fantastic sight of our 350 unwieldy monsters approaching out of a quiet night, with that extraordinary great lump sitting on top (perhaps they thought it carried great explosive charges) had demoralized the Germans. Our infantry had little to do but to receive the prisoners and clear the dug-outs in the trenches.

When *Harrier* had come to the second Hindenburg line, my Sergeant, Callaghan, stopped the tank to adjust its position, I released the dropping gear and our fascine fell to the bottom. But it had fallen askew. Callaghan gently lowered us on to it; but the tracks would not grip it and went round uselessly. We were, as we used to say, 'bellied'. With patience and skill Callaghan put the engine in neutral gear, raced the engine to maximum speed and jerked in the clutch again and again. *Harrier* shuddered and we finally got the tracks in a firm position where they got a bite and we cautiously crawled out of the trench. Then away to our next objective which was the village of Ribecourt. Our speed was not more than 2 mph going fully out and with no stops and obstacles, so time seemed long for the real distance covered.

At Ribecourt the only resistance was by Germans who were using houses for protection and shot from the roof. The Germans were very ready to surrender in large numbers. We stopped and I wrote a report to affix to the leg of one of the pigeons which flew off alright but of course I never knew if it duly arrived at its loft at the Headquarters of the Third Army. That was at 8.55 am. Through the village we turned left to the railway yards, climbed up a bank and bumped over the rails. Then right again into open country and on to the third Hindenburg defence line which was my final objective. It was full of Germans and I was astonished at the vast floor of virgin wire in front of it. Waiting a short time until we saw our allotted infantry, we flew our red and yellow flag to show the path we would crush for the Norfolks to cross. We went over the wire and up to the trench. Looking down I saw the white and inquisitive-looking Germans at the entrance of a deep dug-out. They indicated surrender and the Norfolks obliged in collecting them.

Hassell's tank did not survive the day unscathed, however. His crew had climbed out of *Harrier* for a stretch and a smoke when the Company Commander came up and told him that there was some 'trouble' up a slope to the left:

Another tank had arrived so he said to both of us 'Go and see what it is'. So into *Harrier* again and I followed *Hong Kong*. Near the top I suddenly saw white smoke coming from *Hong Kong* and then more. At once Callaghan and I got *Harrier* round 90 degrees, so that if we had any more trouble it would be behind us instead of being broadside on. But alas I next saw our right track flying and gyrating up to the sky. A second hit blew in the roof and a third took us in the back. 'Abandon Tank' I signalled. (We had a long time ago practised this drill.) And almost miraculously I found no injury to any of us, except shock and dented-in steel helmets. My friend Cecil Edwards, commander, with his crew of *Hong Kong* were all killed. The German gunner who had the guts to stay and train his field gun on us as we climbed to the hill top, and fired with open sights, hit thirteen tanks in all. He was specially mentioned by name in Sir Douglas Haig's Cambrai despatch.

But the action had its lighter moments. As already stated, General Elles had taken personal command in the tank *Hilda*. Writing just after the event Hassell commented:

There is rather a joke out against him about it. The newspaper reports apparently refer to this 'bus' as taking the General, and 'penetrating deeply into the Hindenburg Line'. This was literally true; as his machine unfortunately stuck in the trench, and actually penetrated as deeply as possible.

Despite its hopeful beginning, however, the Cambrai battle ended unhappily; the British failed to exploit their advantage and within days the Germans had won back all the ground the tanks had gained. But the importance of this new arm had been established and in 1918 tanks would play a continuous and crucial part in the final advance.

Americans on the Western Front

United States forces had their first taste of action in France in late May 1918. However, they did not play a major military role until the final stages of the war and when their turn finally came to participate in a full-scale set-piece battle they suffered as heavily as their Allies had before them. Their attack in collaboration with the French in the Argonne region on 26 September 1918 produced the familiar pattern of early success followed by later setbacks and resulted in over 100,000 casualties. However, the American presence alone was a powerful factor in determining the course of events in the war's final year.

Above: An American 14-inch railroad gun firing in the Argonne region, September 1918 (Q81616)

Left: American wounded being treated in an old church by the 110th Sanitary Train, 4th Ambulance Company, 1st Division, Neuvilly, France, on 26 September 1918 (Q 7074)

PART III
The War at Sea

'THERE is great enthusiasm in the British Isles due to the war and recruits are flocking in daily,' wrote Lieutenant Eric Woodruff RN in September 1914 to his brother in Australia. 'If only the German Fleet would come out we would wipe them out in a few minutes.'

This was the standard view not only within the Royal Navy but of the British public when hostilities began. There would be a face-to-face contest between the world's two most powerful fleets and the heirs of Drake and Nelson would emerge victorious. In fact for most of the war the capital ships were inactive, and, though there were occasional sweeps up and down the North Sea or elsewhere, many ships' companies spent months simply 'swinging round the buoy'. Men became used to, and bored with, the sight of lines of anchored warships in Scapa Flow or Rosyth, or their German equivalents, Kiel and Wilhelmshaven. Meanwhile, one of the Royal Navy's greatest wartime successes, almost taken for granted, continued day after day in the English Channel, where not a single troopship going to or from France was lost to enemy action.

The hunger for a great sea-battle was finally appeased, but once only, and that not until mid-1916, at Jutland – and this was not the clear-cut victory that one side expected and the other side hoped for. Jutland remains one of the epic sea stories of the century, however, and is given pride of place in this part of the book.

Before that there were other engagements, of which the Battle of the Heligoland Bight has already been described (see Part I), and two other notable ones are dealt with here. One was a crushing British defeat; the other an overwhelming victory – the second being a return match following the first. At Coronel a small British squadron was decisively beaten by a larger German one; off the Falkland Islands, a few weeks later, a powerful British force exacted a virtually mandatory revenge.

These were old-style gunnery sea-fights, without any input from such new and untried weapons of war as the aeroplane or the submarine. Remarkably, the latter – in the form of the German U-boat – came very close later to inflicting defeat on Britain. The undersea war is therefore also an important theme, with a section on successful submarines and other sections on the means adopted to thwart them. Q-Ships – vessels which were armed but disguised to look like ordinary merchantmen – provided a number of dramatic episodes, of which one is retold here. More effective, however, was the adoption of the convoy system, which required servicing by the Navy's smaller ships, whose contribution to victory was in the end virtually as important as that of the great battleships. This aspect of the war at sea is reflected in a section based on the diary of a young officer who spent many months in convoy duties.

HMS *Iron Duke*, Admiral Jellicoe's flagship in the North Sea (Q 55500)

The War at Sea **Important Dates**

1914

August 28	Battle of the Heligoland Bight
September 22	Sinking of three *Cressy* class cruisers
November 1	Battle of Coronel
December 8	Battle of the Falkland Islands

1915

January 24	Battle of the Dogger Bank
February 4	Germany announces blockade of British Isles
18	Blockade begins
22	Germany commences campaign of unrestricted submarine warfare
May 7	Sinking of the *Lusitania* by *U 20*
September 18	Germany abandons submarine campaign following reaction to sinking of *Lusitania*, *Arabic* and *Hesperian*

1916

February 29	Start of second campaign of unrestricted submarine warfare
March 24	Sinking of the *Sussex*
April 24	Germany calls off campaign – U-boats ordered to work in accordance with international Prize Law
May 31-June 1	Battle of Jutland
June 4	HMS *Hampshire* sunk by a mine off Orkney Islands
5	Lord Kitchener drowned
August 19-October 19	Sorties of German High Seas Fleet

1917

February 1	Germany declares unrestricted submarine warfare
April 27	British Admiralty agrees to adopt convoy system
October 17-December 12	German surface attacks on Scandinavian convoys
November 17	Cruiser action in Heligoland Bight

1918

April 25	Last sortie of German High Seas Fleet
April 22-23	Naval raid on Zeebrugge
May 9-10	Naval raid on Ostend
November 21	Surrender of German Fleet
November 23-27	German Fleet arrives in Scapa Flow to be interned

1919

June 21	German Fleet scuttled in Scapa Flow

Torpedoed Three Times in a Day

On 22 September 1914 three armoured cruisers of the *Cressy* class – *Aboukir*, *Hogue* and *Cressy* herself – were on patrol in a sea area known as the Broad Fourteens off the Dutch coast when they were discovered by the German submarine *U 9*. She sank them by torpedo one by one.

W.H. 'Kit' Wykeham-Musgrave was a naval cadet who had just completed his first term at the Royal Naval College, Dartmouth; sent to the fleet on mobilization along with his fellow-cadets he had been appointed to HMS *Aboukir*. When *Aboukir* was torpedoed he managed to get off and swam to *Hogue*: when *Hogue* was sunk he escaped to *Cressy*; when *Cressy* went down he found himself swimming for his life yet again, to be picked up eventually by a Dutch trawler.

Wykeham-Musgrave wrote several accounts of his ordeal, of which this is the first and most detailed:

Friday 25th September [1914]

Dear Grannie

Thank you so much for your kind letter and for the sovereign you sent me. I had a most thrilling experience. We were steaming line ahead with a distance of three miles between the ships. We were struck first. I was sleeping down below at the time. We were woken up by a terrific crash and the whole ship shook and all the crockery in the pantry fell. Of course we thought it was a mine, and rushed up on deck; we had all the scuttles and watertight doors closed at once, and everything that would float brought up and thrown overboard in as much time as we had. She then started to list heavily. By that time *Cressy* and *Hogue* had arrived and had let down their boats. The *Aboukir* at last went down suddenly and we slid down her side into the water. Fortunately there was not a great deal of suction on the side we jumped off so with difficulty got clear. I swam to the *Hogue* and was just going on board when she was struck and sank in three minutes. I then swam on to the *Cressy* where I was hauled up the side with a rope. I went down into the Sick Bay where I had a cup of cocoa, but directly I had finished she was struck also and we were forced to go up on deck again. We sat on the fo'c'stle and we saw a submarine come as close as 200 or 300 yards off and we fired all the guns at her until we sank. I jumped off again and got clear and after swimming about for a long time found a plank to hang on to. I hung on to it until I was picked up having been three hours in the water. I don't remember being picked up as I was unconscious. But I woke up in the trawler the *Titan* which was Dutch. They had rescued about 300 survivors. They were awfully kind to us and did every possible thing for us. We were taken off on a destroyer called the *Lucifer* which took us to Harwich. I had no clothes on when picked up but was provided with the most funny clothes on the destroyer. I hope I shall see you soon and be able to tell you more about it. It was a perfect miracle how I was saved considering only 50 out of 800 of our crew were saved. With best love from

Kit

HMS *Cressy*. There were six ships in the *Cressy* class, all built in 1902, so that half the class went down in one day. The other three, *Bacchante*, *Euryalus* and *Sutlej*, survived the war and were sold in 1920 (Q 38576)

The principal statistics of the class were: length 472 ft, beam 69½ ft; displacement 12,000 tons; maximum speed 21 knots; guns 2 × 9.2-inch, 12 × 6-inch; torpedo tubes 2 × 18-inch; complement 760

His remarkable ordeal, and the cheerful spirit with which he faced it, was noted at the time by his naval colleagues, among them Sub-Lieutenant Cyril Bower, who wrote in a letter in late September that one of the rescuing destroyers based on Harwich had brought in a 'tiny little snottie [naval slang for a Midshipman] called Wykeham-Musgrave aged 15½'. 'I think', commented Bower, 'I should volunteer for *farming* somewhere as far away from the sea as possible after an experience like that, but he was quite unperturbed and anxious to get another ship after his ten days' leave.' His later naval career was more fortunate. Midshipman, later Lieutenant-Commander, Wykeham-Musgrave survived for another seventy-five years, dying in 1989 at the age of ninety.

The story of the sinking of the three cruisers was much publicized at the time, not least because among the 1500 who lost their lives were a score of young midshipmen of Wykeham-Musgrave's age – 'Winston's war babies', as they were dubbed, with more than a hint of criticism of the First Lord of the Admiralty's rashness in allowing so many young lives to be put at risk. Wykeham-Musgrave himself featured in at least one breezy press story under the title, with accompanying photograph, MIDDY'S ESCAPES. But to one submarine officer – doubtless speaking for many – the real lesson was that the three cruisers should not have been where they were in the first place, which was not so much Churchill's responsibility as that of the Naval Staff at the Admiralty. Lieutenant Ronald Trevor wrote in a letter of 23 September:

Those three old cruisers which were sunk yesterday had been expected to be sunk every day for weeks by us and our commodore had repeatedly warned the Admiralty that it is madness to allow ships to patrol up and down the North Sea practically on the same course and at the same speed. The North Sea is no place for big ships. I only hope the person responsible for putting them there gets hung.

A Defeat Avenged: Coronel and the Falkland Islands

Why our Admiral ever engaged will never be known of course, but he decided to take them on, two guns of ours against twelve of theirs, which was what the fight actually amounted to. The result you already know, in less than an hour, in fact in forty minutes, the *Monmouth* blew up, and ten minutes later, the *Good Hope*, a roaring furnace, did the same. The *Glasgow* escaped with three shot holes on the waterline, and we without a scratch, marvellous as it may appear and really it is absolutely miraculous. The shells were going whistling overhead and falling ahead and astern of us like hailstones and we never got a touch. One would have finished us altogether. However, we put our best leg foremost and legged it for all we were worth.

These terse sentences written by a young Lieutenant of the Royal Naval Reserve, Harry Woodcock, put in a nutshell the story of a naval defeat which shocked the British nation in November 1914. His statement (from a letter to his uncle and aunt) also raises the unanswerable question over what came to be known as the Battle of Coronel: why did it ever happen? Following a chance encounter off the coast of Chile, Vice-Admiral Sir Christopher Cradock committed his small cruiser force to an affray he could almost certainly have avoided with Germany's powerful East Asiatic Squadron under the command of Admiral Graf von Spee. From the start there was no contest. Cradock went down with his flagship, HMS *Good Hope*, taking his motives with him as well as his men. *Monmouth*, too, had no survivors. Only the *Glasgow* and Woodcock's own ship, the armed merchantman *Otranto*, which was not equipped for serious fighting, evaded the carnage.

The sense of shock was summed up shortly after the event by H.W.G. Spencer, Chief Yeoman of Signals in *Otranto*. He wrote to his wife: 'My God it was awful, on account of our helplessness in the face of a vastly superior force.'

Cradock may have felt that British naval tradition required him to do battle; that it would have been cowardice to run away. Or he may have decided that von Spee would probably overhaul him sooner or later and that if he squared up to him resolutely and at once David might at least inflict some damage to Goliath. Be that as it may, all this was too much for the British Admiralty. A substantial squadron as superior to the German force as the latter had been to Cradock's was despatched under Vice-Admiral Doveton Sturdee to exact revenge. Admiral von Spee had won his victory on 1 November; on 8 December, having sailed round into the Atlantic, he encountered Sturdee off the Falkland Islands. British naval pride was duly reinstated, though the task took longer than the forty minutes required at Coronel. Four out of five of von Spee's warships went to the bottom, fighting as fiercely as Cradock's had done before them; only one light cruiser, the *Dresden*, escaped and that was later scuttled at Juan Fernandez Island.

As this action, inevitably dubbed the Battle of the Falkland Islands, was virtually the last fight at sea in the old tradition of warships versus warships with no other elements involved, it is worth recording for that reason alone; it was also a battle richly written about by participants at the time.

The German squadron of five ships was led by two powerful armoured cruisers, the *Scharnhorst* and the *Gneisenau*, with the light cruisers *Nürnberg, Leipzig* and *Dresden* in support. The British force, which was busily coaling when the Germans arrived on the scene, was led by two of the Royal Navy's prized battle cruisers, *Invincible* and *Inflexible*. (Battle cruisers were a relatively new concept – powerfully armed warships which had been given speed at the expense of protective armour.) In addition, Sturdee had four armoured cruisers, two light cruisers, an armed merchant cruiser and the back-up of an old battleship, *Canopus*, beached at Port Stanley and capable of contributing (as she did in the first moments of the action) much like a unit of land-based artillery.

'Yesterday – what a day! Ye Gods and little fishes!!', wrote Petty Officer H.S. Welch in his diary on 9 December 1914; his ship, the armoured cruiser HMS *Kent*, had been heavily involved in the fighting. 'At 8 am while at breakfast we had a signal from the C-in-C "Kent to weigh anchor". I thought we were just to go out on guard at entrance to harbour till others finished coaling, but a few minutes later another signal came through – "Two enemy cruisers in sight". Gee whiz thought I – something doing.'

Lieutenant V.H. Danckwerts was also in *Kent*, with the key role of gunnery officer. As he put it in the account he wrote a few days later:

I was in my bath when I got the signal '*Kent* weigh; two German cruisers reported from the back of Port Stanley'. Naturally that made me sing, but we could not believe it was true. We had had hopes before, but they had always been dashed.

Richard Steele, a clerk in the flagship *Invincible*, was similarly incredulous to begin with; he wrote in a letter home dated 12 December:

Campbell and I were just finishing dressing when the Flag Lieutenant rushed out of his cabin with a signal in hand and said to us: 'You'd better hurry up and get dressed – the enemy's ships have been reported outside the entrance to the harbour.' I thought at first he was pulling our legs.

It was no leg-pull. Soon Danckwerts had the enemy in view:

We got under way almost immediately, and when we got to the harbour mouth I went up to the crow's nest and saw the sight I have been longing for all the war, and for which the whole Navy would give all they have: two German cruisers, the *Gneisenau* and the *Nürnberg* approaching. They went slow, and turned up parallel to us at a distance of 14,500 yards, and we saw them go to 'Action Stations'.

At about this point the Germans, in the words of the distinguished naval historian Arthur J. Marder, 'got the shock of their lives. They saw tripod masts, which could only mean the presence of battle cruisers, the last thing they expected to see in the South Atlantic.'* *Gneisenau* and

*From *The Dreadnought to Scapa Flow*, vol II, p.121

Nürnberg fell back towards the remainder of von Spee's squadron, and within minutes, as Welch put it in his diary account, 'the enemy's ships were bolting for all they were worth.' As quickly as they could the British ships that would take part in the fight – *Glasgow, Invincible, Inflexible, Carnarvon, Cornwall* – followed *Kent* out of harbour. 'At 10.22½' wrote Danckwerts, 'the signal went up on the flagship "General Chase" and by Jove! we did with some zest.'

The action took a long time to develop, for the Germans had made the most of their head start, but as Steele, in *Invincible*, noted in his account – much of it written in a graphic present tense – the British were steadily catching up:

Right ahead away right down on the horizon a little to our starboard bow are five little specks with five little trails of smoke behind them. This is the enemy – soon we shall be within range of them – our engines are doing their utmost to that end – we are deliberately setting ourselves to riddle them with shells until they sink and until we have done that we shall continue firing, unless they first sink us: but the latter idea does not occur to one for one reason or another.

'Our battle cruisers were steaming like the deuce,' wrote Welch admiringly from the viewpoint of the less powerful *Kent*. Then, at last, the enemy came within range and the fight began. Welch continued:

The victors of Coronel on their way to the Falklands. Admiral Graf von Spee's squadron in line ahead off the Chilean coast, late November 1914 (Q 50992)

Above: SMS *Scharnhorst*, photographed at Valparaiso between the two battles (Q 80706)
Length 474½ ft, beam 71 ft, displacement 11,600 tons; maximum speed 22.5 knots; guns 8 × 8.2-inch, 6 × 5.9-inch, 20 × 3.4-inch; torpedo tubes 4 × 17.7-inch; complement 765-850; armour – belt 6 inches, deck 2 inches

Below: HMS *Inflexible*, one of the two battle cruisers which dominated the Battle of the Falkland Islands (SP 3143)
Length 567 ft, beam 79 ft; displacement 20,000 tons; maximum speed 25-26 knots; guns 8 × 12-inch, 16 × 4-inch; torpedo tubes 4 × 18-inch; complement 750-837; armour – belt 6 inches, turrets 7 inches (cf *Queen Elizabeth* class battleships: belt 13 inches, turrets 11 inches)

At five minutes to one the *Invincible* fired the first shot with one of her twelve inch guns. I have since heard that as the first shot went the Admiral signalled by wireless 'God save the King'. All our men on the forecastle gave one huge cheer when they saw the flash of the gun. Everyone seemed full of secret joy at the prospect of a fight. It is hard to describe my feelings at this time. Thoughts of danger found no room owing to the exciting interest of it all. No-one, I think, seemed to give danger a thought. Every man and boy looked like a lot of schoolboys going away for an outing.

The Germans now realized that they could not escape and that the only course was for their most powerful ships to stand and slog it out, in the hope of allowing their weaker ones to get away. Danckwerts observed the crucial manoeuvres:

The *Scharnhorst* and the *Gneisenau* turned sharp to port, and the three light cruisers turned slightly to starboard and left them. The *Invincible* and the *Inflexible* turned to port at once and opened fire with all guns, the *Scharnhorst* and the *Gneisenau* doing the same. We three [in *Kent*'s crow's nest] had the most magnificent view of the finest scrap I shall see for a long time. I have never seen any ship fire heavy guns so rapidly and continuously as the *Scharnhorst* and the *Gneisenau* was not much behind her. They fought absolutely magnificently.

Steele in *Invincible* also admired the enemy gunnery:

It was noticed that they got their shots off in splendid salvoes, all the flashes being almost simultaneous. At 1.42 they were straddling us, i.e. some of their shots fell over us and others short, but none yet hitting us. At 1.45 we all felt a dull thud and the ship quivered slightly – we had been struck for the first time.

The British were handing out even greater punishment, as Welch noted from *Kent*:

I saw one shell (fired by the *Inflexible*) strike the side of the *Gneisenau* amidships and burst. It must have been real hell near that part. The splash and flame seemed to reach quite two-thirds to the height of the mast. What effect it did have I don't know but I thank heaven I was not on the *Gneisenau*.

At this point the battle resolved itself into two main engagements: the two battle cruisers versus the *Scharnhorst* and the *Gneisenau*; the cruisers versus their German counterparts, with the advantage of fire-power in both cases to the British. Steele noted the progress of events:

At 3.28 the third funnel of the *Scharnhorst* was reported to have been shot away by one of our shells. At 4 pm the *Scharnhorst* was seen to be capsizing. At 4.8 '*Scharnhorst* going down by the head'. At 4.17 she had disappeared completely with all on board. No time to think of rescuing those struggling bodies clinging to wreckage, no time for that. The *Gneisenau* is still spitting fire.

Meanwhile HMS *Kent* was beginning a fierce gladiatorial contest with the *Nürnberg*, later to be vividly recorded in Welch's diary:

Now we were at it in deadly earnest. The crash and din was simply terrific – first our broadside going off and shaking our bodies to pieces, deafening, choking and nearly blinding us, then the shells from the enemy hitting and bursting, throwing death-dealing pieces of shell and splinters of steel in all directions and nearly poisoning us with the fumes. Shells were scorching all round us and as they whizzed by the bridge and the deck I could feel the rush of air. One hit the corner of the fore turret casing, glanced off and tore through the deck into the sick bay crumpling and tearing steel plating as though it were paper. Another

burst just outside the conning tower and sent a perfect hail of pieces of shell in around us.

Our shell fire was now telling with awful effect on the enemy. *Nürnberg*'s foremast was shot clean away at 5.58 and four minutes later she caught fire below the foremost funnel and the forebridge. I have since heard (from the statement of one of the *Nürnberg*'s crew we saved) that *one* shell of ours killed fifty of her men outright.

The enemy was still game, but I could see that we were getting the upper hand – several of her guns were smashed clean up and one of her 5.9 inch guns on the forecastle was blown overboard and the other was falling about the deck. Her upper works were a picture – funnels all splintered and torn and jagged pieces sticking out.

Still the German cruiser refused to surrender, and it was another hour before she hauled down her flag; even then it was some time before she foundered:

At 7.26 the *Nürnberg* gave a sudden lurch to starboard and sank smoothly down into the deep amid a mass of wreckage and dense clouds of smoke. The sight was one of fearful awe, and yet she turned over and sank with a graceful gliding motion as would a cup or a tumbler pressed over in a bowl of water. Those who went down in her were game to the end for we saw a party of her men standing on the quarter-deck waving the German ensign (tied to a pole) as she sank and so they went down into their watery grave. One can only feel that they were brave men and died as their beloved Fatherland would have them. They fought well and to a finish.

By this time the *Gneisenau* had also gone down and Steele in *Invincible* was witnessing the picking-up of survivors:

As they're hauled on deck, they're taken below into the Wardroom ante room, or the Admiral's spare cabin. Here with knives we tear off their dripping clothing, then with towels try to start a little warmth in their ice-cold bodies. They are trembling, violently trembling, from the iciness of their immersion. Most of them need resuscitation. Some on coming to consciousness give the most terrible groans as if there was represented to their minds some very awful picture. What frightful sights they must have witnessed, some of them! Our shells did terrible damage, sometimes wiping out an entire gun's crew. One or two are horribly burned and some of their bodies are red where they have been peppered with lyddite. We get what spare warm clothing we can, such as blankets and sweaters. We have three surgeons on board and these do what best they can, relieving suffering frequently with morphia. I will draw a veil over the rest of this. I myself don't like to think of it. The human body is not beautiful in all circumstances! That is all I will say.

Kent's fight had taken them away from the main battle area, and, moreover, a German shell had (in Welch's phrase) made 'an Irish stew' of all the instruments in the ship's wireless room. Danckwerts noted:

As we were out of sight of all the others, they did not know what had happened to us, till we got into harbour next day. They were all very anxious and we could hear them signalling for news of us, and telling ships to search for us.

For Welch the arrival in Port Stanley was a crowning moment:

Didn't they just cheer us when they saw us loom out of the mist and signal that we were the *Kent* and had sunk the *Nürnberg*? Their cheers just about made us feel a wee lump rise in the throat.

Germany's Own Goal: The *Lusitania*

On 7 May 1915 the German submarine *U 20* sank the Cunard liner *Lusitania* – which was en route for Britain from the United States – off the southern coast of Ireland: 1202 people perished, among them 128 Americans. The event produced a notable shift in American opinion in favour of the Allies, and it soured attitudes in Britain and among Britain's fighting forces. (It was even adduced on the Western Front in December 1915 as a reason for refusing a Christmas truce along the lines of the remarkably widespread fraternization of the previous year.)

It was a gift to the Parliamentary Recruitment Committee who attempted to channel the upsurge of anger that resulted from it into persuading more men to join the colours. It produced much mockery of Germany's so-called claim to be a cultured nation, such as the cartoon reproduced here, *Gott mit Uns or German Kultur*, published in a pamphlet by Sir Isidore Spielmann entitled *Germany's Impending Doom*. ('*Gott mit Uns*' – 'God with us' – was the slogan carried on German soldiers' belt buckles.)

There has been much discussion as to whether, because she was carrying certain war supplies in her cargo, she was a legitimate target for submarine attack. However, such historical niceties were not on the public mind in 1915, when the deed was seen as yet more evidence of German 'frightfulness'.

At the age of 102, a survivor of the tragedy, Mrs Jane Lewis, who had been travelling with her husband, recorded an interview about her experiences:

The sea was calm; if the water had not been like that, there would have been many more lost. It happened about lunchtime. All in the daylight.

The most vivid scene of all was when it first started, when the explosion came. We were in the dining room. Everybody was frightened then – they panicked. Had we not been by a door we would never have got out, because a stream of people came down the dining room, there were others following at the back, and people were being stepped on, walked on. That was the most terrible thing – they just couldn't help themselves, the crowd was too strong.

And when we were going down the staircase towards the boats someone fell on top of me – I would never have survived if my husband hadn't got hold of me and had the strength to pull me out.

She had other clear memories: of 'a poor bandsman on deck trying to get out of his uniform; he was so fat he couldn't get out of it; I don't know what became of him': and of 'a little Frenchman on board with his five children and his wife – he kept them all together; he popped up at Queenstown [the port in Ireland to which the survivors were taken] and he had saved them all'.

REMEMBER THE LUSITANIA!

One mother lost all her three young children, one six years, one aged four, and the third a babe in arms, six months old. She herself lives, and held up the three of them in the water, all the time shrieking for help. When rescued by a boat party the two eldest were dead. Their room was required on the boat, and the mother was brave enough to realise it. "Give them to me," she cried. "Give them to me, my bonnie wee things. I will bury them. They are mine to bury as they were mine to keep."

With her hair streaming down her back and her form shaking with sorrow, she took hold of each little one from the rescuers and reverently placed it into the water again, and the people in the boat wept with her as she murmured a little sobbing prayer to the great God above.

But her cup of sorrow was not yet completed. For just as they were landing, her third and only child died in her arms.

BERLIN, MAY 8.

Hundreds of telegrams have been sent to Admiral von Tirpitz congratulating him.

✳ ✳ ✳

ARTICLE IN **COLOGNE GAZETTE.**

The news will be received by the German people with unanimous satisfaction, since it proves to England and the whole world that Germany is quite in earnest in regard to her submarine warfare.

✳ ✳ ✳

ARTICLE IN **KOLNISCHE VOLKSZEITUNG.**

With joyful pride we contemplate the latest deed of our Navy and it will not be the last.

✳ ✳ ✳

NEW YORK, MAY 8.

Riotous scenes of jubilation took place last evening amongst Germans in the German clubs and restaurants. Many Germans got drunk as the result of toasting "Der Tag."

ENLIST TO-DAY.

Poster and cartoon milking post-*Lusitania* anti-Germanism

Mrs Alice Drury (*née* Lines) was ninety-one and the last known survivor of the tragedy when she was interviewed. She had been on board the liner as a nursemaid with an American family. An English girl, she had answered an advertisement in 1914 in the society magazine *The Lady* and had met her future employer, one Colonel Pearl, by appointment at a London club. 'It was the days when we used to wear large hats and he said "Will you take your hat off?" – which I did. I had, to be quite honest, lovely hair, and he said, "Oh my wife will love you, because you've got such pretty hair".'

She joined the family for what was meant to be two years of touring round the world, but war intervened when they were in Denmark and there were considerable difficulties in getting back to the United States. By the spring of 1915, however, Colonel Pearl felt confident enough to travel back to Europe and booked his family on the *Lusitania*; as well as himself and his wife there were four young children, Susan, Amy (known as Bunny), Stuart and baby Audrey, plus two nursemaids – Alice Lines and a Danish girl. The first torpedo struck as Alice was below in the cabin attending to the baby:

While I was feeding her there was a terrific bang – instinct told me what it was – I just picked up the shawl and the baby with it. Stuart was also in the cabin and he was crying 'I don't want to be drowned, I don't want to be drowned', and I crossed over to him and said, 'Hang on to me whatever happens', and he did.

We got up one flight of stairs, and the second torpedo struck. The other nurse called down to me 'What shall I do?' I said, 'You look after Bunny' – I never saw her or Bunny any more.

We eventually got on deck and a sailor grabbed Stuart and threw him down into the lifeboat. I made to jump after, but a sailor said 'It's full – room in the next one', but I got hysterical and yelled out 'You've got my boy' and I just jumped, and a man leaned forward and grabbed me by the hair and I toppled over into the boat. I always said my hair saved my life.

I saw the ship go down. There was this huge lovely liner, and as I watched one funnel went and then the other and the other until the ship was gone and the sea was calm, and all you could see was bodies, and wreckage of furniture and everything that had been in the ship floating in the water.

As well as the Danish nurse and Bunny, a second child, Susan, also drowned. It was deaths such as these, of uninvolved neutrals, which ensured that the event was a German propaganda defeat.

The Battle of Jutland

Expected since the outbreak of war, the battle between the world's two most powerful navies was finally joined on 31 May 1916. There was enthusiasm for a showdown on both sides. As Leutnant zur See Heinrich Bassinge, of the German light cruiser *Elbing*, expressed it in the memoir he wrote half a century later: 'After two years everybody was eager to have a good battle with the hated English.'

The Battle of Jutland involved 250 warships and twenty-four admirals; twenty-four ships were lost and there were almost 10,000 casualties. Writing to his family on 3 June from HMS *Colossus*, Assistant Paymaster Harold Foot tried to describe the impact of the event on eye and ear, beginning with the basic fact of a battle fleet spread over seven or eight miles with numerous small craft distributed in between:

This is as it were the foundation stone. Next you add great wicked-looking tongues of flame which appear four or five at a time in each ship followed immediately by a dense brown fog of cordite smoke which probably eclipses the ship for several seconds. Then comes the most picturesque touch – the tremendous columns of water (thicker at the top than the base) which rise to a height of about 200 feet as each projectile strikes the water, and finally the dull red glow of shots getting home on the target. The latter effect is considerably altered when the point of view is shifted to the ship that is hit. Probably it then takes the form of a blinding flash and sharp heavy explosion, and from a ship near by looks like the destruction of the ship.

We reach the limit of description or realization when it comes to a ship blowing up. The original vast sheet of flame is immediately succeeded by an apparently slow ascending column of fragments and yellow-grey smoke. The slowness however is only apparent at the top of the column which when finally expanded must reach a height of something like 1000 feet.

Noises are in similar proportion. Enemy shells bursting close to the ship have a sharper sound than one's own guns firing, but the passage of large projectiles through the air causes a continuous heavy roaring sound broken up into waves like the passage of an express train and conveys a distinct sense of heat.

At the heart of this gigantic running maelstrom were the two Commanders-in-Chief, Vice-Admiral Reinhard Scheer in the German battleship *Friedrich der Grosse* and Admiral Sir John Jellicoe in HMS *Iron Duke*. Petty Officer Telegraphist A.J. Brister was on the bridge of Jellicoe's flagship for much of the battle:

After 9 pm when signal traffic had thinned out, Commander Phipps asked for a relief for me and was told that there was none available. He therefore suggested that I laid down between the incoming or outgoing of signals, but there was only one place where I could do that – on a leather-seated wooden settee on which reposed the C-in-C's greatcoat. Finding no means of hanging up the coat or placing it elsewhere, I stretched myself out on the seat and spread the heavy garment over me. The excitement of the last few hours began to fade and I was feeling pleasantly relaxed when the charthouse door opened, the trip-catch putting out the light. The door closed slowly, the light came on and staring down at me was the C-in-C. I froze, unable to think what to do or say at the moment.

The Admiral was wearing an old tarnished cap and a faded blue raincoat, his weather-worn face looked tired and strained yet his eyes were clear and penetrating. What would he say to a Petty Officer who had the impertinence to make use of his coat? It seemed ages before I struggled to get up and it was then that the Commander came to my rescue. 'I told him to lie down, sir. He has had no relief.' Admiral Jellicoe nodded, went to the chart table and began dictating signals and conversing in his usual soft-speaking voice. For a while I stayed on the seat looking at the back of the great little man who was carrying such a tremendous load of responsibility. What would the morrow bring him and would he go down in history as the modern Nelson?

Sadly for Britain's hopes this was not to be. Nor would the man who came nearest in public perception to the Nelsonian image – Sir David Beatty, the Vice-Admiral in command of the Battle Cruiser Fleet – achieve all that had been expected of him on this long-awaited day.

Beatty was in contact first over two hours before the C-in-C; in fact the opening phase of the action was the meeting of the battle cruisers of both nations, with Beatty attempting to draw the Germans on to the massive fire-power of Jellicoe's battle fleet coming up behind. Beatty's flagship was HMS *Lion*; in an account written immediately afterwards one of her junior midshipmen, N.G. Garnons-Williams, described the view from *Lion* as the firing began:

The visibility was good, but not abnormal, and we began getting ranges at about 22,000 yards. The enemy was now bearing 45 – I could now distinguish five battle cruisers, with destroyers ahead of them. The rate was a closing one, and it surprised me that we did not open fire sooner. As it was, at 3.47* they opened fire with their leading ship, and we replied immediately, range 18,500 yards. They had the advantage of light and did very good shooting. I could not see much of our shooting for the first half hour, but we appeared to be getting several straddles. Their shorts** did not appear to make any difference to us, as they are generally supposed to, in fact only one salvo splashed the conning tower and that was an over. At 4.0 pm the TS [Transmitting Station] reported no communication with Q Turret and the Captain ordered Q magazine to be flooded. I had heard some hits on the after part of the ship, but they did not make so much noise as our own direct salvoes, and I had no idea that we had been hit so badly.

The flooding of Q magazine – generally credited to the orders of the turret officer, Major F.J.W. Harvey, Royal Marines, who was awarded a posthumous Victoria Cross – saved *Lion* from the fate which was shortly to befall two other ships in Beatty's fleet. Shortly after 4 pm, following hits on her upper deck and fore-turret, two huge explosions put paid to HMS *Indefatigable*, and half an hour later she was followed to the bottom by HMS *Queen Mary*.*** Midshipman Peregrine Deardon was one of

---

*Times given in personal accounts have been moved back by one hour to Greenwich Mean Time to accord with the official record of the Battle.
**ie, salvoes falling short of their intended target.
***Jellicoe, Beatty and others blamed inadequate armour protection for the loss of battle cruisers at Jutland. The fact that the British gunnery system was particularly vulnerable to cordite flash is now seen as the basic cause; in action, magazine doors were kept open and lids were taken off powder cases with a view to attaining a rapid rate of fire.

Battle cruiser HMS *Indefatigable* going into action at 3pm on 31 May 1916. Just over an hour later she blew up and disappeared from view, with two survivors from her crew of 57 officers and 960 men (SP 799)

the latter ship's handful of survivors. This is from a letter he wrote from a German prisoner of war camp a few days later:

About 2.45 pm on the 31st we went to action stations and had everything ready and about 3.45 pm we opened fire and after about an hour and a half of enjoyment [in fact three quarters of an hour] there was a terrific explosion forward and I was sent out on the top of our turret (after turret) to see what was happening, and had to put on a lung respirator owing to clouds of smoke and fire. I could see nothing for a minute and then all cleared away as the foremost part of the ship went under water. I then told the officer of the turret that the ship was sinking rapidly and so as many as possible were got out of the turret. The whole foc'sle was almost blown off and I immediately took off all my gear except my shirt and vest. As soon as in the water I swam clear and astern of the ship about thirty yards when she suddenly blew up completely. I was luckily sucked under water and so all the wreckage chucked about did not come with its full weight on my head. I held my breath for a long time and at last came to the surface and started looking round for something to support me as much as possible. The surface of the water was simply covered in oil fuel which tasted and smelt horribly. I smothered myself all over with it which I think really saved my life as the water was frightfully cold.

Deardon was eventually picked up almost unconscious by a German destroyer.

In line following *Queen Mary* was HMS *Tiger*; Commander E.R. Jones was *Tiger*'s Executive Officer (ie second-in-command). He noted in his normally low-key factual diary:

The *Tiger* being astern of the *Q.M.* we saw their accident closely and a horrible sight it was. First an enormous height of dull red flame, followed by a great mass of black smoke amongst which was the wreckage thrown in all directions. The blast was tremendous. We passed through the smoke and it was very unpleasant for the moment, however no effect to us seemed to result.

Meanwhile *Tiger* herself was sustaining heavy punishment. On board was Father Thomas Bradley, Roman Catholic Chaplain to the 1st Battle Cruiser Squadron; his place of duty was in the ship's distributing station, where the wounded would be brought for treatment. Something of the special awfulness of being cooped up below decks in a major sea-fight emerges from his diary account:

The first two or three hours were a terrible experience. It was a 'bloody Hell'. As this was the first time I had been under fire the first few minutes made one feel a strange sort of funk, but after a time when we became busy with the wounded one grew more used to it. One could see nothing when below. There would be an explosion somewhere aft in the ship and in a few minutes would come the wounded, some groaning and crying. Then the repetition of the same thing for'ard, and we waited not knowing but that the next might come in where we were. One burst came quite close to us and the blast nearly knocked us off our feet. After the *Indefat* and the *Q.M.* had gone there was the fear that we might suffer the same fate and that one of their shells might get at one of our magazines and we would all be entombed in the ship. The hatchways leading from the engine rooms etc onto the gangways and those leading from the mess decks above are all almost buttoned down. Only one was left free so that we had the somewhat unpleasant knowledge that if the ship went suddenly like the *Q.M.* or *Indefat* we would be drowned like rats in a cage.

We also had a very unpleasant list due to the flooded magazines. We did not know the cause and every time the ship turned to port the list increased and we did not know what was happening, there was the dread lest the ship was turning over on to her side.

Next to be involved was the 5th Battle Squadron of fast battleships, *Barham, Valiant, Warspite, Malaya*, and there then followed the second major phase of the action: the meeting – for a few hectic minutes only – of the two battle fleets. Edgar Sharpe, a rating in HMS *Valiant*, found himself drawn to the magnificent sight of the arrival on the scene of the prime force of the British Navy, despite the hammering his own squadron was receiving at the time. He wrote home:

We had eyes for our Fleet only, though. My word (it was the main part of the Grand Fleet – four battle squadrons of Dreadnoughts) they did look fine. Like a picture! It was evening, and though there was no sun, the light reflected on their light grey sides, and huge columns of water were spouting up all about them.

Among the Dreadnoughts of the approaching Fleet was HMS *Vanguard*, from which – while taking a brief respite from his prime task, the oddly un-warlike one of baking bread – one of the ship's cooks, Walter Green-way, surveyed the amazing prospect in front of him. As he put it in a letter home:

While my dough was proving in the tins I went out on the quarterdeck and witnessed a magnificent spectacle, one never to be forgotten. The whole visible horizon was one long blaze of flame. The hulls of the enemy's ships were not visible to the naked eye, but could be seen dimly through the haze with the telescope. And the only means we had of knowing the enemy was there was by spurts of flame from the enemy's guns. I was so intensely interested that I did not realize the risk until observing a cruiser close by on fire. I went back to the bakehouse and endeavoured to save my batch of bread. The dough required at least twenty minutes more proof. But being very loathe to waste the material and labour, I put it in and trusted to luck if it would be possible to save it later. Then

The destruction of HMS *Invincible*, photographed from *Inflexible*, 6.34pm, 31 May 1916. She was struck by a heavy shell on the starboard midship 12-inch turret; the flash from this shell ignited the magazine of the two 12-inch turrets, which contained 50 tons of cordite. The ship broke in half and sank in ten to fifteen seconds, with the loss of 1025 officers and men out of a total of 1031 (see also colour section, p144) (SP 2469)

my superior officer gave me orders to leave everything at any critical time. By the time I got to my station we were in the thick of it. Several minutes later I got out a book to read entitled *The Meditations of Marcus Aurelius*. I had not read much when we received the news that the *Invincible* had gone down and we were passing close to her.

The victor and flagship of the Falkland Islands encounter had indeed gone the way of the other two battle cruisers. Commander T.N. James in HMS *Temeraire* at first mistook all that remained of her for something else. He wrote in a letter home:

I had been keeping my eye open for Zepps, as I felt sure they must be about, and although I couldn't see one in the air great was my joy when I thought I saw one wounded, lying in the water some distance on the bow; as we got closer I found it wasn't a Zepp but a ship, and felt rather elated at seeing the fruit of our labours. Alas on getting closer found it was the *Invincible*, with her bow and stern above water, sticking up in the air at an angle of about 45 degrees, her back broken and resting on the bottom.

What of the German reaction to these dramatic events? Leutnant zur See Heinrich Bassinge noted that in SMS *Elbing* 'everybody was overjoyed' at the blowing-up of the *Indefatigable*, and that when the same fate overtook the *Queen Mary* the joy on board was 'unimaginable'. Later, he was aware of the fate of the *Invincible* – announced by 'a tall pillar of fire and smoke' to the north; Bassinge commented, 'it was a terrible sight for all the Grand Fleet to pass there.'

— Starboard Side —

— Port Side —

Hits sustained by H.M.S. "Tiger"

1	5·9"	9. 10. 11	11"
2	11" Pitched on forecastle · burst in cable locker flat	12	11" Burst on "Q" turret Blew in Centre sighting hood.
3	Two 11" projectiles burst in Sick Bay just before turn at 4·35 p.m.	13	11" Did more damage than any other projectile.
4	11"	14. 15	11" Did not penetrate belt.
5	Hit "A" barbette · 12"	16	11" Burst on "X" turret.
6	Burst in flour store · 11"	17.18.19.20	5·9"
7	Carried away steaming light · 11"	21	12" Broke back of Steam pinnace & No 4 Derrick. Blew away battery door and part of bulkhead.
8	11" bounced off without doing much damage.		

For their part, the Germans were also taking punishment. The battle cruiser and flagship SMS *Lützow* was so badly damaged that she would become the fourth in that unhappy category to fall victim at Jutland. Bassinge witnessed her struggles when returning to his battle station after a period below:

I could not believe my eyes! About 100 metres away I could see the *Lützow* with only the upper deck showing. I could not understand that the ship was still able to float. She must have been badly damaged but she still sailed very slowly. At 6.40 more hits on the *Lützow*. English battle cruisers had spotted her but the courageous *Lützow* tried to fire back. At once our battle cruisers opened up their funnels and there was smoke everywhere. The ship was out of sight, the firing soon stopped, but not without a last hit at the *Lützow*. We followed our fleet to the south west and never saw that ship again. We had tried hard to bring her back but late at night she exploded. The crew was rescued by accompanying destroyers.

In fact the *Lützow* was finally despatched by her own side early the following morning, after 1250 of her crew had been safely taken off. Bassinge's *Elbing* was also to become a victim, being mistaken for British during the night by the German battleship *Posen* and rammed. She was finally abandoned and sunk.

In the event, the prospect that 31 May 1916 would see the ultimate showdown between the two fleets never quite materialized. At 6.30 that

Diagram showing hits sustained by HMS *Tiger* at the Battle of Jutland (Q 56781)

evening Jellicoe succeeded in deploying his fleet of twenty-seven battleships across the enemy's line of advance (known as 'crossing the T'), whereupon Admiral Scheer, sensing a hopeless position, ordered a *Gefechtskehrwendung* – a 'battle turn away' – under cover of a smokescreen and destroyer attacks. Less than an hour later Jellicoe crossed the T again – but again the Germans eluded him. The German destroyer attacks on this second occasion led to Jellicoe's decision – much disputed since – to turn his battleships away from the destroyers, thus allowing Scheer to complete his withdrawal.

Subsequently, fighting continued through the hours of darkness, but it was scattered and indecisive – pithily summed up in a letter to his mother by Assistant Paymaster G.N. Cracknell in the light cruiser HMS *Champion*, attached to the 13th Destroyer Flotilla:

The night was very thrilling, the sky was lit up with flame and intermittent actions were going on all round us. Saw two or three ships on fire and one huge Dreadnought blown up by a torpedo. We had a narrow squeak, ran into some German big ships who turned their searchlights on us and blazed away, but did not touch us although bits of shell were picked up on deck next day.

That next day was not, however, to be another glorious First of June. Dawn broke on a scene devoid of German ships; during the night Scheer had taken his fleet back to harbour, leaving Jellicoe the frustrated master of an empty battle ground.

In terms of the balance sheet of losses during the action, the British suffered substantially more than the Germans. Three British battle cruisers, three cruisers and eight destroyers were sunk; the Germans lost one battleship, one battle cruiser, four light cruisers and five destroyers. The casualty figures favoured the Germans even more. They were: British, 6,784 of whom 6,097 were killed; German 3,058 of whom 2,552 were killed. Immediately afterwards the disappointment at the absence of a clear-cut victory was compounded by a downbeat Admiralty statement of 3 June which was precise about British losses and vague about German ones (see opposite). However, overall the palm could be said to have gone to the British, in that the German High Seas Fleet thereafter played no role in the war. Apart from one or two abortive forays, it did not emerge from harbour until it came out to surrender in November 1918.

Sea battles leave their débris as much as their equivalents on land. Walter Greenway, of HMS *Vanguard*, commented on what he saw as the fleet swept up and down on 1 June hoping vainly for a resumption of the battle:

This patrolling was the most pathetic instance during the whole business for we were constantly passing wreckage and the dead bodies in rafts and floating, comrades and foe. This is what goes home to you, but one does not grumble if they possess the heart of a Briton and one feels proud that they have done their bit and took their chance.

He looked forward to the next encounter, however, confident of ultimate victory:

We are not a bit shaken but more determined than ever to avenge our comrades. The Germans have only scratched Britain's Sure Shield. We hope to strike home next time if the elements are favourable to us.

Postscripts to Jutland

The Admiralty Statement (Press Message No. 193) dated 3 June:

THE SECRETARY OF THE ADMIRALTY MAKES THE FOLLOWING ANNOUNCEMENT. On the afternoon of Wednesday, 31st May, a naval engagement took place off the coast of Jutland. The British ships on which the brunt of the fighting fell were the Battle Cruiser Fleet and some Cruisers and Light Cruisers supported by 4 fast Battleships. Among those the losses were heavy. The German Battle Fleet aided by low visibility avoided prolonged action with our main forces and soon after those appeared on the scene the enemy returned to Port though not before receiving severe damage from our Battleships. The Battle Cruisers "QUEEN MARY", "INDEFATIGABLE", "INVINCIBLE", and the Cruisers "DEFENCE" and "BLACK PRINCE" were sunk. The "WARRIOR" was disabled and after being towed for some time had to be abandoned by her crew. It is also known that the Destroyers "TIPPERARY", "FORTUNE", "TURBULENT", "SPARROWHAWK" and "ARDENT" were lost, and six others are not yet accounted for. No British Battleships or Light Cruisers were sunk. The enemy's losses were serious. At least one Battle Cruiser was destroyed and one severely damaged. One Battleship reported sunk by our Destroyers. During a night attack two Light Cruisers were disabled and probably sunk. The exact number of enemy Destroyers disposed of during the action cannot be ascertained with any certainty but it might have been large.

A note from the diary of Father Thomas Bradley, Roman Catholic Chaplain of the 1st Battle Cruiser Squadron:

A few days after the action I called on the Vice-Admiral – Beatty. He was standing writing at his desk in the corner of his cabin and came across to the hearthrug. He was, I believe, writing his despatch of the battle.

Greatly to my surprise he refused to allow us to have a Requiem Mass in the Dockyard. This is contrary to his usual attitude for he does all to encourage services etc. However, he went on to explain that the sailors as I would probably know were a very sentimental lot and he did not think it good for their morale that they should be encouraged to dwell too much on the losses of the squadron which were so severe. He said he had already for the same reason refused to allow the men to attend officially at a Memorial Service in Edinburgh.

I told the Admiral that we had lost 450 men and all the RC officers. I asked if I might convey his special condolences to the relatives of RC officers. He said yes – tell them that these officers died setting a noble example – that he did not feel so much for the dead for they died in the exaltation of Battle but he felt very much for those sorrowing relatives left behind. After a few more words I left him.

War Under the Sea

On 24 August 1914 Lieutenant Ronald Trevor wrote to his cousin from HMS *Dolphin*, the Royal Navy's submarine depot at Gosport, near Portsmouth, 'I do hope the submarines will have a chance of proving their worth.'

Prove their worth they did, in a number of ways, sometimes contrary ones. The ill-judged sinking of the *Lusitania* predisposed the United States against Germany and therefore ultimately helped to guarantee Germany's defeat. Before that, however, the U-boat campaign against Allied shipping brought Germany very close to victory in 1917.

Submarines frequently sailed alone or in small packs and therefore the 'undersea' war gave the opportunity for individual ships and captains to distinguish themselves.

An example was the British submarine *E 11* (captain, Lieutenant-Commander Martin Dunbar-Nasmyth RN), which had served in the Gallipoli campaign. During the campaign *E 11* and her sister ship *E 14* (captain, Lieutenant-Commander E.G. Boyle RN) had created havoc, even sinking Turkish transports in the harbour of Constantinople itself.

Leading Stoker J.T. Haskins kept a diary in *E 14* during her first patrol in April-May 1915. The following extracts give some idea of the submarine's achievements in this period – which led Haskins to state, in the last sentence of the diary, that he would always be proud to say 'I was with the *E 14* through the Dardanelles'.

27 April: 1.30 am. On our way through the Dardanelles on the gas engine, covered about three miles before being sighted. Enemy guns opened up on us, shots now falling all round us. Captain gave orders for diving stations, and we dived to 90 feet and continued on our course. Travelled for six miles at 90 feet right under minefield, then came up to 22 feet to round Fort Chanak. Sighted a gun boat and Captain gave orders to get the bow tubes ready. Dived to 90 feet and after a few minutes came up again. While awaiting orders to fire one torpedo accidentally went off. We fired the second one a minute or two afterwards, it hit the gun boat and she went sky high. Guns from the Fort opened up on us and with shells falling all round us in hundreds we dived again.

1 May: Breakfast on salmon and biscuits and was ready for anything. At 10.12 am we sighted enemy ship, right under land. We dived and closed in on an armoured minelayer. At 600 yards range we fired our torpedo, it was running true. The Captain saw two men aboard the minelayer, cleaning a gun aloft, they saw the torpedo coming straight at them, and they started to run to tell the officer on the bridge. But they were too late, the torpedo hit her and she blew up; by the explosion she made, she must have been full of mines, there was nothing left of her in three minutes. The blast gave us a good shaking up, but nobody minded, as it meant another enemy ship less.

8 May: At 11.15 am we gave chase to an enemy ship, both engines going at full speed and all hands standing by the guns. We got her at 11.35 am and went alongside, only to find she was full of women, children and sheep. After a look around her, we pulled away and let her proceed.

9 May: Constantinople was just showing up in the distance, and there were two enemy ships in sight on which we kept a wary eye.

10 May: We came up to the surface at 6 pm and sighted two transports and a destroyer. At 6.20 pm we dived and

closed in on them. We attacked one of the transports and fired a torpedo, but it missed, we lined up again, and fired a second torpedo. This time we scored a direct hit. The lads gave a cheer as the troops aboard the transport jumped overboard in their hundreds. (We heard later that she had 6000 men aboard her, of which only 2000 survived.)

By 18 May, with no more torpedoes to fire, *E 14* was on its way back to rejoin the fleet at Mudros. There remained the dangerous passage of the Dardanelles:

When we got to Gallipoli, we received a message to say that there were nets across, so we dived to 90 feet and managed to get clear of them. When we got to the Narrows the enemy opened fire on us, but we were too far down for them to do us any harm. After a very exciting time we got through and came up alongside a French battleship. They wanted to know where we had come from, and when our Captain told them we had just come through the Dardanelles, they gave us three cheers.

19 May: At 6.30 am all hands were turned out and had to fall in on the boat. And then reading out the citations, they informed us that our Captain had been awarded the VC, and that our second and third officer had been awarded the DSC, and that the remainder of the crew had been awarded the DSM each.

Above: German U-boats were to prove extremely effective in the Mediterranean theatre later in the war. Standing on the right in this photograph is the U-boat ace Korvetten-Kapitan von Arnauld de la Perrière, commander of *U 35*. Among his remarkable tallies were in June and July 1916, 41 ships; in August 1916, 50 ships. In April 1917 – the worst month of the war for Allied shipping – he with others sank 94 ships (Q 53024)

Left: A merchant steamer breaking up after being attacked by a German submarine (Q 20839)

Q-Ships: Commander Grenfell's Story

'*We have done it at last*: and it has turned out a success beyond my wildest hopes.'

In December 1915 Commander Francis Grenfell, who had retired from the Royal Navy in 1905 and rejoined on the outbreak of war, was appointed commanding officer of the submarine decoy ship *Penshurst*. He wrote the above sentence in his diary almost a year later, having finally and after numerous frustrations destroyed a German U-boat. In terms of the types of warfare for which the *Penshurst* was intended, it was a text-book sinking. For *Penshurst* was one of over 300 so-called Q-ships employed during the war (the British and the French had been using them since November 1914) whose apparent innocence concealed deadly fire-power. Precisely according to plan, when the *UB 19* discovered *Penshurst* off Portland Bill, the German captain was deceived into believing that he had found an unarmed merchantman ripe for despatch; at the crucial moment Grenfell revealed *Penshurst*'s true identity with stunning effect.

HMS *Q 7*
At sea, 2 Dec 1916

Sir,

I have the honour to report that about 4.30 pm on Thursday, 30th November, 1916 when in Lat. 49° 56′N, Long 2° 45′W, I engaged and sank the German submarine *UB 19*, taking prisoners the commanding officer, two other officers, and thirteen ratings ....

Thus Grenfell began his official report, which he recorded verbatim in his diary, but having done so he retold the story in an extended 'personal narrative', which reads like a gripping adventure of the sea. The extract reproduced here begins at the moment that the U-boat was in the act of surfacing, with the presumed intention of sinking the *Penshurst* (or *Q 7*, to use her naval code name) by gunfire. This was standard practice in attacks on solitary merchant ships – a practice indeed on which Q-ships relied, in that they could only be effective in a surface encounter, but then it was assumed that any self-respecting submarine captain would keep his torpedoes for larger and more obviously hostile targets:

She seemed to come up very slowly at first, and kept turning first in one direction and then in another, for the purpose, we thought, of bringing her gun to bear, as it seemed to be abaft the conning tower. Some of her shots fell pretty close, and all seemed to burst on impact with the water, giving off a black smoke. Some hands were now directed to stand at the rail and point her out to each other, and to move about on deck in view of the submarine. I have a mental picture of Pym and Cox leaning over the rail, watching the sub, and then coiling up some ropes, as calmly as if in harbour.

After a considerable while the sub seemed to make up its mind, and come straight for us, firing as she came. I waited until she came within about 1000 yards and had just fired another shot, and then gave the signal to abandon ship. Harrison, the helmsman, and myself rushed off the bridge, well in view of the sub, Harrison and the helmsman then finding their way by the lee of the hatches into the after wheel house above the engines, while I returned on my hands and knees to the bridge. Here I found Ashton with his notebook and watch, and my camera already open and adjusted, and Conway at the voice pipes, both lying at full length on the deck at the after part of the bridge. I crawled like a worm across the bridge, damning Ashton for adjusting his position and exposing the top of his head above the rail. He greeted my objurgations with a cheerful grin and bobbed down.

I was now close against the canvas screen running round the bridge rails, and called to Ashton for a knife to cut a spy-hole through it. With a dextrous flick he slid the knife along the deck towards me without exposing an arm. A second later and I had a small flap cut in the screen, just large enough for one part of my binoculars. I could now see the submarine steering out to port and watched her coming round in a big sweep towards us. She did not fire again after our boats had left. I could see all her people and sung out a number of particulars of her appearance, which Ashton noted down.

It was clear now that the sub had no suspicion of our deadly character, and I was determined that today there should be no doubt whatever as to the issue – so I waited to let her get as close as she cared to come. I expected her either to come close alongside or to put some shots into us, or to board and bomb us. Either event would suit us nicely. Instead of stopping on our port side, however, she continued her circle and passed close under the stern, so close that White, in the after gun house, was afraid the people in her would be able to see in through the after gun house ports. I passed the word to the guns that she was coming round to our starboard quarter, and then slithered across the deck and had another spy-hole cut in the screen in a moment. Then I saw her coming round the stern, and when she was on the quarter and the guns were all bearing on her I leapt for the signal bell and signalled 'open fire'.

Q-ships were converted from many types of vessel, from tramp steamers to sailing ships. (The painting reproduced in the colour section, p144, depicts the converted tramp steamer *Dunraven* which was awarded the VC for its brave encounter with a U-boat in August 1917.) This photograph shows the Q-ship HM Trawler *Principal* with her gun ready for action; in its normal sailing position, ie upright, the gun was meant to be taken for a foremast (SP 3046)

Inside ten seconds the 3 pounder got off its first shot, which carried a man clean off the conning tower; the second immediately afterwards went through her engine room. The 6 pounder and the 12 pounder took up the game almost at once, and the shells began to burst all over the sub. We hit her mostly in the conning tower and after part. Shells burst all along her water line, and the 12 pounder lyddite did grand work. Most of the conning tower was blown clean away, and one shell blew a great sheet of deck plating spinning into the air. We could see the men running on to her deck, and falling or diving overboard. A knot gathered at the fore and where the shells were less numerous. It was a grand sight – and I must admit I mafficked* – I had to run down and shake old Naylor, at the 12 pounder, by the hand.

All this time the sub was going slowly ahead towards our boats, and we learned afterwards that our second shot, besides preventing her submerging, also prevented them stopping the engines. The submarine was now partly shrouded by the smoke of bursting shells, and a shout went up that the men on her were waving in token of surrender. I stopped the firing, but saw nothing of this myself, and as the submarine continued to go ahead, and as I was mindful of Admiral Colville's injunction to me when we commissioned not to take any chances, but to go on firing till the sub sank, I commenced firing again. A very little more, however, convinced me that all was up with her.

Grenfell headed for Portland with his prisoners, among whom there was a number of wounded, and the order was given to 'splice the mainbrace':

We passed the Shambles Light at 11.30 am and just before picking up the examination boat, received a W/T message from Admiral Bayly which read:
    'Very well done. A year's perseverance rewarded.'
I have never received more welcome expression of approval, nor could the message have been more happily worded. I made it known to all hands at once.

There was more to come. On the following day the C-in-C Portsmouth, Admiral Colville, wired to the Commodore at Portland: 'Request you will give _Q 7_ my best congratulations on their great success'.

The outwitting of _UB 19_ was the high point of Grenfell's war. He achieved a second sinking in January 1917, but on this occasion two of his ship's company were killed and two wounded and there were no survivors from the U-boat. He fought four more engagements in February and March, though these were inconclusive. His efforts were acknowledged, however, with promotion to the rank of Captain, with seniority from 8 March 1917. He relinquished his command of the _Penshurst_ in July, being appointed to the staff of the Director of Anti-Submarine Defence. As for his ship, her notable career came to an end when she was sunk by enemy action in December 1917.

Overall, Q-ships were a clever concept but only a modest success. Eventually the enemy became wise to their techniques, and their existence could give wary or ruthless submarine captains a defensible excuse for sinking unarmed merchant ships without warning. They retain, however, with their hint of legitimized piracy, a faint romantic glow in a conflict characterized by brutal killing on an inhuman scale and by all too little finesse. There were few echoes of the world of Robert Louis Stevenson in the war at sea between 1914 and 1918, but perhaps in the adventures of sailors like Captain Francis Grenfell DSO RN they can be distantly heard.

*From the now disused verb 'to maffick', meaning to celebrate extravagantly, based on the euphoric behaviour of the London crowds following the relief of Mafeking, May 1900.

Convoy: A Sub-Lieutenant's Diary

Between February 1917 and April 1918 Sub-Lieutenant Robert Goldrich RN served as First Lieutenant of the sloop HMS *Poppy*, which was engaged in patrol and – later – convoy-escort duties in the North West and South West Approaches. His ship was based variously on Bucrana in the north of Ireland and Queenstown in the south. This was a crucial period in the war at sea, beginning when U-boat operations against Allied merchant shipping were at their most damaging and ending with the tables successfully turned through the widespread use of the convoy system. In an account written after the war Goldrich summed up his fourteen months in *Poppy*:

Those were the days, and no mistake!

Executive officer of a small ship in the thick of the submarine campaign, with the organization of the ship and the comfort of some eighty men to supplement my regular watch keeping duties.

With a crew drawn from all ranks of the community, including miners, tradesmen, and even a music hall entertainer, the leaven of 'Active Service' officers and men, coupled with the compelling necessity of the times, speedily moulded us into an efficient unit of those thousands of small craft which steamed, fought, swept mines and dropped depth charges, and by their unsleeping vigilance ultimately broke the threat of the submarine menace, which once brought us so near to starvation and defeat.

He added that he and his comrades in the 'small ships' realized nothing of their importance at the time, though they understood that their job was to 'keep going – just keep going'. It is not surprising, therefore, that the diary he kept almost daily throughout these months finds no place for strategic analysis or patriotic sentiment; rather it is a brisk, earthy and at times richly amusing account of the experiences of a young man as much dedicated to getting what he could out of life as to winning the war. Matters other than naval are described – such as escort activities of a different kind during leave in Brighton:

15th Aug: Met one 'Nancy', a lady and a very finely built girl. Did her a good turn on the beach and so home to bed well pleased with Brighton.

16th Aug: Had a fairly amusing PM with Margaret, a talented Yiddisher girl but well chaperoned by a Mother of the Hindenburg type.

On board ship there were other consolations. One entry reads:

> Verily – verily – Death cometh in the morning
> And the wages of gin is breath.

There are numerous variations on this theme:

4th April [1917]: Not full of beans this morning. Alcoholic remorse and fed up with the prospect of patrolling for six days out in the Atlantic. Captain also had a liver as a result of too many free drinks last night.

3rd June: Proceeded to make a night of it aboard and got a horrid shock at midnight when we were ordered to sea to assist oiler *San Lorenzo* zonked outside.

'Zonked', or – an occasional variant – 'zoncked', meant 'torpedoed' in Goldrich's vocabulary and he had cause to use the word frequently in his early months in *Poppy*. Indeed, there are numerous entries which clearly show the hazards and frustrations of the pre-convoy period, when merchant ships sailing independently were easy prey for U-boats and the Navy's many anti-submarine patrol vessels all too often arrived on the scene too late:

27 March: A ship reported having seen another fellow torpedoed off Skelligs so proceeded there at full speed. Sighted her at 10.30 am steering all over the shop. Steamed round her and found she had been torpedoed in No 2 hold just forard of the stokehold bulkhead. Sighted the crew in two life boats under sail and picked them up about 1.30 pm. While I was aft mustering survivors 'Action' was sounded and I dived to the bridge to find a submarine panic on. I sighted the Fritz 8,000 yards off high up out of the water but I did not see him soon enough and only got as far as 'Control' and did not get a round off. I was very sick about it 'cos she must have been watching us for some minutes.
We noted her course and steered full speed for a point over her and dropped a DC [depth charge] but without sending up the Fritz as we hoped.

The convoy system – first established in the Mediterranean – finally reached the North Atlantic in July. Fears that a mass of ships together would simply form a larger and more enticing target did not materialize and the situation soon began to show a marked improvement:

4th Aug: Escorted our convoy to 16¼ W with complete success and left them at 11.30 pm to rendezvous with the *Isis* having a convoy of 22 large merchant vessels.

5th Aug: Picked up convoy at 8.15 and had a rather anxious time as that B.F. in the *Rosemary* made some highly dangerous moves and ordered us to follow him. Got the Captain out of his bed with some difficulty and then received orders from HMS *Isis*.
Took station on the starboard quarter on convoy which is zig-zagging at 9 knots. Formation – six columns in line ahead.
Escort – HMS *Isis*, five destroyers, three sloops.
I have never before seen so many merchant ships together and the marvel of it is that they are keeping station about four cables apart and zig-zagging with almost the precision of a battle fleet.

However, there were still occasional losses – and lapses:

Sept 15th: Getting on pretty well and hope to get in tomorrow. Fair sea running.
At a few minutes before 4 pm the *Idomineus*, the Commodore [ie the command ship] of this convoy, was torpedoed. It is very bad work on the part of the escort as a submarine must have exposed his conning tower to get a shot in this sea.
The *Oxonian* which previously reported that she was unable to keep up 8½ knots immediately took the lead and got to hell out of it. The *Hamilton Grange* a swan bow craft about thirty years old developed a sudden eleven knots.
Rob Roy and *Laburnum* are respectively screening and towing *Idomineus* whilst tug *Milwater* is on her way from Lough Swilly.

Life in the *Poppy* with its long periods 'out' and only occasional days 'in', was never easy or comfortable, and Goldrich did not mince his words in admitting this. 'The sea is getting up a bit,' he noted on 17 October. 'I expect we are in for another sod of a trip.' From his entry of two days later it is evident his expectation was justified:

19th Oct: Spent a miserable middle watch with a bilious attack. Neuralgia and vomiting ad lib.
Passed convoy about 1 pm in a fog and ran another 30 miles W. Now we are crashing E at 15 knots to overtake them. A first class balls is what the S.O. [Senior Officer] in the *Ossory* has made of this joint.

As a final detail, Goldrich noted that he heard that a 'Yank' torpedo boat destroyer had been recently 'zonked', though it had succeeded in making port. It had not been a good couple of days.

Overall it could be said that Goldrich's career in *Poppy* was highly typical of naval experience of the First World War. Set-piece encounters were rare; the steady slog of routine patrol and escort with only occasional flurries of action was far more common. Yet the contribution of *Poppy* and scores of ships like her was a major one. Keeping the supply lines open was vital and the convoy system achieved this. To give one statistic: between 2 July and 10 October 1917 117 wheat ships set out to cross the Atlantic: of eighteen which sailed independently four were sunk; of the ninety-seven which sailed in convoy one was sunk, and she had been separated from the rest. The situation improved even further in 1918, when, in the words of a historian of this subject, Allied convoy escorts, aided by Allied aircraft, achieved 'a war-winning victory'*. A generation later Churchill could rightly state that the previous war had proved 'the sovereign merits of convoy'.

HMS *Poppy*, Sub-Lieutenant Goldrich's Flower class sloop. The class was divided into five types, Acacia, Azalea, Arabis, Aubretia and Anchusa; *Poppy* was Arabis type (Q 70608) Length 267¾ ft, beam 33½ ft; displacement 1,250 tons; speed 15-17 knots; complement 80; guns 2 × 4.7-inch

*John Winton, *Convoy*, Michael Joseph, 1983, p.101

PART IV
The War in the Air

AIR warfare was in its infancy in 1914; by 1918 plans were in train to penetrate into the farther reaches of Germany and bomb Berlin – an aim achieved many times a generation later.*

As it happened, the idea of a specially designed bomber aeroplane to attack Germany was first conceived (in the British Admiralty) as early as 1914, but those controlling British military strategy in the field had in mind a far less independent role for the air arm. Aeroplanes were to help the ground forces; they had no separate validity. (The Royal Naval Air Service was separately constituted until 1918, but many of its pilots and observers served with the Royal Flying Corps as the adjuncts of ground forces.) Their basic duty was reconnaissance and observation with a view to supporting the infantry and the artillery.

Aerial combat developed because the enemy naturally wanted to stop such activities, and the inevitable response was to fight back. This led to the production of a whole range of new and more sophisticated aeroplanes as the belligerent countries tried to outwit and outpace each other. In a war which was short of glamorous heroes, air 'aces' gained great popular acclaim – they were the international sportsmen of their time, except that they almost always played too short a season. (In 1917 the life expectancy of a new pilot on the Western Front was between eleven days and three weeks.)

Generally, warfare was communal; the unit was the ship, the battalion, the company, the platoon, the gun battery. Air warfare had its squadrons and its fierce loyalties, but in some ways it was more individualistic; the crew of most aeroplanes engaged in action in the First World War was either two or one. This part of the book is therefore particularly personal and there are some strong and contrasting personalities. Most relaxed is Lieutenant Collett, a kite-balloon officer in the Middle East – but then he was writing after the war was won, and kite balloons only rarely called for the split-second decisions appropriate to other branches of the flying service. Most sanguine is Lieutenant Oscar Greig, who, after many months of competent if undramatic activity, was shot down and made a prisoner of war; wounded, though not badly, he opted to settle

for POW life – devoting not a little of his time to following up the fact, which plainly fascinated him, that he had been the victim of the German who was to prove arguably the most famous ace of the war, Baron von Richthofen. His story shows how little real animus there was between many of the aerial gladiators whose job it was to seek out and destroy each other.

Most optimistic, most 'gay' in the ancient cavalier sense, is Second Lieutenant George Downing, the epitome of that kind of young Englishman who saw air-fighting as sport and could scarcely wait for his next crack at brother Hun. Most critical of his military superiors – and perhaps most remarkable in that he stood so far from the facile jingoism of the time – is Lieutenant Thomas Hughes, an older man, educated and talented, who had no time for bluster or the kind of unthinking incompetence which could cost other men their lives. It is difficult to say how many others shared his caustic and eloquently expressed attitudes, but certainly his is an important voice which requires to be heard.

An RAF Air Technical diagram entitled 'The Last Loop', showing the successful completion of an aerial dogfight (Q 67834)

*The experience of being subjected *to* air raids is not dealt with in this part but in Part VII, The Civilians' War.

The War in the Air **Important Dates**

1912

April 13 Royal Flying Corps constituted

1914

July 1 Royal Naval Air Service constituted
August 13 First RFC squadrons cross to France
Late August RNAS advance reconnaissance base established at Dunkirk
December 25 Raid on Zeppelin sheds at Cuxhaven by RNAS seaplanes

1915

August 19 Command of RFC taken over by Major-General H. M. (later Lord) Trenchard, the 'father' of the RAF
October 12 Bombing raid on Mauser factory at Oberndorf by RNAS and French aircraft

1917

April 'Bloody April' – the high point of enemy successes against British aircraft on the Western Front
May 7 Captain Albert Ball VC DSO MC, famous British air ace, shot down and killed

1918

April 1 RFC and RNAS constituted into Royal Air Force
April 21 Rittmeister Manfred Freiherr von Richthofen, top-scoring fighter pilot of the war, shot down and killed
June 6 Independent Air Force founded for strategic bombing purposes
July 26 Major 'Mick' Mannock, top-scoring British fighter pilot of the war, shot down and killed
October HMS *Argus*, the world's first aircraft carrier, goes into service with Royal Navy

Shot down by the Red Baron

Captain Oscar Greig, Royal Flying Corps, was shot down behind enemy lines, and subsequently taken prisoner, on 24 January 1917. He appears to have seen it as a mark of distinction that he was a victim of the greatest German air ace of the war – Rittmeister (Cavalry Captain) Baron Manfred von Richthofen, known as the 'Red Baron'. In the comprehensive scrapbook which he later assembled about his experiences he included several cuttings from the German illustrated magazine *Berliner Illustrierte Zeitung*, which he plainly acquired during his time as a prisoner of war. Against the photograph of von Richthofen's quarters, decorated with the numbers of the aircraft the German had shot down (see page 126), Greig wrote: 'My machine was 6997.' Respect is the keynote struck rather than resentment; the respect of one flyer for another and a greater, who, as Greig was aware, had reputedly as many as eighty 'victories' to his name when he was himself shot down, fatally, in 1918.

Greig had been in France as an RFC pilot for eighteen months when his fateful day came and he was to remain a prisoner of war until November 1918 (at which time he and a fellow-POW decamped and after numerous adventures made their way home). He wrote a detailed diary of his experiences, the first pages of which vividly describe the events of 24 January 1917. He and his observer had been sent up to take a series of photographs at 10,000 feet in the area of Fresnoy/Henin-Lietard, east of Lens and not far from Vimy Ridge. Greig was standing on the rudder bar looking from his map to the ground attempting to get the aircraft, with its fixed camera, in exactly the right position, and his observer had just begun to make the exposures:

At this moment I heard a machine-gun firing and saw several holes appear in the left wings. We were taken completely by surprise. I turned sharply to the right, banking steeply, hoping to get the enemy in front of me, but on completion of half a circle the enemy fired another burst from my right putting the engine out of action and hitting me on the right ankle. I continued in circles endeavouring to get a sight of the enemy but he succeeded in keeping below and behind my machine, making it impossible for either of us to fire at him while he continued to pour bullets into my machine. I distinctly saw several tracer bullets pass through the instrument board between my observer and myself.

I had no pain in my left foot, only an unpleasant sensation of warmth, and I could still use my rudder.

I was losing height very rapidly. At about 4000 feet altitude by the aneroid, which was probably really about 2000 feet owing to the descent being too rapid for the aneroid to register correctly, the firing stopped and I straightened out making for our lines which were then only some three miles distant. My observer pointed behind us, indicating another attack, and tried unsuccessfully to raise the back gun mounting. As he could not get the gun in action he sat down again. A second after a very fast small scarlet biplane passed over us and went away to the right front.

An FE2b: the type that
Greig was flying when shot
down in January 1917
(HU 57191)

It was the scarlet Albatross biplane von Richthofen regularly used (see photograph on page 126) that gave him his nickname of 'Red Baron'. Greig was left fighting to regain control of his stricken aircraft:

I then tried everything I could to get the engine going but it would only splutter feebly. Seeing that we could not cross Vimy Ridge even if we threw the guns and everything possible overboard I turned east and landed on a flat plane between Vimy and Fresnoy, gliding through a batch of about a dozen field telephone wires breaking them with the undercarriage, and rolling through some more before the machine stopped. There were several small shell holes about but luckily I did not hit any.

When we stopped I stood up and asked McLennan [his observer] if he was hit. He said 'No, are you?' I told him I had got a 'blighty' one in the foot and was damned sorry to bring him there; at which he asked if we were in Hunland and was not pleased to find we were. I noticed that he had several bullet holes in his coat, as I had also.

By this time there were a number of Germans running towards us from all directions. I said we had better burn the machine, and Mac lit the lighter carried for that purpose, handed it to me, and jumped out. I got out onto the wing and put the lighter against the celluloid of my map case to make sure of burning the maps and got down. Whilst doing this I noticed one of the front centre section bracing wires was shot in two. Also the floor of the observer's part of the nacelle [engine casing] was covered with chips of wood made by the bullets. Directly I got down I saw that there were quantities of oil, petrol, and water, streaming out onto the ground and I wished I had put the lighter in this, but it immediately caught fire making a tremendous blaze and a huge cloud of black smoke.

We walked a few yards away to get clear of the Very lights and Lewis gun ammunition that were being set off by the fire and sat down on the snow at the edge of a shell hole.

It was not until early February, after he had spent some days in hospital, that he learned the identity of his attacker:

Three officers of the German Flying Corps came to see me. One was the man to whom I had given my Sam Browne [ie his belt; he had offered it to one of his new 'hosts' as a souvenir]. They enquired what the machine that had brought me down was like and when I told them they said the pilot was Richthofen. I was his eighteenth victim and he had shot down another since.

After the war Greig collected the details of what happened to the members of the famous von Richthofen circus, adding them to his scrapbook as annotations to the photograph below, also from the *Berliner Illustrierte Zeitung*. They are reproduced here as written.

'The five leading pilots of the Scout Squadron of Freiherr von Richthofen, who together have shot down 132 aeroplanes (HU 57192)
[Front row] *Festner* was killed about June 1917 with 12 victories.
Rittmeister v. Richthofen was killed in April 1918 and claimed 80 victories.
Wolff was killed in Oct. or Nov. 1917 with 33 victories.
[Second row] *Schaefer* was killed in June 1917 with 30 victories.
Lt. v. Richthofen [the Red Baron's younger brother] appears to have survived, after 40 victories. It was Lt. Wolff who got my Sam Browne. In this picture he is wearing a British leather flying coat.'

Below: A page from the *Berliner Illustrierte Zeitung* (Berlin Illustrated Magazine), from Captain Greig's scrapbook – entitled at the foot 'A Day with Cavalry Captain von Richthofen's Fighter Squadron' (HU 57193)

Both these pictures are now in the Imperial War Museum photographic collection (Q 50328 and Q 44797). The top picture is captioned: 'Albatross DIII. Single-seat fighters of von Richthofen's circus. 175hp Mercedes engine, von Richthofen's engine second in line.' The lower picture is captioned: 'Baron von Richthofen's apartment decorated with number plates of British and Allied aircraft brought down.' Greig's was 6997.

Below: Pilot's-eye view: a German aerodrome in Flanders (Q 23907)

Bottom: The remains of the aircraft, a Fokker DRI Triplane, in which von Richthofen was shot down by Captain A. Roy Brown DSC, at Sailly le Sec, Somme, on 21 April 1917 (Q 67112)

Die startbereiten Flugzeuge der Jagdstaffel.

Im Quartier des Rittmeisters Freiherrn von Richthofen. Eine Wand mit Nummern und Abzeichen von Flugzeugen, die er selbst abgeschossen hat.

Ein Tag bei der Jagdstaffel des Rittmeisters Frhrn. v. Richthofen.

**Chivalry of the Air:
Enemies given Honoured
Burial**

The funeral of Baron von
Richthofen at Bertangles,
Somme, on 22 April 1918.
The firing party presents
arms as the coffin passes on
the shoulders of six pilot
officers of No 3 Squadron
Australian Flying Corps.
The padre is Rev George H.
Marshall DSO (Q 10918)

The grave of the famous
British air ace, Captain
Albert Ball VC, shot down
near Lens 17 May 1917.
The inscription reads:
'Fallen in aerial combat for
his fatherland' (Q 22283)

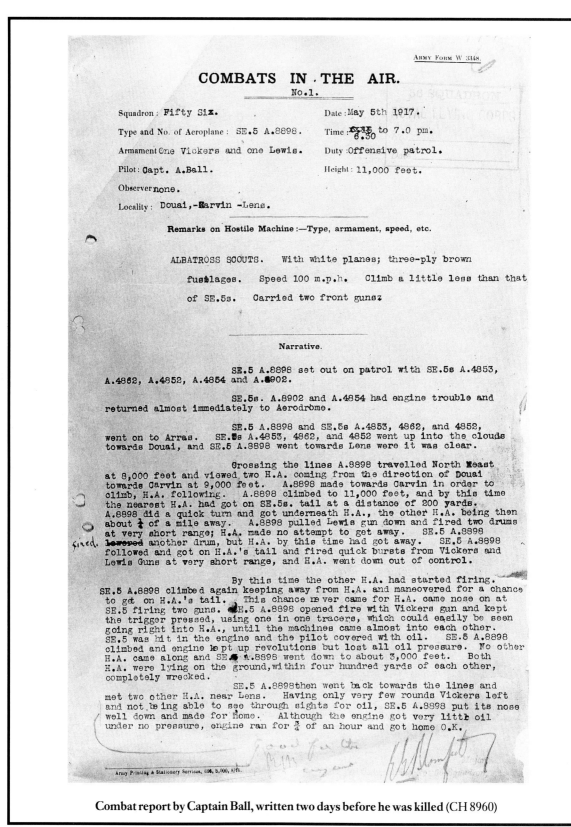

ARMY FORM W 3348.

COMBATS IN THE AIR.
No.1.

Squadron : **Fifty Six.**

Date : May 5th 1917.

Type and No. of Aeroplane : SE.5 A.8898.

Time : 6.15 to 7.0 pm.
6.30

Armament : One Vickers and one Lewis.

Duty : Offensive patrol.

Pilot : Capt. A.Ball.

Height : 11,000 feet.

Observer : none.

Locality : Douai,-Sarvin -Lens.

Remarks on Hostile Machine :—Type, armament, speed, etc.

ALBATROSS SCOUTS. With white planes; three-ply brown fuselages. Speed 100 m.p.h. Climb a little less than that of SE.5s. Carried two front guns.

Narrative.

SE.5 A.8898 set out on patrol with SE.5s A.4853, A.4862, A.4852, A.4854 and A.8902.

SE.5s. A.8902 and A.4854 had engine trouble and returned almost immediately to Aerodrome.

SE.5 A.8898 and SE.5s A.4853, 4862, and 4852, went on to Arras. SE.5s A.4853, 4862, and 4852 went up into the clouds towards Douai, and SE.5 A.8898 went towards Lens were it was clear.

Crossing the lines A.8898 travelled North Least at 8,000 feet and viewed two H.A. coming from the direction of Douai towards Carvin at 9,000 feet. A.8898 made towards Carvin in order to climb, H.A. following. A.8898 climbed to 11,000 feet, and by this time the nearest H.A. had got on SE.5s. tail at a distance of 200 yards. A.8898 did a quick turn and got underneath H.A., the other H.A. being then about ¼ of a mile away. A.8898 pulled Lewis gun down and fired two drums at very short range; H.A. made no attempt to get away. SE.5 A.8898 fired another drum, but H.A. by this time had got away. SE.5 A.8898 followed and got on H.A.'s tail and fired quick bursts from Vickers and Lewis Guns at very short range, and H.A. went down out of control.

By this time the other H.A. had started firing. SE.5 A.8898 climbed again keeping away from H.A. and maneovered for a chance to get on H.A.'s tail. This chance never came for H.A. came nose on at SE.5 firing two guns. SE.5 A.8898 opened fire with Vickers gun and kept the trigger pressed, using one in one tracers, which could easily be seen going right into H.A., until the machines came almost into each other. SE.5 was hit in the engine and the pilot covered with oil. SE.5 A.8898 climbed and engine kept up revolutions but lost all oil pressure. No other H.A. came along and SE.5 A.8898 went down to about 3,000 feet. Both H.A. were lying on the ground, within four hundred yards of each other, completely wrecked.

SE.5 A.8898 then went back towards the lines and met two other H.A. near Lens. Having only very few rounds Vickers left and not being able to see through sights for oil, SE.5 A.8898 put its nose well down and made for home. Although the engine got very little oil under no pressure, engine ran for ¾ of an hour and got home O.K.

Army Printing & Stationery Services, 806, 5,000, 8/16.

Combat report by Captain Ball, written two days before he was killed (CH 8960)

Famous Aircraft of the Great War

The Royal Aircraft Factory BE2c, exhibited in the Museum, with (inset),
the Sopwith Camel 2F1, naval version, 'flying' through the atrium

BE biplane Developed by the Royal Aircraft Factory, Farnborough, between 1911 and 1914. The outstanding flying characteristics of the BE2c variant shown above led to its adoption as the first reconnaissance aircraft to be ordered in quantity for the Royal Flying Corps. However, though an excellent observation machine, its lack of manoeuvrability in combat led to its replacement on the Western Front from late 1916. It was also used in the Middle East, on anti-submarine patrols and was responsible for shooting down five German airships at home.

Statistics: Crew, two (pilot, observer); maximum speed 75 mph; operational ceiling 10,000ft, endurance 3½ hours; armament, rifle or carbine for observer on early models, later up to four .303-inch machine guns, two 112lb or 10 20lb bombs; wing span 37ft; length 27ft 3ins, height 11ft 1in; weight (loaded) 2,142lbs.

Sopwith Camel Introduced in 1917, the Camel was a highly successful combat aeroplane which by the end of the war had accounted for 1,294 enemy aircraft. Most of these victories were over the Western Front but Camels also served in the Mediterranean, Mesopotamia and Russia. The variant shown is the 2F1, produced for the Royal Navy; it could be flown from aircraft carriers or from the short runways built on gun turrets. On 11 August 1918 this particular aircraft, piloted by Flight Sub-Lieutenant S.D. Culley, shot down Zeppelin L53, the last airship victim of the war.

Statistics: Crew, one; maximum speed 177 mph; operational ceiling 17,300ft; endurance 2 hours; standard armament, one .303-inch Vickers machine gun, one .303-inch Lewis machine gun, four 25lb Cooper bombs (though this particular aircraft was modified to take two Lewis guns); wing span 26ft 11ins; length 18ft 8ins, height 9ft 1in; weight (loaded) 1,530lbs.

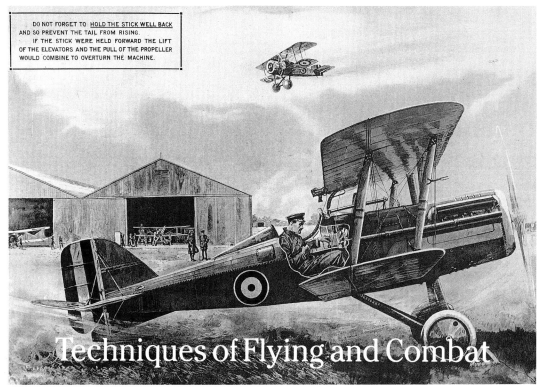

DO NOT FORGET TO HOLD THE STICK WELL BACK AND SO PREVENT THE TAIL FROM RISING.
IF THE STICK WERE HELD FORWARD THE LIFT OF THE ELEVATORS AND THE PULL OF THE PROPELLER WOULD COMBINE TO OVERTURN THE MACHINE.

Techniques of Flying and Combat

From a series of 'Air Technical Diagrams' issued as instruction posters in 1918
Above: 'Position of control stick when running engine on the ground: SE5A Biplane (Q 67837)
Below: 'Getting off – the last look round' (Q 67839)

ALWAYS LOOK BEHIND, ON EITHER SIDE AND IN FRONT BEFORE OPENING OUT YOUR ENGINE TO TAKE OFF.
THERE MAY BE ANOTHER MACHINE ABOUT TO LAND IN YOUR WAY.

Above: 'Right and Wrong Way to Drop a Torpedo' (Q 67846)
Below: 'Beware of the Hun in the Sun'. A Fokker DRI approaching from out of the
sun during a combat between a Bristol F2b and an Albatross DV (Q 67832)

Sportsman of the Air

Second Lieutenant George Downing RFC MC
(HU 59104)

George Downing was a twenty-four-year-old observer with 57 Squadron. He had transferred to the Royal Flying Corps after being trained as an army officer and had taken to the air as though it were his natural element. 'This is the game for me,' he commented in January 1917, when thanking a sister for the gift of a diary, 'which', he told her, 'is specially reserved for the slaying of Huns, or the attempts of same (so far *n' a pu*).'

Within weeks he was participating in aerial combat. He told his story in a general family letter addressed to 'My dearest all':

Now for my little adventure! Hold your breath, shut your eyes, and try to pick out any sense of the following vivid narrative.

Yesterday morning (Sunday) four of our flight set out on a patrol, your humble as per usual with the leader of the patrol. We were peacefully parading about six miles over Hunland, to the accompaniment of sunny little shells, when I suddenly spotted six Hun machines about three hundred feet higher than we were. We went for them, and I blazed away at the beggars with my gun. Soon I saw one of my machines and a Hun go tearing to earth (each had shot the other). The rest of us carried on and chased the five Huns off. About five minutes later we met another batch, and we were soon separated, each fighting about two Huns. My pilot dived straight at one of the beggars and when I was quite close I fired sixty rounds right off into the machine and had the tremendous satisfaction of seeing it depart in flames to Mother Earth. After that it was glorious sport, we fought four different Hun formations for one and a half hours.

Once we were within ten yards of a two seater Hun, when my gun jammed. I could see that bally German gunner glaring over the top of his machine gun as he fired at us, but his nerve was poor, as he should easily have brought us down, but it was a nasty moment. I felt something hit my leg, but it was only the concussion as the bullet went through my trousers. Jove though we had our revenge on the beggar afterwards. We dived on him with both guns firing and he also went west.

What do you think of that for a day's sport?

Having spun his heroic yarn Downing feared it might all seem somewhat exaggerated – 'only I feel so bucked at bringing down two Huns in our very first scrap'. However, he was aware that his breezy exhilaration might produce a more muted response at the family hearth and added this postscript: 'I guess my little mother will think we have started business, but I don't suppose we shall do any work like that again for ages, so there is no need to worry.'

His mother had much cause to worry two months later, when the family received the news that George's elder brother Richard, a Sergeant in the Royal Field Artillery, had died of wounds near Arras. George's birthday message to her in July was especially tender:

A very short note, just to wish you very many happy returns of the day. I am afraid dear this last year has not brought us much happiness, but you have been so wonderfully brave over our Richard's greatest sacrifice. It is just mothers like you that help their sons to play the man's part.

George Downing had a brief respite from the front that summer as he trained to be a pilot. He also achieved the accolade of winning a Military Cross, the news of which appeared in *The Times* on 19 June. On a course at Castle Bromwich he called on a friendly family whose young generation consisted of three daughters:

I went over on Sunday evening to Wylde Green where I found only the three girls. Needless to say very embarrassed, but was prevailed on to stay for about three hours. I promised to pay them an aerial visit next day and at the appointed time came over and stunted for their benefit. It created quite a sensation in the neighbourhood, as I went very low waving to the girls on the lawn who needless to say responded vigorously. Of course all the other people in their various gardens waved also. It was quite good fun.

Dear! dear! These modern times.

For a time there was a possibility that he might stay on in England as an instructor, but then the news came through that he was to be posted back to France. 'I expect the Mater is not so pleased,' he wrote on 27 September. 'Personally I am glad as it is quite time I interviewed brother Boche again.'

On 20 October, now a pilot with 29 Squadron, he was writing in his best graphic style about new adventures:

It is quite like old times. I had quite an exciting experience a day or two ago. You know how misty the weather is nowadays. Well we were cruising about over the lines, when a fellow and myself lost the remainder of the patrol in a fog, and we had not a bit of idea where we were, so we came down to a few hundred feet from the ground. Presently we came to a large town, which puzzled me immensely, and I circled round quite casually trying to locate it on the map. I thought and so did the other fellow that we were our side of the lines. Imagine my amazement when I discovered it to be about twelve miles in Hunland. We were soon greeted with shells and machine gun fire, so of course we frightened everything we met on the roads, diving quite close to the ground on to motor lorries etc, and I bet we scared Huns out of their lives. When we eventually came home, we noticed all the roads quite clear, and lorries etc not moving, so we were immensely bucked with ourselves and enjoyed a jolly good breakfast.

On 26 October he wrote cheerfully to one of his sisters about his recent successes, telling her that the squadron was doing 'pretty good work' and that they had 'bagged quite a lot of Huns lately'. However, on 3 November he reported to his mother that things were rather quiet, allowing ample opportunity for fun and games on the ground:

The weather here is pretty dud now, and not much flying is possible. However we generally manage to scramble up once a day and see if there is a war on.

We had a magnificent dust up with the squadron on the aerodrome last night. They raided us with smoke bombs etc, and some scrap ensued. Some fellows seemed to love the mud, judging from their condition. We had a counter attack later on, bagging their gramophone, playing a triumphant tune on the way back.

Three days later, on 6 November 1917, Second Lieutenant George Downing MC failed to return from a patrol in the vicinity of Ypres. The details of what happened are not known. His body was never found. His name is on the memorial to the missing of the Royal Flying Corps, Royal Naval Air Service and Royal Air Force at Arras.

Disenchanted Observer

Thomas McKenny Hughes was thirty in 1914. Educated at Eton and Trinity College Cambridge, a practising architect who had served his apprenticeship under Sir Edwin Lutyens, he enlisted in the Artists' Rifles on the third day of the war. By November he was out in France. Having no high opinion of his military potential, he decided to remain in the ranks, determined to lead as agreeable a social life as possible despite the occasional interruption of tours of duty in the trenches. However, a meeting with a friend serving in the Royal Flying Corps opened up the possibility of a more challenging career. In the spring of 1915 he trained as an officer and after a brief period with an infantry battalion he secured his transfer to the RFC with a view to becoming an observer.

Hughes was to become an acknowledged expert in tactical reconnaissance and artillery observation and was to receive the accolade of being twice mentioned in dispatches. But he had been caustic about the attitudes and performance of his superiors from the outset and his elevation to officer status produced no overnight conversion. An acute observer in more ways than one, he was to keep a sharp eye on the ways of the war throughout his time in France, recording his comments in a diary many hundreds of pages long in which, although he was always prepared to see the humorous side of things, no item of military incompetence or pretentiousness was spared. It should be emphasized that he wrote for himself alone; he was not writing letters which might be circulated to people who might be puzzled or dismayed by his forthright views. He himself was not exempt, for he could berate himself, too, as he did after a flight in September 1915 for which he and his pilot, Second Lieutenant Balcombe-Brown, had set off inadequately armed. Officially their task was 'close reconnaissance and photography', but this was a euphemistic term as they had no photographic equipment and were therefore reduced to 'trench-sketching', plus a further instruction to look at Courtrai, an important German base in Belgium. 'We went up,' he wrote, 'in an old A flight Morane No 1894 and took 35 minutes to get 6500 feet.' Taking off from Bailleul (Hughes's station throughout almost all his time in France) they flew east from Ypres, evaded the attentions of a German Albatross and then ran into a spirited burst of 'archies' – the standard term for anti-aircraft fire:

I am certain I recognized in our welcome the technique of that beastly hooligan who used to live between Lille and Roubaix and who fires those horrible huge archies with such disturbing accuracy. One of these seemed to burst about ten feet in front of the propeller (it was probably much further) but we went through the thick cloud of it; a nasty smelly thing.

I got some trenches sketched in.

At Gheluvelt we saw another Albatross below us coming from Roulers. Went

Lieutenant Thomas (Tommy) McKenny Hughes working on aerial photographs taken for artillery observation purposes (Q 85116)

on nearly to Courtrai when I noticed two more about 1500 feet above us coming from the west. Called Brown's attention to the phenomenon and we decided that there was really no place like home. So we turned towards dear old Ypres which looked such a long way away. Even detestable Polygon Wood had a homely look from there. We had – very foolishly – only got one Lewis gun and that a fixed one in Brown's seat so we were utterly powerless to shoot upwards or backwards so we were absolutely at the mercy of the two Albatrosses above us, if only they had known it, but fortunately they didn't. Brown put our machine's nose down until our air speed was 75 mph but still one machine above us overhauled us very easily and started letting off a machine gun at us, from about 250 yards.

Brown let off a small burst of firing every now and then, though of course in the opposite direction to the Albatross which was above and behind us, but I pointed my telescope at it in as gun-like a manner as I could so as to give local colour and inspire terror. The result was that after our third burst of mock fire the Albatross sheered off to a discreet distance

It was a fortunate escape, but it carried important lessons: 'Memo. Never go over the lines again without at least one unfixed Lewis gun, and never below 9000 feet if it can be helped.'

Hughes had no love for any kind of drum-beating jingoism. He commented on one artillery unit with which he had to deal that they were 'a fire-eating lot. That vicarious fire-eating which has become such a feature of our national enthusiasm, and which is so gloriously displayed by our Bishops and Chaplains, by the Press, and by the General Staff.' Nevertheless, despite his attitudes, he impressed his superiors sufficiently to find himself being offered substantial promotion of the sort many subalterns would have leaped at. On 21 July 1916 he wrote:

I am becoming more and more in demand. The Colonel rang up and asked if I would like to go to Egypt as GSO3 with rank of Staff Captain.

As I don't care much for the STAFF I said No.

I wrote the Colonel a copy of my 'refusal of preferment' series No 2. This seems the way to become valued in the Army, to refuse its puny honours. They then feel that they are up against something they don't understand and that you must be a devil of a fellow to spurn such giddy heights.

Hughes had no great opinion of his Colonel, at least with regard to the latter's relationship with his officers. A few weeks earlier his erstwhile pilot Balcombe-Brown and another officer had got back to base after a successful but highly dangerous sortie against some German kite-balloons – carried out in full view of the aerodrome. Hughes commented: 'Wild enthusiasm prevailed, even the Colonel, who arrived from Mt Rouge where he had watched the Show, partially broke through his grim reserve and stayed to dinner, during which he spoke several times.'

It was another attack on enemy balloons some months later that produced one of Hughes's angriest outbursts. Under 7 April 1917 he wrote:

No 1 Flight were sent out to destroy balloons this morning and found them protected by about four aeroplanes each, so none were brought down. Bevington was lost though none saw what happened to him – another good man thrown away by muddle-headed red tape methods by the authorities. Instead of allowing pilots to snatch an opportunity for bringing down a balloon they forbid attacks on balloons until one day a 'general balloon strafe' is ordered from Brigade, no matter whether it is a suitable opportunity or not, so that the pilot has to do his best to get the balloon under the circumstances existing however adverse.

And so I suppose our GREAT GENERAL STAFF will continue to muddle away lives until there are no more left to muddle away, or until we too have a revolution, against our Military Bureaucracy.

Generals could amuse him mightily, except that underneath his comments on their behaviour lay a deep scepticism as to whether they were really up to their job. Of one general who was given a guided tour of the aerodrome Hughes wrote that he 'showed quite a childish pleasure and ignorance in everything and asked questions with the privileged imbecility of a judge'. Of another he remarked that 'he was the man who, on hearing that several of the aerials of his batteries had been destroyed by shell fire, actually sent round the order that "in view of the danger of ground stations being put out of action, all aerials will in future be buried".'

In early January 1918 he recorded an account of a lecture he was giving (being now an acknowledged expert on his subject) which, thanks to the unexpected arrival of senior staff on the scene, ended in virtual mayhem:

I started my 'course' on 'Interpretation of aeroplane photographs' this morning. After a bit of business getting the light to work, I got under way with my celebrated lantern exhibition and was getting along quite nicely when the door behind the screen opened and the Corps Commander and the BGGS [Brigadier General, General Staff] shuffled in, tripped over the electric light wire, put the light out and fused the arc light.

The Corps Commander then fell over a chair and I felt it was time to pull up a blind, which I did. He then told me to carry on as if he wasn't there, which was difficult as we should have a light working if he hadn't been there. However, it was eventually got going again and I continued.

Afterwards, the BGGS came in and said it might have been a good thing if I had done this and that. Most of the things I had done.

A few days later, he took a post-lunch walk with a fellow-officer, Beverley, to the top of Kemmel Hill, a noted vantage point near Ypres:

continued on page 153

'The Kensingtons at Laventie' by Eric Kennington

There was no British official war art until 1916, but this painting by a soldier who later became a war artist is a notable precursor of what was to become a distinguished *genre*. Eric Kennington (1888-1960) enlisted on 6 August 1914 in the 1/13th Battalion, London Regiment – generally known as the 'Kensingtons' – went with them to France and was in the line with them between mid-November and January 1915, when he returned to England to be later discharged as physically unfit. His picture – worked up from sketches and painted in reverse on glass – portrays not idealized but actual soldiers: Private Todd is the exhausted soldier in the foreground; the one turned away left is Private McCafferty; Kennington himself is the figure just beyond McCafferty in a black balaclava.

The picture created a remarkable impression when it was first exhibited in 1916 at the Goupil Gallery, London. (It was subsequently purchased by Lady Cowdray, being finally transferred to the Imperial War Museum from the Cowdray Estate in 1983.) When the Department of Information was looking for likely war artists in 1917 Campbell Dodgson, Keeper of Prints and Drawings at the British Museum, recommended Kennington in glowing terms, stating: 'I consider *The Kensingtons* the finest picture inspired by the war produced as yet by an English artist'. Similarly William Rothenstein wrote: 'No one has so marked a gift as he for drawing and understanding the magnificence of the Tommy.'

However, it is perhaps not any sense of 'magnificence' that strikes the observer today so much as the picture's air of documentary reality, its masterly and stylish portrayal of cold, exhausted men only temporarily relieved from a grim ordeal.

Raising the Armies: British Recruiting Posters

Appeal to love of the homeland

Appeal to the desire for companionship and adventure

Appeal to the hope of martial glory

Appeal of the promise of a glorious victory

Funding the War Effort: Foreign Posters

German poster: 'Help us Conquer! Subscribe to the War Loan.' 1917

Austrian poster: 4th Austrian War Loan 1917

French poster: 4th National War Loan 1917

'Oppy Wood' by John Nash, 1918

'It was supposed to be a quiet sector. It was our introduction to the front. I remember it was a very eerie place. Any explosion of any kind resounded all round you among those trees, or what was left of them. It was a very ingenious trench system which I think had been dug by the Norfolks, who were there before us, by skilfully tunnelling out under vast trees. They were nearly all beeches as far as I can remember, and I think perhaps in one or two cases they felled a tree or two so as to lie parallel with the trench, so they could get some sort of shelter under it. Mind you, they were no use as shelters in the case of direct hit or anything like that.'

From an interview with the artist in 1974. John Nash served in France with the 1st Battalion Artists' Rifles 1916-18, rising to the rank of sergeant, and was commissioned as second lieutenant to be an official war artist in May 1918.

'No Man's Land' Detail from the bas-relief by
Charles Sargeant Jagger

Born in 1885 and trained as a sculptor at the Royal
College of Art, Jagger served as an officer both at
Gallipoli and on the Western Front. He was
wounded three times and gassed twice; his war
wounds contributed to his early death in 1934. *No
Man's Land*, made in two versions, the earlier of
which is held by the Imperial War Museum, was
begun while he was convalescing in 1918. He was
later to become famous for his great public war
memorials, such as that to the Royal Artillery at Hyde
Park Corner, but this sculpture relates more directly
to his own experience and to his awareness of war at
the sharp end.

The inscription: 'O little mighty band that stood for
England/That with your bodies for a living
shield/Guarded her slow awaking' is from *To the
Vanguard* by Beatrix Brice-Miller

**Overleaf: 'A German
Attack on a Wet Morning'
by H. S. Williamson**

A Q-Ship Episode. 'HMS *Dunraven* VC in Action against the Submarine that Sank Her, 8 August 1917' by Charles Pears

A Jutland Episode. 'The Last of the *Invincible*', by Robert H. Smyth, RNVR

'British Scouts Leaving their Aerodrome on Patrol over the Asiago Plateau, Italy'
by Sydney Carline

'Handley-Page Aeroplane Bombing Nablus by Night' (Palestine Campaign) by Stuart Reid

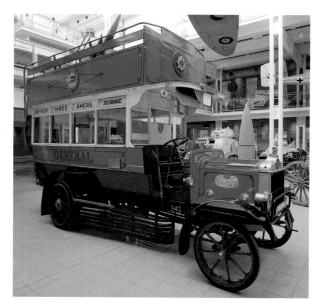

A famous IWM exhibit: the London omnibus 'Ole Bill', used for taking soldiers to and from the line, restored to its civilian colours and with its 'battle honours' – Antwerp, Ypres, Ancre, Somme – inscribed on the windows. At one point there were over 600 such buses at work behind the Western Front

Below: 'A VAD Motor Driver' by Gilbert Rogers

led Leave Ships, Boulogne' by Charles Bryant. Boulogne was also used by ships taking wounded men back to 'Blighty'

Above: 'In the Gun
Factory at Woolwich
Arsenal' by Sir
George Clausen
Right: *'La Réception
des Zeppelins'*: An
impression of the
first Zeppelin raid on
Paris, by Robert
Bonfils, from his
portfolio *La Manière
Française*

Opposite above:
'War Allotments in a
London Suburb' by
Dorothy J. Coke
Below: Letters to
Billie from Salonika,
written and
illustrated by his
father, W. L. Britton
(see p 235)

My Dear Billie

Many thanks for your nice
post cards that reached me quite safely, Mamma
tells me you saw some performing elephants
at a theatre during your Christmas visit to
London, Did you see anything like the above.
You must tell me all about it when you
have time to write, Has "Logo" & his pal,
reached you yet. Don't forget to do me
some nice pictures now you have some
paints. Lots of Love & Kisses from
Your Loving Daddy

x x x x x x

149

T. E. Lawrence (1888-1935), also known as
Lawrence of Arabia, served with Arab forces in the
Hejaz and Syria for two years from October 1916.
When he entered Damascus on 1 October 1918 he
removed the gilt-bronze wreath (left) which had been
presented to the Turks by Kaiser Wilhelm II, from the
tomb of Saladin – the great Kurdish Sultan of Egypt
and Syria who had fought against the Christians
before and during the Third Crusade. Lawrence
subsequently gave it to the IWM, whose first Curator,
Charles ffoulkes, was a close friend.
Shown below is Lawrence's rifle, a Lee Enfield
magazine rifle mark 3. Pesented by the Arab leader
Emir Feisal, and inscribed on the butt 'T.E.L.
4.12.16', it had been given to Feisal by the Turkish
politician Enver Pasha before the Arab Revolt, after
being acquired at Gallipoli. In a letter dated
December 1917 Lawrence stated that the Arab
inscription read 'Part of our booty in the battles for the
Dardanelles.' Lawrence gave it to King George V who
in turn presented it to the IWM.

'A Street in Arras' by John Singer Sargent, 1918

'A Group of British Generals, 1918' by William Roberts

'The Battlefield of Ypres' by Sir David Young Cameron, 1919

There was not much of a view and we only stopped a minute or two. We had a difference of opinion on the subject of war aims. Beverley is fighting in order that 'his kiddie won't have to fight it again' but with truly English inconsequence he is all for continuing the war in the form of an economic boycott against Germany for ever, so I fear that if it is left to Daddy the kiddie will have to fight after all. I thought it best to switch on to some other subject and we soon got round to Beverley's married happiness, which subject carried us back to the Château, Beverley's voice soon becoming a soothing murmur which hardly disturbed my own reflections at all.

Sunday January 27 1918 was a red-letter day for Lieutenant Hughes:

THE SQUADRON IS MOVING

The dreaded summons has come at last and the squadron* goes to Abeele and I shall probably leave and go with the Corps. Anyhow it seems probable that I shall at last leave Bailleul after 3¼ years of mental and bodily stagnation. It is true that there is not much left of the bright youth in khaki who charged into the town on Guy Fawkes Day 1914 to expel the licentious Hun, well knowing the L.H. had already left; the youth who gallantly retreated on All Fools Day 1915 – as the method chosen by an all-knowing staff of celebrating their festival – only to surge forwards again into the old town at the end of the following June, there, as it seemed probable, to end his days.

It is only an old dotard who is left to totter out of the place, babbling of the great days of Bailleul, when Battiscombe was Town Major and de Wynter wore the Mayoral chain.

If by prayer, or by a life of vice, or by any such simple biblical expedient I could bring down fire and brimstone upon the town of Bailleul, I think I would do it.

On the following day Hughes went to Corps Headquarters 'to find out what all this moving meant' and to discuss the question of leave. Suggestions that as much as a month's leave might be possible in certain cases had been recently bandied about, but when Hughes raised this prospect with a senior staff officer, he was met with a firm rebuttal:

Grassett again quoted to me the Corps Commander's dictum at a conference when he turned on a Divisional Commander and said 'Now as to this question of a month's leave, there seems to be a good deal of misconception as to the class of man for whom this privilege is intended. Now I have before me an application for a month's leave for a captain. He has been in the trenches for 2½ years and commanded a company for some time and I dare say has done excellent work – but that is not the sort of man for whom the month's leave is intended.' So if a man like that poor devil does not deserve this month, God knows who does – anyhow my chances are pretty poor. I believe the Corps Commander went on to explain that the month was intended for tired Brigadiers and such like.

However, I hope and expect to get a fortnight.

There is one further entry, under 29 January, and then the diary ends. Hughes had undertaken a considerable number of operational flights during the previous weeks, carrying out his original task of aerial photography, but in this final entry he expresses his satisfaction that 'there are not a great number of shoots to do as a rule now and the Corps are quite exemplary in the smallness of their demands for photographs'. However, he went on a 'shoot' some days later on 5 February, and while taking oblique photographs in the vicinity of Bailleul, he and his pilot were shot down and killed.

*Hughes was a member of the 53 Squadron RFC

Kite Balloon Officer in the Middle East

Before there were aeroplanes there were balloons, and kite balloons (so called because they were not free-flying, but flown from the ground like kites) were used for artillery observation in most war theatres. Lieutenant Thomas Hughes (see previous page) was concerned with shooting down German ones; Lieutenant H.R.P. Collett, RFC and, later, RAF, was concerned with operating British ones in Palestine. As an observer officer with 21 Balloon Company, he took part in the successful attack on Gaza in 1917 and was also present at the opening of Allenby's final offensive against the Turks in September 1918. The following extracts are from a breezy post-war memoir which he wrote under the title of *A Balloonatic in Palestine*. 'Balloonatic', it should be added, was a generally accepted term – and in respect of their vulnerability to attack by enemy aircraft or artillery, balloons were scarcely the safest or most sensible place to be. It was in recognition of this fact that kite balloon personnel were issued with parachutes (but for which Collett's memoir would not have been written), although these were not made available to aeroplane crews:

One feels somewhat helpless in the event of attack by hostile aircraft when aloft, and thus, when on the 19th February [1918] while in the basket I heard the 'Archies' open fire, I immediately studied the sky for their burst to see where the 'plane was, as one had to be on the qui vive in case the parachute must be resorted to.

On this occasion I soon spotted the 'plane at a great height, and almost immediately, according to standing orders, the winch started to haul me down. Then suddenly the 'Archies' ceased fire and in the instant quiet that followed I could hear the unmistakable rattle of machine guns, away up aloft. There I saw one of our 'planes chasing the Hun, so feeling more secure was let up again, just in time to see the Hun plane crash into a tree and turn over, a crumpled wreck.

The pilot who brought the Hun down – Major Stent MC – came quite close to the balloon afterwards, circled round once and waved to me before going back to the aerodrome to report.

Observer officers in the basket of a kite balloon. Palestine Front. A parachute case is attached to the front of the basket. One of the officers is wearing headphones, indicative of the fact that, being static, balloons were in telephone contact with the ground (Q 12502)

In May 1918 Collett was less fortunate, however. His balloon was attacked and shot down and he had to take to his parachute:

It felt, I remember, like jumping from a great height into icy-cold water – altogether a most unpleasant sensation. Many observers who were in France and elsewhere have numbers of parachute descents to their credit and got quite used to it, so I was told.

As soon as I saw that the parachute had opened alright, I looked about me and saw the 'plane pass over the balloon, firing as he came. Our 'Archies' opened up and the air seemed full of explosions and whistling bullets and bits of shell. On looking up I saw a thin stream of smoke drifting from our balloon – easy to see, for I had started the most sickening swing, thus seeing the balloon at the limit of each swing. Shortly afterwards, with a hissing roar, the flaming gas-bag shot past me, crashing finally in a cloud of smoke some 400 yards from where I landed. On looking down I could see men running underneath me and then, owing to vertigo, remembered nothing more until I found myself struggling to my tent supported by a fellow officer, who told me that thanks to half a bottle of whisky, I was revived enough to insist on walking along with him.

Portent for the Future: The Bomber

A Handley-Page 0/400 Bomber at Couderkerque airfield near Dunkirk, 20 April 1918. The 0/400 and its predecessor, the 0/100, were produced following a request from the Director of the Admiralty Air Department, Captain Murray Sueter, for a 'bloody paralyser of an aeroplane' to bomb Germany. On 6 June 1918 an Independent Force was formed from the 41st and 83rd Wings of the RAF to carry out strategic bombing of German war industry sites and airfields. By the Armistice it had carried out 239 raids, but the sudden cessation of hostilities ended what would have been its most ambitious coup, the bombing of Berlin (Q 12033) (See also painting 'A Handley-Page Aeroplane Bombing Nablus By Night' in the colour section, page 145)

PART VI
The Sideshows

THE Western Front was the principal war theatre for the British and French from the first campaigns of 1914 onwards. But powerful voices – Churchill's and Lloyd George's for example – were raised in favour of attempting an alternative strategy to that of hammering away constantly at the enemy's front door. The result was a number of initiatives elsewhere, some failures, some successes, which ultimately affected the outcome of the war to only a marginal degree. Collectively these have come to be seen as 'sideshows'; and one notable effort, the Arab Revolt, in which T.E. Lawrence played an important role, has been called a sideshow of a sideshow. They are, nevertheless, significant parts of the fabric of the First World War.

One of these minor campaigns became, however, a major drama, and could have had significant results given better planning and leadership. In early 1915, despite severe misgivings on many sides, an attempt was made to drive an Allied naval force through the Dardanelles, the idea being to bring Germany's eastern co-belligerent Turkey to a fatal confrontation; when the sailors failed to provide the hoped-for success soldiers were despatched to take the Gallipoli peninsula in order to cover and support a further attempt. Such at least was the theory; the upshot was a bloody, hard-fought campaign which ended in long casualty-lists and a humiliating, if brilliantly executed, withdrawal.

Meanwhile, almost within eyeshot, another sideshow began at Salonika in Greece which was to tie down many thousands of men and vast amounts of resources while producing little significant fighting until the last weeks of the war. The situation was complicated by tangled Balkan politics and the ambitions of the French, so that not for the first or last time military wisdom succumbed to political pressure. Salonika was in effect a lavishly sustained defensive operation against an enemy who was not proposing to attack.

Further east another dramatic story was developing in Mesopotamia where an expeditionary force raised by the British Government of India advanced up the Tigris with the intention of seizing Baghdad. That city was eventually taken in 1917, but not before one of the longest sieges in British military history had taken place with the expeditionary force trapped by the Turks in Kut-al-Amara. Unsuccessful attempts to relieve Major-General Townshend's starving garrison in Kut led to many casualties, and the story ended tragically with the survivors of the siege being taken off to captivity, many of the 'other ranks' perishing in a prolonged death-march across the desert.

Palestine was a more successful theatre, particularly after the arrival from France of General Allenby, who took Jerusalem in 1917 and Damascus in 1918, while the Arabs, with Lawrence as principal liaison officer and military tactician, played a notable part as a highly effective guerrilla right wing. This theatre is not dealt with here but is featured briefly in Part IV on the air war (see also colour section, page 150).

Men of the Lancashire Fusiliers before disembarking at Gallipoli, May 1915 (Q 13219)

The Sideshows   **Important Dates**

1914

November 2	Russia declares war on Turkey
5	Britain and France declare war on Turkey
22	British Indian Army force occupies Basra

1915

February 3	Turks occupy Sinai
19	Combined British and French fleet begins attempts to force the Dardanelles
March 18	Attempt to force the Narrows
April 25	First landing of Mediterranean Expeditionary Force on Gallipoli peninsula
August 6	British landings at Suvla, Gallipoli
October 5	First Allied troops land at Salonika
November 22	Battle of Ctesiphon (Mesopotamia)
December 7	Siege of Kut-al-Amara begins
December-January 1916	Evacuation of Gallipoli Peninsula

1916

April 29	Kut falls to Turkish forces
June 5	Grand Sherif Hussein of Mecca launches the Arab Revolt
December 6	Bucharest falls to the Central Powers

1917

February 24	British retake Kut
March 11	British take Baghdad
26	First Battle of Gaza, Palestine Front
April 17	Second Battle of Gaza
October 24	Start of Austro-German offensive against the Italians at Caporetto
October 31	Third Battle of Gaza; Beersheba captured
December 9	Capture of Jerusalem

1918

June 15-18	Battle of the Piave
September	Successful Allied campaign in Macedonia (Salonika Front)
September 19	Final offensive (Battle of Megiddo), Palestine Front
30	Bulgaria sues for peace
October 1	First Allied forces enter Damascus
24	Battle of Vittorio Veneto (Italy) begins
30	Turkey signs armistice with the Allies
November 3	Austria-Hungary sues for peace

The Dardanelles and Gallipoli

We went into the jaws of death today, but owing to God's mercy we returned without loss of life, although the majority of the sailors did not think it was God's mercy, they put it down to having three black bats on board this ship.

So wrote a British Able Seaman about the major naval initiative undertaken by Britain and France against Turkey, on 18 March 1915. The intention was to make a determined attempt to force the Narrows, the vital 'neck' of the Dardanelles – that stretch of heavily guarded and turbulent water between the Gallipoli peninsula to the west and the Asiatic shore to the east which provided the only access to the Sea of Marmara and, ultimately, the Turkish capital, Constantinople. Progress depended on the attainment of two targets: the silencing of the enemy's on-shore forts and batteries and the removal of his numerous minefields. Earlier efforts had failed; it was hoped that this one would provide the crucial breakthrough.

Able Seaman Cemm was in HMS *Prince George*, a *Majestic* class pre-Dreadnought battleship whose duty was to support the leading line of four warships, which included the brand-new *Queen Elizabeth*, completed only two months before and later to become the flagship of the Grand Fleet. Eight other British and four French capital ships followed astern, while also present were cruisers, torpedo-boat destroyers and minesweepers, all adding up, according to Cemm, to 'a magnificent Armada'. But there was an important weakness; the minesweepers, described by one historian as 'a motley collection of fishing trawlers', were less than adequate for their task. More, there were mines in areas thought to be devoid of them. The operation might look impressive but it had its Achilles' heel from the start.

At first the Turkish fire was not returned, but then, wrote Cemm:

About 11.15 am the first angry shot was fired and after bombarding for about twenty minutes, the *Queen Elizabeth* went ahead of the whole fleet, letting rip for all she was worth. The bombardment was getting very fierce, shells were moaning and whining all around us, and the noise of our gunfire was something terrible. We have not up to the present had a very good opinion of the French Navy, but after what we saw today, I say 'Hats off' to the Frenchmen. Two of their cruisers now passed up the lines, and took a position ahead of our ships on the Asiatic side, and in direct line with the Dardanos fort close to Chanak, and if anyone went over into Hell, those two cruisers did, at times it was impossible to see them, for the spray that was thrown up by the shells falling all around them, the fort was firing like Hell. In the meantime the remainder of the fleet was not idle, it was one continual deafening roar caused by the firing of our ships, and the moaning hissing noise of the enemy's shells – how some of our ships lived through the hail of shells was a mystery to me.

Some ships, however, did not survive – presumably there were no black bats in them. A little after midday the second line of battleships, four

French, two British, passed through the leading line to engage the forts at close range. Almost at once the French battleship *Bouvet* was seen to be in trouble:

The *Bouvet* passed under our stern, and had gone about three or four hundred yards away from us, when we saw her suddenly heel over and turn upside down and she sank in two and a half minutes, taking the best part of her crew with her. Where the *Bouvet* sank, there was a huge upheaval of water, caused by the air escaping from the sunken ship.

Whether she was hit by mine or shell was never established, but both those weapons played decisive roles that day. *Irresistible* and *Ocean* struck mines and followed *Bouvet* to the bottom, two further French battleships, *Suffren* and *Charlemagne*, were crippled by gunfire, and *Inflexible* (one of the victors of the Falkland Islands battle) was so damaged by shells and by a later encounter with a mine that she had to be towed to Malta for a refit.

After this 'disastrous day' (as 18 March was described by Admiral de Roebeck, the naval commander), it was decided that the next step should be for land forces to seize the Gallipoli peninsula – which was now seen as the key to the whole venture – following which the ships would try again. But the peninsula was not taken and the ships did not try again.

They still had a crucial role, however, in that they would have to put the soldiers ashore. Plans were set in train for what was to become, indeed, the most ambitious combined operation of the war. Within a month another, even larger armada was assembling in Mudros harbour in the nearby island of Lemnos, ready to transport a hastily assembled Allied army to the Gallipoli beaches. Arriving on 15 April, Captain K.M. Gresson, an infantry officer of the New Zealand Expeditionary Force, was immensely impressed by what he saw:

First we passed the huge *Queen Elizabeth* with her eight 15-inch guns tilted slightly upwards like a greyhound sniffing the air. Then the slightly less formidable *Cornwallis* and the *London*. Then for an hour we passed warships and transports, English, French, Russian. It was a magnificent sight. This army of 100,000 gathered together in ships from all parts of the world guarded by the magnificent *Queen Elizabeth* and other battleships of England and France, and attended by submarines, torpedo craft and aircraft, lay quietly at anchor in the beautiful harbour of Mudros until the word should be given for the greatest turning-movement ever attempted in the war to begin.

The task-force left Mudros on 24 April, with a view to effecting the landing on Gallipoli in the small hours of the 25th. Gresson noted:

At 3 o'clock the Australian Division who land first sailed out preceded by the convoy of warships, first the magnificent *Queen Elizabeth* flying the Admiral's flag and receiving the salutes of every ship she passed. Then followed the

Nelson	*Prince of Wales*	*Goliath*
Agamemnon	*Cornwallis*	*Majestic*
Swiftsure	*Formidable*	*Bacchante*
Triumph	*Implacable*	*Dublin*
Queen	*London*	

and a host of destroyers and smaller craft.

In their wake came the transports carrying the Australian Division who will effect their landing at daybreak. The 29th Division (English) who are to land at Cape Hellas have already gone with their escort of warships; and the French are drawn up in the outer harbour with their cruisers and destroyers ready for their descent on Kum Kale.

We – the N.Z. Division – leave soon after midnight. I turned in early so as to get a good night's rest before tomorrow when the Allies shall attempt the landing on the forbidden shores of Gallipoli.

'Left Mudros on the great adventure, weather propitious with bright sunshine and a pleasant breeze.' So wrote Surgeon Duncan Lorimer RNVR, in one of the ships whose departure was noted by Gresson, the cruiser HMS *Bacchante*. But Lorimer had no doubts about the hazards the troops would face:

The soldiers in the advanced guard will have a very trying time, embarking in picket boats, pinnaces, cutters, etc, about one in the morning, in pitch darkness, and silence, then steaming for about two hours in the cold and the silence, to a shore it will be impossible to be sure of, to splash ashore and then, wet, chilled and cramped from their long sitting in the boats to advance against an invisible enemy, probably on the alert, and certainly guarded by barbed-wire entanglements, and possibly land-mines. They have a most heroic part to play.

'Heroic' is certainly an appropriate description for most of what took place at Gallipoli on the first day, but that heroism had to compensate for numerous failures and inadequacies elsewhere. As a recent historian of the war has written, 'The events of 25 April 1915 bore witness to what an invading force must suffer when surprise is lacking, improvisation has been substituted for preparation, and no calculation has been made of its needs in manpower and fire power.'* Moreover, on landing, troops met a furious and well-led resistance stiffened by German expertise – in fact the overall commander of the Gallipoli garrison was a German, General Liman von Sanders. Additionally the Turks were fighting for a piece of their homeland and were as eager to repel as the Allied forces were to land.

Among the latter the Australian and New Zealand Army Corps (known forever after as the ANZACs) fought so gallantly that for their two countries 25 April was to become a day of permanent national pride. Their difficulties were compounded by the fact that the Navy landed them a mile north of their intended beachhead – not on a spacious shore as they expected but at a point where they met formidable opposition from geography as well as the Turks. As a staff officer, Captain Guy Dawnay, put it in a letter written some days later:

The landing place was a difficult one. A narrow, sandy beach backed by a very high intricate mass of hills, those behind the beach being exceedingly steep. However, as soon as the pinnaces were forced by the shallow water to cast off the boats they were towing, the men in the latter – all ready with their oars – rowed in; and the moment the boats landed they jumped out and rushed straight for the hills rising almost cliff-like only fifty yards or so beyond the beach. It must have been a magnificent rush. I went ashore there yesterday, into their position, and it seemed almost incredible that any troops could have done it. It is a stiff climb even up the zig-zag path which the Engineers have now built! How they got up fully armed and equipped over the rough scrub-clad hillside one can hardly imagine!

*Trevor Wilson, *The Myriad Faces of War*, Blackwell, 1986, Polity Press 1988. The quotation regarding minesweepers on p. 159 is also from this source.

An earthy Australian account, unfortunately anonymously, gives some idea of what that climb was like as the men fought their way up and inland from what was to become famous as Anzac Cove – under the guns of a Turkish strong-point on the headland of Gaba Tepe to the immediate south:

IWM diorama depicting the hotly contested landing on V beach, Cape Helles, 25 April 1915, showing the prow of the *River Clyde* (Q 63667)

Well we reached the first trench, but not a Turk in it, they had cleared for their lives. The rifle fire became much less but instead there was an awful tornado of shrapnel from Gaba Tepe fort, which could enfilade us and shell the sea shore as they unmercifully did. We made a sort of irregular line, in places three or four deep, and chased the flying Jackos [ie Turks] out of the next two trenches. Fortunately for me I did not have to use my bayonet. I did not much relish the idea of sticking a man through although quite ready to do so. We dared not fire because of our own often being in front of us through the irregular method of advance, the very nature of the ground making it impossible to get into anything like a line and charge. But on we went, when we got half way up we thought we could get a bit of a spell, so we sat down for a bit, and those who were lucky to find their pipe, tobacco and cigarettes dry had a good smoke; I much enjoyed a pipe myself, having kept the tobacco in my haversack. Then the shrapnel harried us and we went up, up, forever it seemed, up this chine to the summit, which at last we reached, and then we dashed along after the Turks who we could see clearly now in the rising of the sun-light. Here a tremendous report echoed all around, we for a moment wondered what had happened, then it dawned on us, it was the warships that had commenced to back us up. That made the Turks hasten a bit and we also took a faster run – now we were on comparatively flat ground and we found it easier work getting along, but as we got further in so our line got thinner and thinner, then we found that we could not hold the third high ridge which we had now reached, and we were forced to retire back to the second ridge. We were very loath to do this after winning all this ground but it was unavoidable, and it was then that a German officer, who I well remember received about 20,000 more Australian bullets on his back for calling out to us, shouted 'Come on you Australian Kangaroos' and managed to rally the Turks, they thinking that we were retiring through some cause or other, but NO, we were not going back any further than the second ridge. And that was the commencement of that tremendous rifle fire, from both sides – I had never imagined that rifle fire could make so fearful and everlasting a roar, it was wonderful in its awfulness.

Anzac Beach, showing the steep terrain up which the Australians advanced on 'Anzac Day' (Q 13603)

Below: Photograph captioned: 'The irrepressible Australians at Anzac. An Australian bringing in a wounded comrade to hospital. The men were cracking jokes as they made their way up from the front' (Q 13622)

Meanwhile Gresson's New Zealanders had been following up, meeting as they climbed the steep sandy bluffs a steady stream of Australian wounded making their way down to the beach. To their eager enquiries as to how the battle was going they got the terse reply 'We're driving 'em to Hell', but when Gresson, in command of an ammunition party, reached the top he found his first task would be to help the Australians, now under heavy enemy pressure:

On making enquiries from a Staff Officer I found that ammunition was urgently required by the 3rd Australian Brigade who were lining the next ridge. I accordingly directed my party across there and making our way down from the plateau we tackled the ascent of the next ridge eventually arriving there exhausted but with the ammunition which they were in desperate need of at this point. Throughout the remainder of the day we were engaged in strengthening this position, getting up water and repelling Turkish attacks.

The Gallipoli peninsula protrudes south-west into the Aegean Sea roughly in the shape of a dragon's head. The Australians' strike was on its western side some miles up, while much further north there was a diversionary feint by the Royal Naval Division towards Bulair on the dragon's neck. The British made their attack, as it were, right on the muzzle at Cape Helles, landing on five beaches code-named respectively (west to east) Y, X, W, V, and S., while the French went ashore opposite Cape Helles at Kum Kale on the Asian shore.

Fortunes varied. At some beaches there was little resistance; at others the invaders were met by a devastating response from artillery, rifle fire and machine guns. The most dramatic and celebrated episode of the day took place at V Beach, where the British had planned to run ashore a specially adapted collier, the *River Clyde*, with a 'cargo' of 2000 men, who would then exit through a number of openings cut in her side in a manner not unreminiscent of Greek soldiers pouring into ancient Troy – a classical allusion not lost on some of the participants, particularly since the reputed site of Troy was only a few miles away across the Dardanelles. Captain Guy Dawnay's letter of 29 April describes the outcome as he observed it from the flagship *Queen Elizabeth*:

The tows going in were met by a terrific fire from rifles, machine guns and pom poms, and though landing was actually effected that is all that can be said. The enemy's fire was all at very close range, and the men who got ashore seemed unable to get off the beach. At the same time as the tows made for the shore, the collier ('the wooden horse of Troy') was turned towards the beach and run ashore. She went right up on the beach fair and square, and so close up to the shore that landing from her would have been quite easy but for the enemy's fire. As it was she was *plastered* with shells bursting round her, and a hail of rifle bullets and it was quite impossible for the men to disembark.

Major G.B. Stoney had been appointed a Military Landing Officer on V Beach, but there was clearly no immediate prospect of carrying out his duties:

Our tow got to the steamer [the *River Clyde*] and the firing was so hot that the beach master, whom I was with, decided that there was no object in our going ashore so we came on board the steamer that lay aground. I nipped up the ladder pretty quickly as we were under the fire of a maxim from the shore. One could hear the bullets hitting the ship's side all around us. From then until dark there was nothing much for me to do. Very few of the troops on board had left because they were being bowled over just as quickly as they left the ship. After dark I was sent out to stop them bringing in the wounded before the troops had been put ashore. Not a pleasant job with wounded men calling for help and groaning with agony. However we had to insist on it. After I had been getting men ashore for about five hours suddenly a very hot fire was poured on us. I was in the bows of a cutter. We all lay as close as we could below the gunwales of the cutter while the firing continued. It must have lasted for about two hours and to add to our comfort it began to rain. Many of the men were so tired that they fell asleep. This I discovered when the firing ceased and I again had to start trying to get them ashore. I got back to the ship at 4 am, and had an hour's sleep not having had any for forty-eight hours.

Overall the events of 25 April were not an auspicious beginning and they set the tone of subsequent events. The battle for Gallipoli was to become a struggle that never really looked like being won. It very quickly took on some of the characteristics of Western Front warfare, with

Below left: British troops returning from the trenches photographed in Gully Ravine – a deep, precipitously sided feature inland from Cape Helles which was gradually wrested from the Turks between April and June 1915 (Q 13315)

Below centre: Australians and men of the Royal Naval Division sharing the same trench. One soldier (left) is using a trench periscope for observation, the other a 'sniperscope' (periscope rifle) (Q 13426)

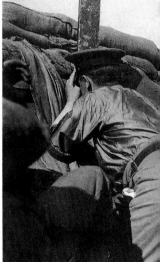

Below right: The great blizzard of November 1915: frost-bitten soldiers at Suvla Bay, lying in shelters made of store boxes (Q 13644)

ill-planned attacks launched against heavily defended positions resulting in ever-longer casualty lists and with few lessons learned from previous failures. As early as 13 May the commander of the Royal Naval Division, Major-General Sir Archibald Paris, could write: 'It seems probable that we have finished with general attack and are now reduced to the silly old game of trench warfare. Clearing the Dardanelles at this rate will mean some years work.'

In August that year, recuperating in England after being wounded, Major H. Mynors Farmar, Staff Captain, 86th Brigade, wrote incisively about the Gallipoli fighting:

When I was there, in every case, attacks were ordered rather lightheartedly and carried out without method. The men on the spot were not listened to when they pointed out steps to be taken before entering on a special task. The Turks had sited their trenches very cleverly and it was often useless to attack one set before another had been taken. The Turks dig like moles and prepare line after line for defence: seven or eight close behind the other. The great difficulty is in making attacks and supporting them. The trenches become congested: the telephone wires get cut by shrapnel: and the whole show gets out of control.

Almost always in Gallipoli the attacks were made by men in the trenches and not by fresh troops. The men are kept too long and too thick in the trenches: they become stupefied after five days.

Attacks seemed always to be ordered against very long strips of line at once without any weight anywhere. It all seemed very amateur. But I suppose it couldn't be helped, the idea was always to get through with a rush and to disregard losses.

A new initiative was tried in early August when another landing was effected to the north of Anzac Cove at Suvla Bay, but there was a delay in exploiting the beachhead, thus allowing the Turks to offer their usual robust and effective response. There were other hazards. Endemic sickness took increasing toll as the weeks went by. Flies swarmed everywhere in the crowded insanitary trenches and, with concepts of food hygiene virtually non-existent, dysentery became rife. Arrangements to

cope with the sick and wounded were hopelessly inadequate. When Surgeon Duncan Lorimer of HMS *Bacchante* went on board a transport bringing casualties from Cape Helles to Mudros, he found 'the whole ship packed with wounded, lying about anywhere, no order, nor anybody in charge. The wounds had not been looked at for forty-eight hours at least, and in that climate were in an awful state, live maggots in many.' He commented angrily, 'It made one ashamed of the Medical Organization of the Army: if they were short of doctors, as they obviously were, they could have had help from the Navy long ago, as I know it was offered.' Extremes of weather presented a further problem – fierce heat in summer, storms in the autumn and then, in November, a two-day blizzard which wreaked havoc on men in trenches with no protective clothing and whom it was often impossible to relieve or supply. From this one snowstorm there were over 16,000 cases of frostbite and exposure and almost 300 deaths.

Well before then a debate had begun on a question unthinkable in the hopeful early weeks: should more men and resources be committed or should defeat be acknowledged and the campaign abandoned? The matter could not be seen in isolation, in that thousands of soldiers and many units of the Navy were being occupied by what in the end, certainly now that the first high hopes had faded, was only a sideshow. Almost inevitably withdrawal became the only option. In October the original Commander-in-Chief, Sir Ian Hamilton, was recalled. When his successor, Sir Charles Monro, took over he saw as his principal, indeed only, mission the successful carrying out of an evacuation, an operation inevitably complicated by the necessity to deceive the enemy into believing that no such thing was taking place. Suvla and Anzac were abandoned in December and by early January 1916 the decision was taken to withdraw the remaining Allied troops from Cape Helles. On 8 January Major-General Sir Archibald Paris, Royal Naval Division, wrote:

To do it properly and to take away all stores would mean a month's careful preparation and they gave us a week. Bad weather would make it impossible and this is the time of year when storms prevail. Not a cheering prospect as it blew hard for two days. However Providence looks after fools and the last three days have been splendid. A good deal has been removed and about half the Army. We now have left only the men who can get away the last night.

Paris's deputed representative on that last night, 9 January, was Lieutenant-Colonel Norman Burge, Royal Marines Light Infantry, who was in command of the 'RND Rendezvous' – to use the official description – in the ultimate stage of the evacuation. The following is from the final pages of a long letter to his mother which he began on the peninsula and concluded immediately after arriving at Lemnos (having admitted in its first section that once he had 'put the last man on his right road, I can promise you that you won't see *my* heels for small pebbles'.)

The plan was to send down as many of the Firing Line and Supports etc. as could be spared and these people began coming through me soon after 9 pm. They came all right – somehow there didn't seem to be any loitering on the way – and then came the anxious time. If the Turks attacked or found out that we were going, we, the last ditchers would of course have been done. The line was to be left clear at 11.45, and it would take them a good hour for the men to get down to me and after them were all the oddments, who were connecting up mines, blocking communication trenches, etc. That means there was a gap of about two hours for me with nothing to do – no one coming through, and dashed cold into the bargain. At last about 1.30 everyone was through – so even if we, the last 600, *had* been collared, the evacuation would have been a great success as we formed such a small proportion of the total numbers. But I don't think any of us last folks had any such high and uplifting thoughts. I hadn't anyway.

We got away about 3.30 and started for Lemnos. About 5 am our fires began to blaze up on the peninsula – all stores we could not get off and which we knew we couldn't get off had been prepared with oil etc and time fuzes set. When these started – Clismas! what a hullabaloo. The Turks thought we were going at last and opened every gun they could on roads, communication trenches, beaches and everything else they could think of. Some of us had thought they wanted to *let* us get off – but this fire showed they had meant to make it as uncomfortable for us as possible.

Burge ended his letter with a tribute to the enemy, couched in the phraseology of the time: 'Well, well – I'm sorry to part with the Turk – he's a whiter man than many I've met and all of us would be only too delighted to join up with him and give the Greeks and Bulgars what they thoroughly deserve and ought to get.' This was a clear reference to a second major sideshow which had already opened some months earlier in the same theatre of war – at Salonika.

Preparing the evacuation, W Beach, Cape Helles, 7 January 1916. The explosion is caused by a Turkish shell fired from the Asiatic shore falling just short in the sea (Q 13692)

Off-Stage to a Sideshow: Commander Forbes RN

Midshipman Wykeham-Musgrave (see Part III) was one of the youngest to serve afloat in the Royal Navy during the First World War; undoubtedly the oldest officer to go to sea was William Forbes, who had been born in 1845 and had been placed on the retired list with the rank of Commander as far back as 1888. Although almost seventy in 1914 he promptly offered himself to the Admiralty at the commencement of hostilities. He was given a curious appointment which he cheerfully accepted: to take command of a dummy battleship, a liner adapted to look like HMS *Orion* (see page 18), the purpose of the exercise being to persuade German submarines to turn their attentions to the impotent dummy rather than the genuine article. His express function, in a word, was to be bait, to be attacked and if necessary sunk so that his effective 'lookalike' should survive to wage war with the enemy.

In February 1915 he was appointed to command a Special Service Squadron of three dummy warships which was to be sent to the Eastern Mediterranean to act as submarine decoy during the forthcoming operations against the Dardanelles. He sailed in the 'flagship' of the squadron, *No 14* – the former 11,000-ton transport SS *Merion*, which had been converted to the likeness of the 35,000-ton battle cruiser HMS *Tiger*. While the fighting ships attempted to force their way through the Dardanelles to the Sea of Marmara, his job was to patrol outside – and to keep on patrolling. 'Here we go down, down

South and up again,' he wrote to his wife on 14 March, 'while the *real ones* go in and *pound away*. It is very tedious and folk are growing discontented. I wish I could get them ashore and set them to play football and cricket. There are no real hardships but I would like a taste of food that has not been frozen and fresh vegetables.' Yet a fortnight later, even though he was engaged in that most loathed of sailors' task, coaling ship ('and a long dirty job it is'), he could write: 'It's weary work but "Are we downhearted?" "No!"'

In mid-April his squadron was given the task of guarding the transports arriving at Mudros prior to the landings at Gallipoli:

I am now away from my lot on a *difficult and delicate job*, but hope to carry it out successfully and then return in a few days and *see great things*. It is a job after my own heart and I am *very* pleased. When you see in *the papers the deed has been done*, you may divulge all you know I think, at least that I was there.

But the St Crispin's day satisfaction he craved was denied him:

April 28th, patrolling. I have been very low for the last two days for the Great Day has come and we were away on patrol thirty-five miles from the scene of action. After all our weary beats up and down, generally in hateful weather, off *the* place, it does seem hard not to be there now and see what *I* feel sure will be the end and victory. But *events happened* which made *this* a locality which had to be well guarded so I was sent with my lot to do it.

The Two Faces of Commander Forbes's 'Flagship'
Left: SS *Merion*; displacement 11,000 tons (SP 3236)
Below: SS *Merion* transformed to the design of HMS *Tiger*.
Tiger's displacement being 35,000 tons, the converted
merchant ship was effectively pretending to be a
warship over three times her actual size (SP 2350)

It was an unfounded alarm that enemy U-boats were
about which had removed him from the central
scene: 'The danger has been over two days and more
and I fear we are forgotten! still I can't leave the work
I am set to do.'

In May, however, the situation changed. The
presence of U-boats in the Eastern Mediterranean
was now proved and the prospect of the proffered
bait being taken became very real. 'It will not be an
inglorious ending, really, if we are caught,' he wrote,
philosophically, on 27 May. His next letter, dated 31
May, was written from another ship, at Mudros:

I was writing to you last night at 8 p.m. when they got me
with a torpedo and finished poor old *No 14* and my job.
Excuse my breaking the news so abruptly – but it's best I
think. Thank God we only lost four men out of 117 – two
engineer officers and two firemen. Both men and officers
behaved quite splendidly, there was no panic and every
man got into his own boat without confusion and very little
noise: we were patrolling twenty miles south of here. We
pulled away from her thinking another torpedo *must* come
but the submarine never showed or fired again. We pulled
towards this (the base) till 2 am when we were picked up by
a tug and towed here: four boats full of half clad folk. I have
lost *all*, only a jacket, shirt and trousers: all my photos, and
diaries, money, everything. We will be sent home soon.
I am *not* surprised, as once we knew the submarines were
up the straits, I knew they would get us in time. Both
Admirals and everyone are so kind and nice. When the
shock came I was in my deck cabin addressing a letter to
you and was nearly lifted through the ceiling. She did not

sink though half full of water, and I got leave to take a party
from *here* to see if she still floated, but they managed to get
the tug aground, and so I never got there. I can't write
more now. We got in here at 6 am and I have not yet had a
lie down 8 pm. We are to be sent home in a few days.

Forbes had done everything that could have been
asked of him. He had sent a wireless message to the
Admiral to inform him that *No 14* had been
torpedoed, he and the operator having to break open
the door of the wireless room which had been
damaged in the explosion. Subsequently, in the high
tradition of the Navy, he and the captain (Forbes's
command had been of the squadron, not of the
individual ship) had been the last to leave the stricken
vessel. He returned to England in the *Tunisian* with
other Royal Navy and Army officers who had served
at Gallipoli, and in July was given command of the
thirty armed drifters based on Ramsgate which
formed part of the Dover Patrol. But failing health
caused him to relinquish his command soon
afterwards. Forbes was promoted to Captain on the
retired list in August 1915 as a mark of the
Admiralty's appreciation of his services.

Earlier in the year the real HMS *Tiger* had taken
part in the Battle of the Dogger Bank and she was to
be heavily involved in the Battle of Jutland in 1916,
but her good fortune was to continue; she survived
the war and was sold and scrapped in the early
1930s.

A Wild Goose Affair: Salonika

In November 1915, towards the end of the Gallipoli campaign, Second Lieutenant Cuthbert Aston went for a walk with three fellow-officers. They climbed to the top of Karakol Dagh, a hill 500 feet high to the north west of Suvla Bay across which ran the British second line trenches. 'One gets the most magnificent views,' he afterwards wrote, 'of the whole Gallipoli coast round the Bulair lines, the Turkish coast, and the Bulgarian coast right round to Salonika with some topping mountain islands behind which the sun sets.'

Salonika – over 200 miles to the west across the Aegean – was to be the setting of another of the war's major sideshows, though unlike Gallipoli, the Salonika Front was to go on and on, its camps and trenches occupied by many thousands of men who for months on end had no idea when they might next be called upon to fight. By comparison with most other fronts, it was an inactive volcano. In October 1916 Captain Tommy Martin, 5th Battalion, Connaught Rangers, one of the infantry battalions in the 10th Division, wrote in a letter home, 'Two of my new subalterns are from France recently so think this is a great joy-ride.'

Salonika's initial significance lay in the fact that, as a major port in northern Greece, it provided a means of access for the Allies to intervene in the Balkans in support of their ally Serbia. In the second half of 1915, the Central Powers (Germany and Austria-Hungary) judged Serbia ripe for conquest, and when Bulgaria – Serbia and Greece's next-door neighbour – came in on their side, Serbia stood little chance. Her outnumbered army made a desperate retreat through the mountains to the Albanian coast, from which Allied shipping took the survivors off to Corfu. An Anglo-French force despatched to Salonika on Serbia's behalf now stayed on to parry any further enemy ambitions in the region, and in particular to do battle with Bulgaria. After some initial exchanges it became increasingly clear that Bulgaria was not overly anxious to do battle in return.

However, once they had put their men ashore at Salonika, it became extremely difficult for the Allies to extract them – even though they were in a country, Greece, whose pro-German neutrality made her a less than benign hostess. When the British, fearing decreasing dividends from the campaign, began to lose interest, the fact that French enthusiasm remained undimmed made it politically unacceptable to withdraw. An extra twist to the story came from the fact that the French had a senior commander, General Maurice Sarrail, who had been dismissed for

*(see opposite page) The geographical as opposed to the political name of the area in contention (at this time the territory known since 700 BC as Macedonia was divided between Serbia and Greece). A useful thumb-nail definition of the situation is that the British in this theatre were the British Salonika Army engaged, with their Allies, in fighting the Macedonian Campaign.

incompetence on the Western Front and who had to be assuaged with an important command elsewhere. Offered Salonika, he accepted provided the French commitment there was increased. He got his way. An apt German description of Salonika dubbed it 'the greatest Allied internment camp' of the war. Equally dismissive, the British Prime Minister until 1916, H.H. Asquith, called the Salonika campaign 'a wild goose affair'.

A memoir by Ifor Powell, formerly a captain in the 6th Battalion, Leinster Regiment, also in the 10th Division, spells out what this stalemate meant for the soldiers involved.

The 10th Division spent nearly two years in Macedonia.* First came the period of waiting, then the brief period of war, or near-war, in the South-Eastern corner of Serbia, and thirdly the long period of anti-climax enlivened by only short periods of action. During these long months we had to contend not so much with the malice of the enemy, as with homesickness, dearth of leave, surfeit of bully beef and biscuits, absence of feminine society, the attentions of mosquitoes, flies and other insects, dysentery, septic sores, malaria, and last, but not least, senior officers. There was exhilaration for some in the nearness of ancient Greece, in the reality of what had been mere names before. Was it nothing to stand on a high ridge, on a clear and cloudless day, and such were many, and look on snow-crowned Olympus, most noble of mountains, and Pelion and Ossa beyond? Yes, and then turning northwards, to marvel at Rhodope, pink-tipped in the setting sun.

Of the various hazards listed above, the mosquito was perhaps the worst. According to Powell it was particularly active in one of the main operational areas on the Salonika Front, the Struma Plain:

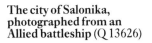

The city of Salonika, photographed from an Allied battleship (Q 13626)

**The Enemy on the
Salonika Front
Right: German Hussars
crossing the River Dvina
into Macedonia (Q 56992)
and (opposite) Bulgarian
infantry in action
(Q 56995)**

The valley of Death, it was called locally, and not without reason, for in places
the fever was of a malignant type. Yet we of the 10th Division rushed boldly in
and lined the very river banks, vainly trusting to the prophylactic qualities of
daily potions of quinine. Scarcely able to believe their good fortune, with in-
furiating, high-pitched buzz, the cohorts of anopheles mosquitoes ('miskitties'
to the Irish) alighted on every square inch of exposed anatomy, and caroused
from dusk to dawn on the heaven-sent consignment of fresh untasted human
blood.

Illness was in fact a prime belligerent on this front – and its incidence
gave rise to some remarkable statistics. Overall, there were at one time
or another 400,000 British troops here; the official figure for men falling
sick throughout the campaign was 481,000.

The funnel through which this massive army reached the front was
Salonika itself, a striking sight when seen from approaching ships.
Private William Knott of the 32nd Field Ambulance was an early British
arrival, being transferred there from Gallipoli in the autumn of 1915. He
noted in his diary under 11 October:

Rose at 6 am to find that we were in a wide gulf bordered by high mountains to
right and left. For the first time we found our destination was to be the historic
city of Salonika. It was a magnificent sail, the glittering sunshine showing up the
snow-capped peaks of Grecian heights on our left. As we approached the city, at
the terminus of the gulf, we could see the tall towers of innumerable Greek
churches and these and the white buildings all presented a radiant picture of
splendour seldom seem in England. Sailing close to the quayside, we could see
trams, hotels and other attempts at Westernizing the sea-front, a very different
aspect to the barren Turkish territory we have just left.

Second Lieutenant Owen Rutter, 7th Battalion, Wiltshire Regiment,
was equally impressed by his first sight of this teeming polyglot city when
he arrived there a year later, in November 1916. Its impact produced an
eloquent passage in his diary:

It was a clear sunshiny morning, the air rather sharp and the harbour and town
looked very lovely in the morning sunlight. Men of war English, French and
Italian and their destroyers were there and many transports, and the city clus-

tered together on the hill with the old castle on the summit, its white tower and minarets rising like candles to the blue sky.

They put us ashore very soon and we formed up on the quay. We marched off through the town, quaint and eastern with its pavé streets and mosques and minarets, western in its trams and shops. There seemed to be every nationality under the sun, never even in Singapore or Yokohama have I seen such a mixture of East and West. English soldiers and French and Greeks, the Greek officers (the only ones not at war) with their swords, Jews, Armenians, beggars of every kind, Greek ladies in most wonderful costumes and a sprinkling of every Balkan nation. It would take an abler pen (or pencil) than mine to paint it, for there was colour everywhere. Through the town we marched, crowds of people watching us (with interest but without enthusiasm) and we eyes lefted to a Greek guard while our band woke Salonika up.

For Captain Tommy Martin of the 5th Connaught Rangers, the Salonika scene – as observed on a brief social visit – provided a mixture of amazement and amusement. He wrote in a letter home in April 1916:

The variety of types both military and civilian in town here are absolutely bewildering and beat Egypt hollow. The view from the swell restaurant must be one of the most extraordinary the world has ever seen. Musical comedy seems to have got mixed up with real life as far as uniforms are concerned.

There was little of musical comedy, however, in what had taken place in the first weeks of British involvement. Private William Knott had arrived early enough to be sent up-country into Serbian territory at a time when the Serbian Army was still engaged in its fighting retreat, which had drawn with it a tide of civilian refugees who had fled their homes in panic and were endeavouring to make their way to safety. A compassionate and deeply religious man, Knott was clearly moved when, writing in his diary on 18 November 1915, he tried to describe what he had just witnessed:

In the afternoon a long line of refugees passed under military escort. What a heart-rending sight it was, thin, half-clad, starved women and children dragging their weary way, many with sore bare feet not daring to stay lest they felt the lash of the soldier's whip. Their probable husbands drove little skeletons of donkeys loaded with all their belongings, consisting of a few old tins and spare clothing; almost pushing some of them, in fact some lay down and died. It has opened our eyes, how much the country we love and serve needs men to defend the rights of a smaller power and praise God it is not our own country and homes being pillaged and loved ones turned out. It encourages us to defend them till peace shall reign. The night was bitter cold, so I got fifteen fellows to sacrifice their issue of cocoa and off we went (four sergeants, Bert and I) up the hillside where we found some stragglers who, absolutely exhausted, had dropped helpless at the wayside. We first gave drink to women and children, then the men, all of whom were chattering away, probably trying to thank us. We then returned to camp praising God for such an opportunity of giving a little succour to those in great need.

A British machine gun post on the Struma front (Q 32313)

The Allies' brief incursion into Serbian territory was followed by a strategic withdrawal as the Serbian campaign closed down, after which the Salonika initiative mutated into its long stalemate. Knott witnessed little more action in the remaining twenty months he spent there, while many who arrived later and then were moved on elsewhere saw virtually no fighting at all. For example, Desmond Allhusen, a young infantry officer in the 3rd Battalion, King's Rifle Corps, who had fought hard in France and would do so there again, found himself for months in a position about fifty miles east of Salonika, 'holding the right of the long British line against an enemy who would not attack.' He took part in a great deal of shooting, however, but not at the enemy:

The day's amusement began with dusk. About six o'clock the woodcock began to flight, and for the next half hour the whole gorge was unsafe. Everybody seemed to have a shot-gun; fearsome local weapons which seldom hit anything they were meant to. The woodcock came over in hundreds, and though the whole gorge rattled with pellets, the bag was never very big.

There were occasional flurries of action. In the few months Lieutenant Holroyd Birkett Barker, Royal Garrison Artillery, spent on active service at the front there were some fierce duels with the enemy, after one of which, he noted, 'we inspected the damage caused by our opponents and found that in addition to large craters round most of the guns, near the cookhouse and behind the battery, the mess had suffered heavily – one shell in particular having burst within two or three feet and covered the table with earth and stones, overthrown the tables, broken our entire stock of drinkables, jam, pickles and other luxuries and generally leaving it in such a state of disorder as in normal times would have testified to an exceptionally convivial evening.' At other times, however, there was so little cause for firing in anger that the guns were used for purposes which Barker thought quite pointless:

2nd July 1917: Calm still reigns on the front and to relieve the monotony our batteries fire on hay-makers and – worse still – bathing parties for which I really see no profitable excuse. We saw them all clearly in the ravine below us and when the shells came over several of them bolted for cover and left their clothes behind. If Bulgarian Quartermasters resemble ours these men will have to risk another trip across the open for their kit or finish the campaign *en costume d'Adam*!

This was to be virtually the last entry in Barker's diary. Earlier he had suffered a bad attack of malaria and had spent six months recuperating

in Malta; now the disease struck again, dysentery followed and Barker died in hospital in Salonika on 15 August 1917 – a wasteful sideshow fatality typical of many.

Indeed it was the fact that so high a proportion of the Salonika force was disabled by sickness that prevented Sarrail's efforts to break the log-jam in 1917, and it was not until September 1918 that, under a new French commander, Marshal Franchet d'Esperey, the hoped-for routing of the Bulgars took place. In the end Bulgaria was hustled out of the war in a fortnight. A vivid picture of this last phase emerges from a letter of Captain R.W. Townsend MC, 10th Battalion, Devonshire Regiment, written in odd moments during this hectic period. Earlier he had complained 'We seem to live right outside the war here', but this was no longer the case, as the following extracts make clear:

22 September: We really are on the move after the Bulgar who stole away in the night. Our patrols were in their line by nine last night and now we have followed them up and infantry and guns are well inside. It was a very hurried flitting as two deserters told us they got the order to move at 8 at 7.30. I visited a bit of their line this afternoon. They have blown up a lot but there are still some wonderful dug-outs. The wire is tremendous everywhere and we have been blasting a way through it this afternoon for our transport.

26 September: It has been a tremendous day. We started off on sudden orders about 9 and have marched hard over two tremendous passes and down to a village called Strumnica which is at the head of the Struma Valley and we are well into Bulgaria at last. The Bulgar has gone quickly but it has been a fearfully hard march and I didn't get in until 10 o'clock absolutely beat. However it is all part of the day's work and we are finishing off the Bulgar in great style. Still more guns today. It is very pretty country but the dust on the road has been simply awful.

29 September: At present we are absolutely held up. The Bulgar evidently intends to make a stand and has got a wonderful position. He has been shelling hard all day but fortunately there have been very few casualties. It is going to be a very difficult job to turn him out. This evening we have had a real Balkan thunderstorm and got wet to the skin so no one will have a very pleasant night. We try to attack again tomorrow.

30 September: At 5.30 this morning the wire was brought to me to say that Bulgaria had made peace. It came just in time to stop our attacks today which would have been very costly. So the despised Salonika Army is the first to finish off its job. It has been a wonderful fighting campaign though our bit of it has only been tremendous marching and other people have been doing the fighting part of it especially the Serbs. Our Division and especially the Brigade have done especially well. This afternoon we have moved back about five miles to a place called Dabilja for rest and re-equipment. I am quite glad of a pleasant spot with plenty of water under trees. I shall be glad of two days' rest as I have got a mild dose of Spanish Flu and am feeling utterly bored with life. Peace is very good and I think Austria and Turkey will follow Bulgaria's example.

Despite this striking success, those who served at Salonika were never to feel that their contribution to the war was appreciated or even acknowledged. They could draw comfort, however, from the words of Winston Churchill, who was later to write – if perhaps somewhat optimistically: 'The controversies were silenced by the remarkable fact that it was upon this much abused front that the final collapse of the Central Empires first began!'

The Siege of Kut

On 4 April 1916 Lieutenant L.S. Bell Syer, an officer of the 104th Wellesley's Rifles – a unit of the 6th Anglo-Indian Division, Indian Army – noted in his diary: 'The 121st day of the siege, we have now beaten the siege of Ladysmith, as they were relieved at the end of 120 days.'

Since the previous December Bell Syer and some 11,500 other officers and men of the 6th Division had found themselves bottled up in a squalid little township on a bend in the River Tigris deep in Mesopotamia, at that time part of the Turkish Empire. Their lines of communication had been severed and a much larger army of Turks was harassing them on all sides. By the time he wrote those words the garrison (3000 of whom were British, the rest being Indian troops) was steadily losing casualties to disease and starvation, while the Turks were becoming ever more optimistic that, with the Gallipoli campaign now over, another victory over the Allies was within their grasp. The township in question was Kut-al-Amara, a place – as Bell Syer's gloomy comment foreshadowed – that was to win a melancholy footnote as the setting of one of the longest sieges in British military history, outstaying Ladysmith. And whereas Ladysmith was relieved, Kut was not.*

The disaster at Kut stemmed from a feeling common to the British Cabinet, the War Office and the Government of India that a major success was required in the East. If the Gallipoli venture was failing surely something might be achieved in Mesopotamia – why shouldn't the substantial Anglo-Indian force which had already established itself in that country seize her supreme trophy, the capital city, Baghdad? Also enthusiastic for this idea was the Commander-in-Chief in Mesopotamia, General Sir John Nixon, who in October 1915 received his go-ahead from the British Cabinet through the Viceroy of India in terms which put the responsibility deftly on his shoulders: 'Nixon may march on Baghdad if he is satisfied that the force he has available is sufficient for the operation'. Nixon judged that he was so satisfied and passed on the task to the 6th Division, which by then had pushed far up the Tigris and, following some spectacular and inventive river fighting, had reached – that same name again – Kut-al-Amara. However, Kut on the way up was a very different matter from Kut on the way down.

The 6th Division's commander was Major-General Sir Charles Townshend. He was much less convinced than Nixon that he had the capability to carry out the mandate given to him, but nevertheless advanced as instructed towards Baghdad. On 21 November, still twenty miles short of the city, he launched a major attack against newly reinforced Turkish defences at Ctesiphon. After a promising start the attack broke down. With a third of his troops killed or wounded,

*The siege of Ladysmith (1899-1900) was one of the two most famous sieges of the Boer War, the other being that of Mafeking, which lasted 217 days.

Townshend turned back down river. By early December, exhausted and with many of his casualties requiring rest and attention, the depleted force was back in Kut.

Townshend had emerged successfully from a siege early in his career, and confidently expected to get out of this one. He decided to sit tight, defend the town and await the arrival of the inevitable relief. Meanwhile life could continue more or less as normal. Major E.G. Dunn, a Staff Officer seconded from the Royal Irish Rifles, wrote in his diary for Christmas Day.

A very good dinner today – what price this menu – mutton scotch broth; salmon mayonnaise: chicken conflets: roast duck and green peas: plum pudding (A & N* tinned); pear tart: Italian eggs; chocolate, and of course we toasted all our dear ones at home.

On the last day of the year Dunn was still in buoyant mood: '1915 passes leaving us very confident of being able to hold out till relief comes – what will 1916 have in store for us?'

One aspect of what 1916 had in store for him and his colleagues was a swift reduction in the standard of high living that they had enjoyed at Christmas. By late January he was noting: 'First issue of horse flesh today. Last issue of white bread and sugar'. Bell Syer's comment at this juncture was, 'We started eating horse flesh, it's not bad but I prefer

Below left: An observation post in Mesopotamia (Q 24237)

Below: A wood-foraging party in Kut. As fuel ran short, anything that would burn was commandeered (HU 51395)

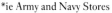

*ie Army and Navy Stores

beef'. More ominously, he continued: 'that damned relief force is only twenty miles away and unable to move for want of men, guns and water transport, which ought to have been supplied months ago by the Indian Government.'

Even more heated at this time was Captain Reynolds Lecky of the 120th Rajputana Infantry. News had been received that General Nixon, whose over-confidence – and incompetence – had been significant factors in bringing about the present impasse, had been dismissed for his pains. Lecky's diary comments were far from sympathetic:

Things seem to be getting towards the limit. No chance of Aylmer [commanding the relief force] doing anything until the weather improves. Bad luck seems to have followed us since 22 November, though I suppose we have asked for it, having 500 miles of Lines of Communication unguarded. Nixon has been recalled, hope they strangle the blighter. This makes the fifteenth General returned from Mespot under a cloud.

Another regular chronicler of the siege was Lieutenant-Colonel H.S. Maule, one of Townshend's senior artillery officers; fearing possible seizure if matters went awry, he wrote his diary – cast in the form of a long-running letter to his wife – in microscopic handwriting on thin paper and subsequently concealed it in his uniform. The following entries give some hint of the deteriorating situation as the weeks went by:

9 February: We have gone on to barley bread which though not so good as the brown bread is quite eatable. We are going to try starling on toast tonight.

11 February: Our starlings were not over-successful, being overcooked, but we had a tin of Milkmaid cream for tea yesterday.

25 February: Aeroplane dropped us some papers and gramophone needles yesterday so we got a little news from the outside world and had a concert from the gramophone after dinner. Jam reduced to 1 oz per diem.

2 March: All our mess sugar is finished.

4 March: No tea and cheese left now.

Throughout all this time the garrison was also suffering from sporadic attacks and bombardments at the hands of the besiegers, who were now being assisted by German air-power. Bell Syer noted on 14 March: 'We have been shelled and bombed and our life has been made a general hades, but we are still keeping the flag flying in spite of it.'

On 20 March Lecky summed up the month to that date:

On 8th Aylmer made his big attack and failed to get through. This makes his fourth effort and we now hear that he has been recalled; Gorringe his Chief of Staff reigns in his stead. We have now rations up to the end of this month so hope Gorringe will make a big effort soon. Ration again reduced, bread down to 8 oz and meat to 1¼ pounds, no vegetables, tea, butter or any luxuries. Turks have produced from nowhere a grand new battery of eight inch guns and are mounting them on timber baulks. On 18th Fritz dropped two 100lb bombs on British hospital, one exploded and killed five and wounded twenty-six, the other stuck in the roof and was gently removed to the river by Sappers.

'It's a weary show this, old girl', Colonel Maule had noted in his ever-lengthening letter to his wife on 10 March. By the end of the month he was even more depressed:

21 March: I am beginning to feel the strain of all this a bit. There is always some problem to be competed with.

28 March: Many happy returns of the day. Next birthday I hope I shall be with you and not in this beastly country.

Meanwhile, particularly among the other ranks – and especially among the Indian troops whose beliefs restricted their already depleted rations – the fatalities had begun. Captain Lecky noted:

1 April: The men are dying off fast now from starvation, scurvy, pneumonia etc. The Tommies are sticking it better than the Indian troops who refuse to eat mule or horse.

2 April: Fox rejoined from hospital on 31 March, having recovered from his wound. Wood, after doing splendidly on Xmas Eve and recovering after having his arm blown off, has died of jaundice, a good fellow.

The guns of the relief force could be heard from down river, and there was still optimism, if not in all quarters, that Gorringe would break through the stubborn Turkish defence lines before it was too late. Colonel Maule wrote on 9 April:

The General had us all out of bed at 5 am this morning to watch the bombardment, and was quite stuffy with me because I didn't agree that the shells were bursting nearer to us. It's pretty sickening to know Gorringe is seventeen miles off and yet can't get through.

Among Gorringe's officers were Second Lieutenant Cuthbert Aston, already a veteran of the Western Front and Gallipoli, and Captain Harold Davson, a Company Commander of the 82nd Punjabis. Their accounts (from a letter in one case, a diary in the other) counterpoint the increasingly pessimistic comments from their comrades inside Kut during the last weeks of the siege:

11 April: *Second Lieutenant Aston, relief force*
The Turks hold their line with a good many machine guns and are well equipped with Very lights. We have superiority of guns and numbers and it's just those infernal machine guns that make one man as good as a battalion on this level coverless country. If it weren't for these forever damned machine guns we'd be in Kut now!

21 April: *Major Dunn, Kut*
Good Friday; a wonderfully quiet day – only seven rounds gunfire into the town and sniping hardly noticeable. A message today to say that relief is certain and everything goes well – but we have learnt how much faith to put in the promises from below.

21 April: *Captain Davson, relief force*
Apparently we are for it tomorrow. A real good biff at the Turks. Oh for the men we had at the beginning of the war. We should go through them like paper. We will anyhow, but some of us will probably have met dear old Beauchamp Clerk, who left us at Neuve Chapelle.
It is in the hands of the gods.
If alive I will write a full description afterwards.
We must go through.

23rd April
But we did not. We marched at 7 p.m. on the 22nd and marched until 2 a.m. when we got into some trenches. The next morning the attack started at 7 a.m.

One hour's bombardment. We were in the 3rd line.

It is always the water that defeats us. We got into the Turkish two front lines and then could not use our rifles as everything was under water.

22 April: *Major Dunn, Kut*

Relief force attacked the Sannaiyat position today and failed so we are put off again, unless something happens unexpectedly and soon our fate is sealed.

22 April: *Lieutenant Bell Syer, Kut*

We are down to starvation rations now, 4 oz of meal and 9 oz of horse meat per man. The Arabs of the town are in an awful state and absolutely starving. We are supposed to be able to last out until the end of the month, but we shall be in a very rocky state by then.

26 April: *Major Dunn, Kut*

General Townshend received instructions from the War Office to surrender and accordingly a flag of truce was sent out to treat for surrender. All firing was stopped by Khalil Pasha [the Turkish commander] on receipt of the letter.

28 April: *Captain Lecky, Kut*

We hear terms asked are full military honours and safe conduct to our own people down stream on parole.

29 April: Terms of surrender evidently refused by Constantinople as we can hear them blowing up the guns again. What next I wonder?

Later, white flag up, unconditional surrender, so it is all over.

29 April: *Colonel Maule, Kut*

Well dearest the end has come, we destroyed our guns this morning, burnt everything we can and are waiting for the Turks to come and take over. We have no more food. It's the saddest day of my service.

30 April: *Captain Davson, relief force*

Heat is appalling, and only just begun. Fleas bite hard – are in thousands. Cholera has started so things are very cheery. I was inoculated yesterday against it and then had to march in the heat of the day to relieve trenches. Great fun.

We lie and gasp all day under a blanket, which we put up to keep off the sun which it does indifferently.

Kut has fallen. With our forces we could not have got through, and 24,000 casualties since December is a lot.

In fact you may say I am pretty fed up with Mesopotamia.

2 May: *Captain Lecky, Shamran*

Left village at 6 p.m. and embarked with 110th and 120th on S.S. *Basra*, proceeded up stream to Turkish camp at Shamran where we found the rest of the Division.

Half the inhabitants of Kut were either shot or hanged, and before we left the trees were dangling with corpses.

3 May. Whole of Division is rotten with cholera, and men are dying like flies.

The siege of Kut was a double disaster: for the garrison who were taken off to a long and humiliating captivity – though many of the other ranks did not survive a horrific forced march to Turkey conducted with the utmost brutality, and for the relief force, which lost considerably more men in casualties than the total complement of the besieged garrison. All this was a long way from the striking success for which the British and Indian Governments had hoped. Baghdad was eventually taken, in March 1917, but its capture was to have little impact on the progress of the war, except that for the Allies it was one positive if minor gain in an otherwise largely disappointing year.

PART VI
Women at War

THE First World War revolutionized the role of women in British society. The chronology overleaf listing the dates on which various women's organizations came into being to assist the nation's cause reads like a stirring roll-call; by 1918 there were numerous avenues away from the kitchen or the drawing-room that were unimaginable four years earlier (so many in fact that only a small number can be represented here). Not that it was all plain sailing. While the government mobilized men, women largely had to mobilize themselves, and when they appeared in certain key industries they sometimes encountered a vigorous male backlash. In May 1915, for example, the Manchester Tramway Workers passed a resolution against the employment of women, while in July that year there was the strange phenomenon of a women's march through London in support of the 'Right to Serve'. Nor was the revolution a permanent one; in the majority of cases when the national emergency was over, women were expected to relinquish their status and skills and withdraw to their traditional areas of society. But they did so with the vote in their grasp – provided they were over thirty – and their contribution was not one that could be lightly dismissed. As the authors of a recent study of the subject have written: 'Although many of the transformations were to prove temporary, the movement of women from the private to the public world and the acknowledgement of a new relationship with the state would become permanent. Women might return to the domestic sphere, but the door to the outside remained open.'*

The common – and largely correct – understanding is that countless men were in acute danger during the war while women, unless they were extremely unlucky, were at least physically safe. The first story in this section concerns two remarkable ladies who did not believe in any doctrine of feminine immunity; indeed they went as nurses to Belgium in September 1914 on the express understanding that they would be prepared to work under fire, and did so selflessly and with amazing courage until they were gassed in 1918. Similarly, professionally enlisted nurses such as Sister Mary Brown and Nurse Elsie Grey could find themselves in situations of high risk; there are nurses, too, who have become part of a foreign field, as their numerous war graves around the world testify. Women who worked in munition factories faced other dangers: explosions could and did take lives and there were also serious hazards to health. But danger was not the most important factor; what binds together virtually all the women referred to in this section is a sense of energy, determination and fortitude that makes one almost breathless. They may not have started with many cards in their hands but they certainly seized their opportunities, leaving the nation, and their own sex, much in their debt.

Girls operating cranes in the Chilwell shell-filling factory (Q 30038)

*Working for Victory?: Images of Women in the First World War, 1914-18 by Diana Condell and Jean Liddiard, Routledge and Kegan Paul, 1987.

Women at War **Important Dates**

1907 First Aid Nursing Yeomanry (FANY) founded

1910 Voluntary Aid Detachment (VAD) founded

1914

August Establishment of Women's Emergency Corps, Women's Interests Committee, Women's Volunteer Reserve, Women's Defence Relief Corps, Central Committee on Women's Employment

September Women's Hospital Corps founded

October National Union of Women Workers' Police Patrols recognized by Home Office

November Women's Police Volunteers founded

1915

February Women's Police Service founded

July Ministry of Munitions formed
Women's Legion founded

1916

January Women's National Land Service founded

February Women's Forage Corps founded

July London County Council Ambulance Corps staffed entirely by women

1917

February Women's Land Army founded

March Women's Army Auxiliary Corps founded

November Women's Royal Naval Service founded

1918

April Women's Royal Air Force founded, simultaneously with Royal Air Force

December General Election: women over thirty given the vote

Nurses at the Front:
'The Madonnas of Pervyse'

In August 1914 Mairi Chisholm, aged eighteen, travelled from her well-to-do home in Scotland to London in search of war work. She did so on her own motor-cycle, which fact, remarkable for its time, was to be the open sesame to an amazing wartime career. In London she became a despatch rider for the newly formed Women's Emergency Corps whose headquarters was situated in the Little Theatre in the Strand, and which was entirely staffed by suffragettes who had called off their campaign on account of the national emergency and had put themselves at the government's disposal. As she explained in an interview recorded in 1976:

It was while I was riding for them that Dr Hector Munro who was then organizing a Flying Ambulance Column to go to Belgium saw me riding in London. My motor-bike was a strict racing motor-bike with dropped handlebars, and I think he was deeply impressed with my ability to ride through the traffic. He traced me to the Women's Emergency Corps and asked to see me, and he then said 'Would you like to go to Flanders?' and I said 'Yes I'd love to' and that's how it started.

There followed some three and a half years as a nurse working close to the Belgian front line, most of the time at a tiny shell-battered village called Pervyse, during which time she and another of Dr Munro's recruits, having struck out on their own, became justly and honourably famous. Her colleague was a fully trained nurse aged almost thirty called Elsie Knocker; a widow, she was eventually to be wooed and married by a Belgian aristocrat, the Baron de T'Serclaes. Asked what was the attitude to them of the countless wounded who passed through their care in those years, Mairi Chisholm replied: 'That we were madonnas; we were dealing with a Catholic country and they called us "*les deux madonnes de Pervyse*". They felt if they fell into our hands, you see, they had every possible chance.'

Dr Munro was a man of advanced views in relation to women and their place and competence in society:

He was a great feminist at a time when that wasn't popular amongst men. He felt that women should have more say in things and he wanted to prove that he could take four women on to the battlefield and they would not fail, they would stand up to it. So he selected four, of which one was an American; he said he wanted to show America that if they were not coming into the war one of their women should cover herself with glory. She was Helen Gleason, whose husband was a free-lance American journalist who was out in Flanders already, and she was naturally anxious to get there too; and he also chose Lady Dorothy Fielding, one of the daughters of the Earl of Denbigh, Mrs Knocker, and myself – and of course a whole male outfit too, four doctors and two men drivers, and two ambulances, and we went off.

Of course the Belgians had not expected war and their medical arrangements were mixed, and obviously their men were in a terrible state; and so it was a rescue affair and a great emergency.

The Museum is rich in the 'relics' of these two outstanding women. In addition to Mairi Chisholm's recorded interview there are detailed diaries written by both of them – though regrettably covering the first phase of the war only – and numerous photographs, many taken on private cameras in the early months but also others taken by the British official photographer Ernest Brooks in 1917. Among a wealth of papers and documents there is a handsomely printed list of awards for 'gallantry and devotion to duty in action', dated 10 October 1917 and issued in the name of General Sir Henry Rawlinson, Commander of the British Fourth Army; the recipients of the Military Medal named on it include:

Baroness Elsie Blackhall de T'SERCLAES, British Red Cross Society, attached Belgian Army
Miss Mairi Lambert Chisholm Gooden CHISHOLM, British Red Cross Society, attached Belgian Army

Most remarkable of all is the Baroness's autograph album, in which over the years many people wrote messages and drew or painted pictures in tribute to the work of the women of Pervyse. Including Bruce Bairnsfather, Heath Robinson, Fortunino Matania and Louis Raemaekers among its artist-contributors, it is both a minor treasure in its own right and also eloquent proof of the high regard in which its owner and her companion were held.

For the first two months they remained with Dr Munro's team. Eventually, however, Elsie Knocker decided that what they were achieving was not enough. She saw that men with superficial wounds were dying from shock while being evacuated in the ambulances to hospital. She proposed therefore to set up a first-aid post immediately behind the front line; she chose Pervyse for its location and asked the young Mairi Chisholm to assist her. Apart from visits home the two women were to remain in and around Pervyse from November 1914 until they withdrew after being gassed early in 1918.

The understanding from the outset was that if necessary they were to work under fire; both their diaries contain vivid accounts which show that they did not flinch from fulfilling this condition. This is by Elsie, dated 5 October 1914:

What a wonderful and terrible day. I shall never forget it. We started at Berlaese and were there during the bombardment. Then on to Appels for some wounded. Left the car by the roadside and walked four miles over meadows to the trenches by the river. Germans other side of river. We saved the Major and a soldier – the latter with foot blown off and back shot – both very bad. Had to sneak back in the dark under fire – a terrible journey in the rain and with two men so bad. Found Tom with the car had also been under fire – Germans fired Berlaese village, a great glow in the sky – a long weary ride back, very tired and cold. Both wounded arrived safely but soldier died later. After operations.

The following, by Mairi, was written on 24 October 1914, while she was literally under fire:

We are now at Carskerke and the shrapnel is screaming over our heads and the big guns are booming all at once. The German shells are falling quite close and

Above left: Baroness de T'Serclaes and Mairi Chisholm outside their sandbagged 'poste' at Pervyse (their third because of German bombardment) (Q 2663)

Above right: Mairi Chisholm on the roof of their first-aid post at Pervyse in 1917, spotting British aircraft crashed in No Man's Land before going out to retrieve the dead and wounded crews (Q 105955)

Below: The women of Pervyse and a Belgian orderly, wearing gas masks, giving artificial respiration to the victim of a gas attack, Pervyse, 1917 (Q 105948)

it is just like hell itself – one's head is absolutely splitting with the din. Oh what a life. To think we could ever be here in the midst of things like this. The noise is too bad to continue – we are waiting here for wounded.

Having been forced to withdraw ('We had to leave Carskerke because it was too hot to hold us'), they drove back to Oudecapelle picking up wounded men who were subsequently despatched to hospital. Later after a brief respite for lunch ('biscuits, cheese, corned beef and claret in the car'), her colleagues drove off with another badly wounded soldier, leaving Mairi behind in charge of the stretchers. Her diary account of what followed provides not only an insight into the thoughts of a remarkable young women in genuine danger but also a vivid impression of the kind of emergency she and her colleague would have to deal with throughout their many months at the front:

I am sitting on the wall in Oudecapelle – with only a few soldiers and one or two peasants to keep me company. The German fire is working up this way and now one can see the German shells bursting about a mile away. It is a queer feeling knowing that I am absolutely alone, and here I have got to stay till one of our cars happens to come back to fetch me and my charges. The firing becomes heavier every minute – the French guns are literally screaming – and the Belgian batteries to the right of this village are putting in good work. I wonder how long I shall have to remain here in the midst of this. Mrs K. will probably be worrying about me. However, it is the fortune of war, and one must get accustomed to being left on one's own. An aeroplane has just passed over but I do not know which one. Probably English.

Just as I had finished writing about the aeroplane some soldiers came up and told me that the German shells were advancing. They went further down the road, but I went into the room we had prepared and got ready all the Red Cross bags and stretchers for the ambulance when it returned. Just as I had finished doing that Dr Van der Gisht [a Belgian doctor who had been working virtually alone in the embattled town of Dixmude nearby] brought in a load of wounded men in a car and asked me to take charge of them for him. I got them all into the room and a Belgian military doctor came in to see to them. I helped bandage and patch up – one man had had a bullet through his nose which was pouring blood – he was partly delirious too and struggled a good deal. Mrs K. came back just as we had fixed them up. However, almost immediately another batch of wounded came in and we had to see to them. Our ambulance returned and we loaded that with wounded, five sitting and two stretcher cases. The man with the wounded nose proved most obstreperous. When we got the stretcher in he climbed up in a sitting position and fought to get his bandages off. We took him out and Mrs K. and I tied him down to his stretcher – the doctor refused to allow us to give him morphia. Mrs K. and I had wounded men coming in the whole time – quite a hospital.

The 'poste' (their own word) which the two women established in the village of Pervyse was not only a medical station, it was also a source of warm human contact, and of warm sustenance to match. On 21 November 1914 they provided, for the first time, soup for the troops: 'It was very much appreciated and a huge success', Elsie wrote in her diary, while two days later she noted: 'Kept hard at it all day giving the soldiers hot chocolate – cup after cup – without ceasing from 6 a.m. till dark.' The last cups were taken to the night sentries who were within 500 yards of the German trenches: 'It is a lonely walk – one may not speak or have a light of any sort.'

From the Baroness de T'Serclaes's autograph album: an original portrait of the Baroness by Fortunino Matania

Their principal concern was, of course, with Belgian casualties, but their part of the front was to be frequently overflown by British aeroplanes, against whom was inevitably turned the full fury of the German anti-aircraft defences. In her interview Mairi Chisholm recalled:

We worked a lot too for the Royal Naval Air Service and the Royal Flying Corps which were behind us, and they used unfortunately to be brought down in No Man's Land and we used to have to make expeditions to try and get the pilots out. That's where we got the Military Medal, you see. It was really for our work in getting hold of these pilots who came down in front of the trenches.

We went on foot, not always with stretchers, just hoping to be able to get them with their arms around our necks. In fact I strained a valve in my heart by humping men on my back. Although I'm small I was extraordinarily strong physically and I could heave somebody on my back and carry him.

The Belgian Army ambulances were three miles behind us, they weren't allowed to be situated so close to the trenches, but we actually kept an ambulance up at our post hidden in a sandbag shelter of its own, so that we had one available on the spot. And I used to take that ambulance out and drive the length behind the trenches sometimes to get people out. And it was exactly like being a grouse because I'd stop here and I'd spurt there, and it was absolutely a case of trying to get through, and always depending on timing.

It was a game, was it?

It was a game. You don't think of death when you're young, you know, it's not with you.

What about the day-to-day work at Pervyse?

If the trenches were quiet there was generally a young medical student or somebody in the trenches with them; and if for example a man had a boil he'd give him a chit and say 'Go to the ladies and they'll attend to that boil for you'. We used to have – perhaps for an hour if the lines were quiet – people coming in with beard disease, VD, boils, sore feet, anything you like, for ordinary treatment.

We ran a surgery as well, and then of course a certain amount of work was done at night. That was why we slept with our clothes on – at any moment you'd hear a roar of '*blessés, blessés, blessés*' (ie 'wounded men') and the door would be flung open and the soldiers would bring in one of their companions. And also we went into the trenches a lot ourselves, and poked our noses around to see everybody was all right, and occasionally we went out into the advance trenches, which were within twenty-five yards of the Germans. I think one had an enquiring mind and if some adventurous officer would say 'Mademoiselle, let's go for a walk up through the advance trench to so-and-so', I said 'I'm on'. And so I had a slight reputation for doing things.

There must have been so many decisions that you were faced with?

Oh, tremendous decisions, and some of the wounds were pathetic; men emasculated and things like that, and we wondered so much when they got back what lives were ahead of them.

Recognition from the Belgians came remarkably early – a tribute to the quality of their service and the humane attitudes which informed it. They were visited by King Albert of the Belgians on 26 November 1914; Elsie Knocker noted that the King expressed himself as being 'very pleased with our work'. And there was more to come. Elsie began her diary entry for Wednesday 27 January 1915 by writing the day and date in huge letters, and later added like a headline at the top of the page: 'Decorated – and my feelings'. Her account of what was for both women plainly a quite overwhelming event, reads as follows:

What a great day. We had breakfast at the usual time and everything looked the same and we all went into the *Blessé* room to tidy up and Mairi and I sat down to pad splints. Suddenly a motor car drove up. It turned out to be General Jacques and his staff – he had often been up to see us before so I was glad to see him. He suddenly opened a long paper and said, 'Madame Knocker and Miss Chisholm, His Majesty the King has commanded me to inform you that he has seen fit to bestow on you the Order of Leopold and that you are from this day forth

"Chevaliers de l'Ordre de Leopold".'

I never felt so foolish in my life. I stood like a stuck pig and gazed at him too dumbfounded for words – and yet in spite of all I felt awfully happy and cheery. I could hardly believe it. If I had been given a simple medal, a silver, gold or bronze medal I could understand – but to be made a Knight and to receive the highest order of all – that which is the equivalent to our VC or DSO – was wonderful and overpowering. General Jacques, after having shaken hands and complimented us again, left, and Mairi and I faced each other with the great news. We sat down to go on covering our splints and we thought we would drink our health and warm ourselves at the same time with a cup of Horlick's Malted Milk. We could not help smiling to think of how we were drinking our own health – what a splendid advertisement for Sir Joseph Horlick. We of course had endless callers in all day long to congratulate us and everyone was so kind and nice – and were genuinely pleased at our great bit of luck.

It was during an intense forty-eight-hour bombardment in March 1918 that the two women received a substantial dose of gas. They had been working in their concrete pillbox wearing gas-masks throughout that time and had just decided to remove them, when, as Mairi recalled, 'in that moment of pulling them off the Germans lobbed a salvo of gas shells into a broken down passage-way which blew straight back into the pillbox'. They had stuffed the air vents in the pillbox with their Aquascutums (raincoats) to keep out shell splinters, and because of this they both took 'a jolly good mouthful'. They were evacuated to hospital. Mairi recovered and returned to the 'poste', but the Baroness (as she had now become) was sent home to England badly shocked. When after some three weeks it was realized that she was no longer fit enough to return to Pervyse it was decided that Mairi (who had taken a second but lesser dose of gas in the meantime) could not continue by herself. So to their great regret their remarkable adventure came to an end.

Looking back on their experiences Mairi Chisholm emphasized that this was the last war in which anything like that could happen. She was also anxious to stress that they were not the only ones: 'You must remember that there were a lot of people who went out here, there and everywhere. The Duchess of Sutherland took a posse of people out to Namur; and Mrs St Clair Stobart had a hospital in Antwerp, and so on.' In a letter written many years later Mairi summed up her war:

Three and a half years of packed incidents; of being privileged to work in danger alongside brave men, and to recognise their immense decency to two women in exceptional circumstances. It is I expect the reason why the Baroness says that only in time of war has she found any sense of purpose and happiness. The cause was greater than ourselves.

The route march through London, of which the high point was passing Buckingham Palace. Captain Roberts is at the head of the column (HU 59105)

Uniformed Volunteer: Captain Roberts

Men who volunteered for the forces entered into a long established and highly ritualized system with its accepted ranks, uniforms and terminology; there might be variations but the theme was set. Women eager to rally to the cause started with no such standards or traditions, but the example of the events around them was so powerful that it was almost inevitable that many of their leaders should choose to follow almost exactly in the steps of their menfolk. Quasi-military organizations with ranks and uniforms – none of them official at this early stage of the war – were coined out of the air, so that, for example, almost as soon as she got back from her badly affected holiday in Switzerland Miss Winnifred Adair-Roberts (see page 30) had mutated into Captain Roberts of the Women's Volunteer Reserve.

The WVR grew out of the Women's Emergency Corps, founded on the second day of hostilities, 5 August 1914, by two notable ladies, Decima Moore and the Hon Evalina Haverfield. The standard uniform, khaki coat, skirt and felt hat, with shoes and puttees, cost £2.10s. The WVR's purpose, in the words of one of its pamphlets, was to create 'a trained and efficient body of women whose services could be offered to the country at any time'. The Hon Miss Haverfield, a former suffragette, became its leader while Miss Adair-Roberts, who had joined three days after recruitment began, took on the role of a senior captain with a company of her own which she ran from her home in Hampstead. In July 1915, feeling that the WVR appealed to too narrow a social class, the Marchioness of Londonderry launched the Women's Legion, which was soon to claim many thousands of members. In October Captain Roberts's company became part of this larger organization.

According to the 'strength return' for 31 May 1915 'A' Company of the WVR consisted of eighty-two members: three Officers (Captain Roberts, Lieutenant Sturges, Second Lieutenant Henderson), eleven NCOs, fifty-nine Trained Ranks and nine Recruits. By the end of August that year the hundred figure had been passed. The Company drilled weekly on Thursday, route-marched every three weeks, and undertook all kinds of useful tasks and initiatives in the London area, such as staffing YMCA canteens at railway stations and elsewhere, ambulance work, Red Cross work, or knitting woollies and socks for Lady French's Fund.* They also raised monies for various causes. Their finest achievement in that context was

the purchase of a YMCA Hut – funded through bazaars, jumble sales, concerts, carol singing, even playing barrel organs around the streets and sweeping snow – which was put up at La Calotterie, near the Army training base at Étaples, France. A letter to Captain Roberts dated December 1916 from the London headquarters of the YMCA states: 'The Hut is greatly appreciated and crowds of our brave men use it day by day. It is very prettily decorated and evidently well cared for. There is much of the atmosphere of home about it and that is greatly appreciated by these men who are so far from their own homes.'

Her war-work came to an end suddenly in February 1917. Never strong, she found that her efforts since September 1914 had seriously affected her health. There was also the fact that *official* women's organizations were about to be set up, which meant that, as she put it in a memorandum to her Company explaining her decision, 'we can give a greater aggregate of work for our Country by being disbanded'. She continued: 'I know that you will each volunteer for the work that you are able to do, and at the time and in the place where you can do it most suitably, and in this way the Country will get the benefit of the utmost capacity of the Company.' However, when she herself was asked to join the newly established Women's Army Auxiliary Corps – the WAACs – she refused; apart from the matter of her health the new force was to be run from the War Office, and she had come to realize that she was 'nine-tenths pacifist'.

But she was fiercely proud of what she had done and in a letter of 1955 she wrote:

I don't think anyone realises or remembers – that *before* the WAACs were started Lady Londonderry and Dame Gwynne-Vaughan consulted *me* as to uniform, discipline, drill, etc, etc, etc, for the proposed new Women's Army and that, in the earliest days after the WAAC came into being, it was seven of the women I had myself trained who gave the instruction and drilled the recruits.

Later on when the first batch of WAACs went to *France* ... it was *my* girls who got the responsible positions.

Her letter ends with a restatement of the reasons for refusing to come into the new 'Women's Army' herself (she adds a further reason that she had 'a lifelong reluctance to joining committees etc where I am only a "Yes-man"'), and a reference to another cause for pride: that when the battalion went on a route march past Buckingham Palace in 1915, she had been chosen to lead it.

*Lady French was the wife of the BEF's first Commander-in-Chief, Field Marshal Sir John French.

TO THE YOUNG WOMEN OF LONDON

Is your "Best Boy" wearing Khaki? If not don't <u>YOU</u> <u>THINK</u> he should be?

If he does not think that you and your country are worth fighting for—do you think he is <u>WORTHY</u> of you?

Don't pity the girl who is alone—her young man is probably a soldier—fighting for her and her country—and for <u>YOU</u>.

If your young man neglects his duty to his King and Country, the time may come when he will <u>NEGLECT YOU</u>.

Think it over—then ask him to

JOIN THE ARMY TO-DAY

Mobilizing the Nation's Women

The duty of men was evident from the outset: they were to volunteer to join the armed forces to fight for King and Country. The duty of women evolved, progressing through numerous distinct, if frequently overlapping, stages. The poster shows the first stage: the prime function of women was to persuade, cajole, threaten, moralize, until their man – or as here their 'best boy' – got himself into uniform. The photograph below shows another instantly recognized obligation, that of 'substitution'. While father or husband went to war, daughter or wife would take over until (to adapt the words of Ivor Novello's famous song) the boys came home.

The second stage is exemplified in the poster and photographs opposite; women were needed because there were not the men to do the necessary jobs. It was not enough that they should hold the reins against a male relative's return, they must keep the sinews of the nation in good repair. They must also be won by the offer of reasonable recompense; an interesting contrast to the situation of the ordinary infantryman, who was considered adequately paid at one shilling a day.

Left: Early poster issued by the Parliamentary Recruitment Committee

Below: 'O'Yez! O'Yez! The girl of Thetford who is carrying on her father's appointment of Official Bill Poster and Town Crier' (Q 31030)

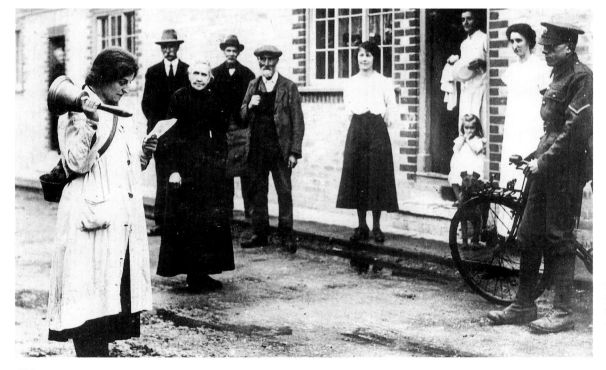

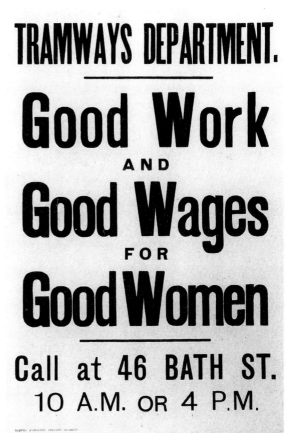

Woman tram conductor collecting the fare from a soldier (Q 109772)

Right: Recruitment poster

Below: Women cleaning an express engine of the Lancashire and Yorkshire Railway, Horwich Running Shed, Manchester. Ten women cleaners were employed here, all of whom appear in the photograph, taken 15 May 1917 (Q 107142)

The final inevitable step, given the length of the war and its rising human cost, was that women themselves should be recruited for full-time, paid and even uniformed national service, though conscription was not legally enforced until the Second World War. One major requirement which women fulfilled magnificently was the role of the munition worker (see next section). But they were also persuaded to undertake work on the land and to don uniform, as nurses and as auxiliary soldiers, sailors and members of the air force.

Above left: Munition poster

Above right: Land Army poster

Right: Poster calling for volunteers for the 'WAACs' – the Women's Army Auxiliary Corps

VAD Ambulance Driver:
Alice Proctor

My father was secretly rather proud. He had no sons to send, the boy was only a nipper, and he was secretly rather proud. Mother was horrified, like all Victorian ladies she had never mentioned the facts of life to any of us, it wasn't done, and because of that she thought we should get into all sorts of trouble. We soon learned.

Thus Alice Christabel Remington, née Proctor, in an interview about her experiences as a wartime ambulance driver in France.

From 1910 the Army's less than adequate nursing services had been supplemented by what was officially described as the 'War Office Scheme for Voluntary Aid Detachments to the Sick and Wounded'. 'VADs' – as those who responded to this new initiative were generally known – were enlisted by the two medical charities, the Red Cross and the Order of St John. There was to be no remuneration and volunteers could be of either sex. In the event, however, the great majority were women, for when hostilities began the scheme was seen as offering an instant avenue into war service for women who were of independent means or who could rely on the financial support of their families. If pay was not provided, however, uniform was, so that when Alice Proctor, then aged nineteen, went to France as a Red Cross VAD all she took with her was 'a change of clothing and towels':

My uniform was so loosely fitting you could wear lots of woollies and things underneath, and we did have very good topcoats, but we seldom wore them for driving because we only had one of everything and we were so horrified of having to get out and change our wheels and things and spoiling our nice uniform.

We had rather a mixed collection of clothes which we wore on top when nobody was looking. I remember a Canadian officer who gave me a most magnificent leather flying coat all lined with fur and of course I put this on with great joy and was considerably ticked off – but I was warm.

She was already a competent driver; the only medical training she received before going to France was a brief first-aid course, in which she learned a few basic techniques:

How to stop bleeding with a tourniquet, and if it was a fracture you'd put a couple of broomsticks down the side of the leg and fasten them above and below the wound, and offer hot sweet tea for shock, which of course is quite wrong. And for burns, most astonishingly to put flour on or bicarbonate of soda, which of course is quite wrong, you now just put it under the cold tap. And if somebody fainted, to loosen their collar and give them plenty of fresh air, but it was very rudimentary. You picked up the rest as you went along.

Their base was an enormous stone barn in the grounds of a fashionable golfing hotel at Le Tréport (on the coast between Abbeville and Dieppe)

Line of motor ambulances with their VAD drivers at Étaples, 27 June 1917 (Q 2441)

which had been transformed into an officers' hospital. The barn had been a garage for the smart cars of the hotel's guests; now it housed a fleet of ambulances, while the drivers lived in a flimsy wooden structure that had been constructed on its flat roof. Entirely unheated, with only thin board partitions to offer a semblance of privacy and with insufficient insulation to keep out fumes from the vehicles below, this was home to some thirty young women. They had canvas camp beds, on which they constructed as comfortable a habitat as they could with army blankets – no sheets for the first two years – a thin palliasse as mattress, and layers and layers of paper above and below, all this topped up by their own clothing:

As for washing they did eventually put in a couple of basins, and if the orderly was fairly spry he would stoke the boiler underneath and we got a little hot water, but it was a little sketchy. Hair washing was difficult because most of us had long hair. There were two in particular that had short hair, I remember now I envied them so. But it never struck me that I could have short hair; some instinct told me that my parents would be horrified I suppose, but when I come to think about it what a fool I was, nowadays I should have insisted on having it cut off, it would have been so much easier.

If you went down to Le Tréport town, you could have your hair done there occasionally, but it was very expensive and not easy to get an appointment. So if we washed our hair once a month we were lucky. There was a stove, not an open one, in a room downstairs where we ate and where we sat, and you would have everybody kneeling there with their long hair and their towel rubbing away trying hard to get it dry.

The vehicles at their disposal were mainly Buicks, but there were also others with a special advantage:

We had two Wolseleys which our section leaders had and they had *windscreens*. I was full of envy, I did so hate getting my chin and nose cold. Now our Buicks were slow and solid and they were for taking the wounded off from the trains to the hospitals, but the Wolseleys were better sprung and better equipped, and if we had some special case that had to be taken to Rouen or Le Havre or Boulogne or somewhere for some special hospital they were used, they were smoother and quicker and could do long distances better. They had self-starters too.

The drivers' chief task was to meet the trains bringing casualties from the front:

VAD drivers running to their vehicles when an ambulance train was signalled, same location, same day. (That this was a simulated emergency for the camera is clear from the attitude of the second driver from the left.) (Q 2452)

There was an officer known as the RTO – Railway Transport Officer – who was stationed down the line and he passed the message that a convoy had started and was expected to arrive at Le Tréport at such and such a time. All being well it would come straight through and then he would ring up our little office and sometimes we got more information to say if they were all stretcher cases or if there were some sitting up, to give us some idea. It took us only five minutes to get from the hospital down the hill to the railway station. If we were in bed a most awful whistle went and I think that's why I hated whistles all my life. This frantic shrill whistle went in the doorway and my little cubicle happened to be next to it. And then, it was up and out.

At the station there were no refinements like waiting rooms. In fact, sometimes when things went wrong we were waiting down there for perhaps two hours because the train got held up, bombed or something further up the line. It really was priceless, we knew all the little dark corners and the little dark alleyways. There were no facilities at that time.

Medical orderlies came down with the trains to look after the wounded. They were responsible for lifting the stretchers up into the ambulances, but there were times of course when they were desperately short of men and those of us who were moderately strong used to help. I always used to get into my ambulance and go to the far end of it, and as they were pushing the stretchers in I would try to stop them from hitting the other end and giving a jolt. These orderlies were sometimes so tired that it was a case of, oh let's get rid of this lot, whoop, like that! Well, if you have a broken shoulder or something like that ...

The men that had dysentery, poor things, that was really terrible because they couldn't be looked after and they were in a shocking state. I used to feel so sorry – they were so ashamed of themselves, they couldn't help it, but sometimes the smell was simply frightful. I used to feel very sorry for them, particularly the ones of a slightly higher intelligence and education, to feel that they were in that state and that we girls were doing things for them. They wouldn't have minded the nurses, but we weren't the same thing, we were different.

And of course they were so lousy. As soon as we'd finished we took all our blankets and we went to a room where they were defumigated, and then you had to wash out your ambulance otherwise it would have been in a frightful state.

The ones that had trench fever and the ones that had dysentery were the most depressed. The ones that had a clean wound they were in the top of their form, but the ones who were very badly wounded, they just lay there inanimate and just hoped that they weren't going to cry too much, that's what they were so afraid of. If they'd been badly wounded for three or four days their morale had got so low because there is nothing more horrifying and depressing than continual pain, it gets you down.

Did they realise when you met them that this was the last stage of the journey and that they were going into a proper hospital?

Yes I think they did. They were astonished, the ones that weren't too badly wounded, you could see them getting up in the ambulance off their stretcher and sort of peering round the corner ... 'Eh, it's girls'.

Did any of the drivers have to leave because they couldn't really stand it?

One unfortunate girl threw herself over the cliffs, committed suicide. If they did go it was because they were worn out with the mental part of it, the strain. If you had a lot of wounded people, you know, groans of people in pain are very distressing and you know that there's not much you can do except get them there without making their wounds even worse, because if you drove fast besides giving pain, which they might have stuck, you had to be so careful if there were any fractures that the fractures didn't jag into anyone, particularly if it was a chest wound. You couldn't have any ribs or anything puncturing lungs.

Another of their functions was to transport the dead to the nearby military cemetery for burial:

How often we did this depended very much on how the war was going at the front. If they were having what they used to call a push – absolute slaughter I called it – and we had a lot of badly wounded men down you might have five or six a day. Then you could perhaps go ten days without any.

If your hours of duty happened to be when there were funerals you had to take the coffins. Sometimes when things were bad they couldn't supply wood and then it was just a question of blankets. We had to go up to the mortuary, which was just an ordinary hut, and they had the bodies named and numbered, and whoever had been dead longest had to be buried first. That was one job I did not like at all but it had to be done.

If I had the time and I wasn't to go back and do anything I always tried to go and stand with the padre beside the grave because there was no other woman there for these chaps.

There were, however, up-beat occasions in the young VADs' lives as well as many sad and depressing ones. There were numerous love affairs ('quite a lot of them came to fruition in the end') and, among other memorable occasions, she recalled one particularly buoyant, even happy, Christmas:

It was a really beautiful starlit night, it was Christmas Eve and a very big convoy came in but they weren't badly wounded, and they were all very cheerful at the idea of getting into a bed with clean sheets; and we started singing, I think it was 'Hark the Herald Angels' or something like that. Anyway they all sang and it was such a very quiet still night and you could hear as we were going up and down the hills these boys singing their heart out in Christmas carols. It was really a lovely thing, the moon shining and the stars shining and these boys all singing carols as they went up to the hospitals. They were so thankful, they knew they'd get a bath and be clean. That was wonderful, I shall never forget that night.

Leave was very difficult to come by; if it was desperately needed for either health or family reasons a week's absence might be granted, but there was nothing definite or planned. Alice Proctor managed a visit home after she had been in France a year, but this was sick leave because she had damaged her hand – and as soon as she improved she was under pressure to return. During her convalescence she never discussed with her parents the gruesome details of her life overseas:

They never even asked. I think, you know, in my generation you were taught not to boast about what you did or talk about yourself, and therefore unless some-body asked you a question you didn't sit down and say 'I must tell you what we've been doing'. It wasn't done.

Since they were volunteers without contractual obligation VADs could leave their service at any time. Early in 1918 Alice Proctor returned home to England and shortly afterwards married. Her bridegroom was an officer whom she had met in one of the hospitals to which she had been delivering patients for so many months. Commenting on the lack of social life of any kind available to her friends and herself she recalled:

He [her future husband] managed to wangle with two others a car and a bit of petrol, and we went to Rouen and had a meal together but I think that was the only time I ever went out. There was nowhere to go, there was no petrol.

The Nightingale Tradition:
Sister Brown and Nurse Grey

Mary Brown described her wartime experiences as a member of the Queen Alexandra's Imperial Military Nursing Service in three well-filled diaries covering the period May 1915 to January 1918. Between those dates she worked first as a staff nurse and then as a sister in the Mediterranean theatre, India and Mesopotamia. She was closest to the realities of war when she found herself in hospital ships off Gallipoli, where she was present for two crucial episodes – the major offensive of August 1915 and the evacuation of December 1915-January 1916. Her accounts of the August action and its results are particularly memorable, both for the vividness of her description and for her obvious compassion. 'What a wild and useless bit of country so many lives are being lost for, it's nothing but rocks', she wrote on 9 August on the hospital ship *Devanha*, then anchored off Anzac Cove: 'The whole thing is too ghastly to write about.' But write she did, even in the midst of a bombardment. 'As I am writing this the shells are going whistling over our heads, they don't worry me, the noise of the guns so close worries me more, we saw the shells going up and exploding by the hundred to-night. I am dead tired, it has been a nerve-trying day for everyone. Some of our men had no food for three days, and no proper sleep for weeks and as for a wash and change some not for twelve or fourteen weeks.'

Nevertheless she had found the prospect of leaving the ordered safety of Alexandria for the battle zone an exhilarating one when the opportunity had first arisen two months earlier, shortly after her arrival from England in the troop-ship *Orsova*. She wrote on 3 June 1915:

Great excitement, I have been chosen for transport duty tomorrow, I am going somewhere in the Dardanelles, three of us are going, also Matron. Did some shopping, got back to the Hotel at 6 p.m. where we were met by a very excited Red Cross lady, who told us to pack up and be ready to join a ship in twenty minutes. I bundled in all my things, took all my kit and was ready in less than twenty minutes; I joined the other two and was taken to the docks bag and baggage in an ambulance.

By going to the Dardanelles Mary Brown was following virtually in the footsteps of that great pioneer of the nurse at war, Florence Nightingale, whose reputation had been established not many miles away at Scutari. But even if she realized this Mary made no mention of such historical niceties in her diary as she and her fellow-nurses prepared for what was soon to prove a harrowing task. On 7 June, at Mudros, she wrote:

This morning as I left my cabin one of the ship's officers told me that the hospital ship *Somali* was coming alongside with 390 serious cases on board. Sure enough before we finished breakfast she was alongside, we had a scramble making another hundred beds, but after all our rush we only took thirty-two slightly wounded, the others were too ill to be moved.

Photograph taken during the outing of 21 February 1916 described opposite, and captioned: 'This print is taken from one of Captain Cane's films. We had a donkey ride the day we were at Montaza. I have Mr Stanley, ship's officer on my right and Matron on my left.' (HU 59107).
Another photograph taken the same week (inset) is captioned: 'Having lunch at the Pyramids. We do look busy don't we?' (HU 59108)

Matron and I were invited on board by their senior medical officer and I never will forget the awful sight of that boatload of shattered humanity and not a murmur from one of them, several were dying. We went into the Officers' wards and discovered two of our *Orsova* friends, one a Captain Masterman wounded in the arm and leg and another boy wounded in the leg. They told us that Captain Smeeton was wounded too. The *Somali* has naval sisters on board, one of them told me that they had twelve deaths on the way down and three more waiting burial this morning. They are going to Malta, lots of them will never reach there.

In the afternoon we saw a very sad sight, our Tommies rowing one boat having another in tow, with eight dead bodies in it covered with a Union Jack, they were taking them ashore to bury at Lemnos. Poor fellows, there are no coffins for them here, they are just sewn up in a blanket or sail cloth.

These were first impressions, and written away from the actual fighting. Some weeks later she was within sight and sound of it:

S.S. *Devanha* Aug. 8th Anzac
Arrived this morning. Great news. 2000 men landed on the Peninsula on Thursday night: 3000 Turks taken. We sail for *there* [ie Gallipoli] at 3 p.m.

Left at 4 p.m. sailed close up Imbros then the darkness came down just as Cape Helles appeared in sight, we sailed by the much talked of Achi Baba [the mountain that dominated the southern end of the Gallipoli peninsula], the

shells were flying thick, we could see them bursting in the air and hear the boom boom of the guns. As we got higher up we got to the place where the Australians first landed, their lights were twinkling on the shore and over the hill there was a continual crack crack of rifle fire, then on our left there was the sound of very fierce fighting right on till midnight. About 10 p.m. a boat slipped out from shore with about a hundred wounded to us, so the firing didn't interest us further, we worked on till after midnight, and when we finished there was dead silence and black darkness all around us except for the red and green lights of the Hospital ships; one would hardly think that such a cruel war was waging within a short distance of us.

S.S. *Devanha* Aug. 9th Anzac
Up early this morning, began dressings before 7.30. The men are nearly all Australians, they are badly wounded, but all very plucky. I was on deck at 5 a.m., the guns woke me up then, the Turks were doing their morning hate, it was a continual boom boom and crack crack the whole morning. We watched the fighting through field glasses, we saw about fifty of our men leave their trench and make for the Turks.

Some of the battleships beside us kept up a continual fire with big guns. The noise was awful. We could see the shells bursting, several fell in the water, and during the forenoon shells fired by the Turks went right over our ship into the sea.

Before we got breakfast a boat load of wounded came alongside, and all day the boats were bringing them over. We dressed nearly a thousand and were hard at it all day.

The *Devanha* sailed for Lemnos with a full load of wounded early the next morning. 'I was not sorry to get away from the awful din,' Mary wrote: 'We are all feeling quite stupid we are so tired. Already we have had twenty-three burials at sea and there will be more before we reach Alex.'

Mary Brown's diary covers many aspects of the war, not all of them as grim as her experiences at Gallipoli. There were numerous lighter moments, some of them recorded both by her pen and by the camera, as the clutch of tiny photographs which have survived with her diaries testifies. Alexandria in particular – if all was quiet elsewhere in the Mediterranean area – was a great place for trips and outings. On 21 February 1916 Mary and a group of other nurses, including the Matron, and with one of the ship's officers as escort, travelled by train into the country to a station called Montaza where they were met for a picnic lunch by an RAMC officer, Captain Cane. Afterwards they walked to Aboukir, where events took a distinctly hilarious turn:

Natives pestered us with donkeys to ride, we each got on to one and then the fun began. We rode to the top of a sandhill then on to the old fort and got a good view of Aboukir Bay then we went back to Montaza riding by the sea all the way. As we neared the station we saw the train coming, the donkey boys lashed up our fiery steeds and Captain Cane galloped on and kept the train waiting for us. I will never forget that last ride, my brute galloped all the way and I had just to hold on, he jumped ditches etc and each time I expected to find myself sitting on a sandhill, but to my great surprise I was still on his back, I think it was the most enjoyable day I have had since coming out here.

Elsie Grey was a qualified nurse in her late twenties at the outbreak of war but when she travelled from her native New Zealand to England in mid-1916 she did so as a companion to her aunt, whose husband was a

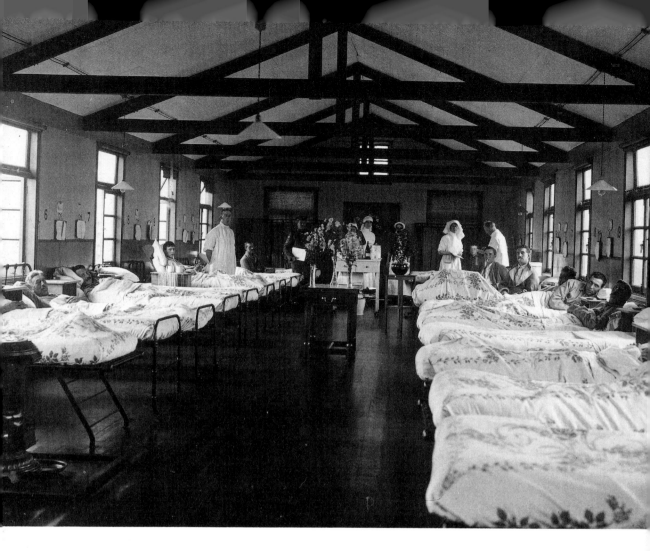

No 13 Stationary Hospital; surgical ward (Q 29155)

Opposite above: Operation for a stomach wound, by Henry Tonks

Below: Canadian sisters searching the ruins of their quarters which had been hit by a bomb, in a raid in which two nurses were fatally wounded (CO 3823)

serving soldier. Before the year was out, however, she had decided to return to her chosen profession. She wrote in her diary: '30 December 1916. I was attested and signed on to serve with the New Zealand Expeditionary Forces for the duration of the war. I wonder how I will like it.' She had at least an inkling as to what she was letting herself in for, having seen some of the more obvious results of modern warfare for herself. In October 1916 she had written in a letter home:

On the way to Walton we passed the Roehampton Hospital, where they fit up artificial limbs. In the streets round about here we saw dozens and dozens of returned boys with arms or legs off – two we saw with both arms and legs off. They look quite happy but it must be deadly for them.

In due course she found herself in France, with a contingent of lively compatriots:

At 1.45 p.m. we left Boulogne for Amiens where the New Zealand No 1 Stationary Hospital is. We were not allowed to tell anyone of our destination, and felt quite mysterious. All the way up we passed the camps. At Étaples there were New Zealanders and we waved frantically at them through the carriage windows. We had great difficulty in keeping Huddleston's legs in – she was nearly head first several times.

To begin with their duties were relatively light, but there were harder times to come:

The New Zealand stunt* on 7 June ended our ease. On the night of the 9th (at midnight) the wounded poured in. It was simply ghastly. Most of them were head cases (our hospital is a special hospital for head cases). They were all operated on and the MOs never stopped day or night for four or five days.

It is terrible to see them wounded in the head – numbers of them became paralysed and quite a number were minus arms or legs or eyes. For the first few days they were quite silly – lost their reason and some speechless. Oh it was ghastly and very busy – we just went on and on doing dressings with no hope of finishing. The doctors and padres were awfully good in the wards – taking the men drink and so forth. I don't know what we would have done sometimes without them. Crowds died of course and eighty were down on the dangerously ill list. We worked hard in the daytime and oh the nights they were terrible. Matron put ten of us out to sleep in two large marquees. We didn't like it of course but we had to pick up our camp beds and get into them like lambs.

The reason why they disliked being under canvas was that they were apprehensive about air raids – a fear that was immediately justified:

I will never forget that first night as long as I live. Wakened up suddenly, shot up in bed and then realised what was happening – the Hun aeroplane was directly overhead and the anti-aircraft and machine guns were thundering up at it with terrible force. Oh it was terrifying – the shrapnel was falling in all directions – first on the trees knocking off the boughs at the side of our tent then on the tent itself. The bullets were whizzing through the air and sounding like dozens of dogs howling and the flashes were reflected into our tent. I was speechless and absolutely terrified.

There were raids on subsequent nights but Elsie and her friends felt somewhat less vulnerable: 'Fortunately Matron brought us in from the tents – there didn't seem to be enough between ourselves and glory with just a canvas roof and I am sure that I would have got shell shock if I had stayed out there much longer.'

Nurses were sent to the battle zones to help the wounded, not to become casualties themselves, but war was no respecter of such distinctions. Bombers could probe far behind front lines and whereas hospitals were usually beyond artillery range this was not always true of Casualty Clearing Stations, as Elsie recorded in August 1917:

Tonight there is great excitement. Eighty nine nurses arrived here from their various C.C.S.'s shelled out. They had a most awful experience. One English sister was killed instantaneously. The shell burst just outside the tent – a piece of shrapnel shot through her tent piercing the subclavier artery – she died ten minutes later. Three orderlies were also killed and several wounded. At the Canadian [C.C.S.] one sister lost her right eye. Goodness knows what is going to happen. It was awful seeing these sisters when they arrived just collapsing on the floor – some fast asleep with their heads resting on their kit-bags just like the boys. Several of the sisters have had to be evacuated because of shell shock.

Elsie Grey's brief but vivid diary stops abruptly in September 1917; it is not known why. She was to survive the war, however, dying in 1949. Similarly, Mary Brown's diary comes to a sudden end in January 1918, when she was based in Mesopotamia. A later hand has added: 'It is known that Mary Brown was unwell in 1918 which is presumably why she ceased keeping her diary.'

*A 'stunt' in military parlance was any kind of offensive operation from a trench raid to a major attack; clearly the latter meaning is intended here.

The 'Canaries': Women Munition Workers

Black and white photographs taken in munition factories obscure one important fact, that the hair and skin of many of the workers would have been markedly discoloured. Caroline Rennles, who later moved to the more famous Woolwich Arsenal, began her munition worker's career at the factory at Slade Green:

The Manager wanted us all to look like nurses, and he would say 'Look, tuck that hair under'. It was all bright ginger, all our front hair, and our faces were bright yellow. They used to call us 'canaries'.

It was the task of filling shells with the high explosive trinitrotoluene (generally known as TNT) which produced this bizarre coloration. But the acute shortage of shells and other ammunition which the Ministry of Munitions – launched in early 1915 under Lloyd George's dynamic direction – was created to overcome, meant that many thousands would have to undertake this vital, if uncongenial, form of war-work. Most of these thousands were women. Before the war only a handful of women had been employed in the Royal Ordnance Factories; four years later there were over 24,000. In addition, new National Shell Filling Factories were established around the country, which by 1918 employed another 50,000.

The 'canaries' had no effective disguise, which fact could lead to unfavourable reactions, for example when travelling to and from work, as Caroline Rennles recalled:

Sometimes the trains were packed, so of course the porters knew that we were all munition kids, and they'd say, 'Go on, girl, 'op in there', and they would open first-class carriages. And there'd be officers sitting there and some of them used to look at us as if we were insects. And others used to mutter, 'Well, they're doing their bit.'

Some people were quite nice and others used to treat us as though we were the scum of the earth. We couldn't wear good clothes because the powder used to seep into them. You couldn't wear anything posh there really.

When your hair and skin turned yellow could you wash it off?

Oh no, it just wore off. Of course the conductors used to say on the trains 'You'll die in two years, cock.' So we said 'We don't mind dying for our country'. We were so young we didn't realise. I was very patriotic in the First War, everybody was. If you saw a chap out in the street you'd say 'Why aren't you in the army?' Oh we thought it was marvellous to go to war.

Lilian Miles left her native Devonshire to work in White and Poppe's munition factory in Coventry, later moving to the Royal Ordnance Factory in the same city. Discipline in the factories was strict. The girls never spoke to each other when they were working: 'It was dangerous work. And we had to keep our mind on what we were doing.' Safety regulations, too, were carefully observed:

When we went into White and Poppe's we had to go into a room, we were searched, there had to be no grips in your hair, no brooches, no nothing, no shoes. We had to have special shoes, and we had a special overall and a cap on our hair, which had to be *under* our cap. And no wedding rings – women couldn't wear a wedding ring. And there were special buttons on the overalls. We knew before we went in that we couldn't wear anything with metal.

I knew a girl who had been out the night before with me, and because of the blackout someone gave us a couple of matches to light the candle when we got to our room. She used one match and I don't know what she did with the other. The next morning she went to pull out her handkerchief and out flew this match. And of course the foremistress saw it. She fetched the bosses and they suspended her right away. I tried to tell them it was quite accidental because someone had given us a couple of matches to light our room, but they said it didn't matter what I said, proceedings would be taken against her. She was brought into court next day, and she had twenty-eight days without the option of a fine. They took her away to prison, to Winston Green. And she never got over it. Within a few months she died. She was twenty years of age.

Lilian Miles's friend was particularly unfortunate, but that safety was considered of paramount importance emerges clearly from the diary of Miss Gabrielle West, who served in munitions factories as a member of the Women's Police Service. This, like numerous other women's initiatives, was a product of a pre-war suffrage group, in this case the Women's Freedom League. Despite its name it was an 'unofficial' force at first; it was not 'adopted' (ie subsumed into an accepted professional organization) until 1918. Over 1,000 women joined this service during the war, of whom 985 worked in munitions. Gabrielle West was assigned to a factory at Pembury in South Wales, about which she wrote the following stringent comments in April 1917:

The girls here, and the men too for that matter, are very troublesome about bringing in matches and cigarettes. A week or two ago one of the Women Police actually caught a girl smoking outside a danger building. Last week a girl just going off duty came to the W. Police office and asked me to please rescue her coat from one of the danger building lobbies, as she had not time to go back for it and catch her train. She told me I could recognise her coat because her pay slip was in the pocket. When I went for it I found the pockets full of cigarettes! Of course the poor wretch had to be prosecuted, though it was obviously an oversight or she would not have sent me for the coat.

If Gabrielle West was critical of the workers, she was also extremely critical of the conditions in which they had to function:

This factory is badly equipped as regards the welfare of the girls. The change rooms are fearfully crowded, long troughs are provided instead of wash basins, and there is always a scarcity of soap and towels. The girls' danger clothes are often horribly dirty and in rags, many of the outdoor workers, who should have top boots, oilskins and s. westers, haven't them. Although the fumes often mean sixteen or eighteen casualties a night, there are only four beds in the surgery for men and women and they are all in the same room. There is another large surgery but it is so far from the girls' section of the factory that unless it is a serious case girls are not taken there. There are no drains owing to the ground being below sea level, but there could be some sort of incinerator, but there isn't. The result is a horrible and smelly swamp. There were until recently no lights in the lavatories, and as these same lavatories are generally full of rats and often very dirty the girls are afraid to go in.

Inevitably there were accidents. Caroline Rennles recalled that one girl had her eyes blown out when some TNT exploded in her face. Lilian Miles remembered no major crises in her Coventry factories, though there were many occasions when people suffered minor injuries – 'I've seen the ambulance fetch people out lots of times' – and she herself was slightly hurt once:

When I was soldering one of the bullets it sort of went back and then, bang! And my fingers – you see, those three fingers have always been a bit funny. I couldn't

Girl worker in the largest shell-filling factory in Britain, Chilwell, Nottinghamshire. (Q 30031)

work for about six weeks with it. I couldn't use my arm; they put my arm in a sling. But I couldn't stay at home. I had to go to work every day to get my wages. I had to go to work although I didn't do anything.

There were, however, some extremely serious large-scale accidents. The factory at Chilwell in Nottinghamshire was often called the 'VC' factory because of the bravery of some of its staff in the wake of an explosion which took many lives. While Gabrielle West was at Pembury a disaster overtook the factory there, as she noted in her diary:

Such a day! I came home at 3 to our rooms. At about 6 o'clock there was a tremendous explosion and then a whole succession of little bangs. I rushed upstairs and from the window saw flames and smoke coming from the factory in volumes. The landlady wept and flapped and said poor Miss Buckpitt was no doubt already dead, and all the poor dear girls blown to atoms, and all the women police and so on.

I flew into my uniform with the old girl clinging round my neck and bolted off to the bicycle shop. Here I hired a bike (my own was of course punctured just when I wanted it). When I got near the factory I met several girls running for their lives. One of them stopped me to say that she had left her case containing her food in the dining room, would I please be sure to rescue it as soon as I arrived at the factory! When I did arrive I found the danger gates barred, and all the girls huddled just inside them. A large shed behind the G. Cotton section was in flames, and going off in small explosions now and then. All the policewomen on duty were busy pacifying the girls, and attending to various cases of fainting and fits. After about half an hour of this performance the fire was put out and we were told to get the girls back to their sheds. This was easier said than done. However after another half an hour of persuasion one girl announced that she was going back and she hoped if she perished the policewomen would remember that she had left all her money to her mother, we should find the will under the drawing room carpet. Of course when one started all the rest followed and back they marched singing

What's the use of worrying
It never was worth while
So pack up your troubles in your old kit bag
And smile, smile, smile.

There were lesser-scale, but also distressing, casualties in this essentially women's theatre of war. Lilian Miles's elder sister lost her life, because of throat cancer:

When she went to the doctor he said she was under the influence of alcohol because she was falling about, and he told her to come back when she was sober. Well, I went down to the doctor and I said to him 'She doesn't drink'. He said, 'Well, I think she was under the influence of drink.' So anyway my landlady said, 'Don't go down to him again. I'll send for him.' So she sent for the doctor, and he got a specialist to her, and they took her to hospital. She died in terrible agony. They said the black powder had burnt the back of her throat away. She was only nineteen. She died before she was twenty.

The *News of the World* put it right across the front page 'Pretty Devonshire Girl Dies in Tragic Circumstances'. But they brought in an open verdict because they said they didn't know whether it was the work she was doing or what it was that caused her death.

The 'canaries' – or the 'munitionettes' as they were also called (a conscious reference back to the militant suffragettes who had made no small impact on pre-war Britain) – could be exceedingly forceful if they

'Dangerous work, packing TNT'. Sketch by Archibald Hartrick from a sequence on women's work

felt they had a genuine grievance. Gabrielle West recorded a lively occasion at Pembury in September 1917:

A great and terrible strike, as usual for more pay and less work. The girls stormed around, yelled, shrieked, threw mud, and so on. Then they discovered a wretched little creature who had dared to come to work; being timekeeper's clerk and not in the sheds at all, she really had known nothing about the strike. She was well reared though. They chased her from one end of the factory to another and she fled for protection to the W.P. [Women's Police] office. The strikers threw water at and knocked down a police woman who prevented them from getting at the 'blackleg'. The men police eventually came out and helped drive them away. Then they went to the main office and broke all the windows, demanding to see the manager. He said he wouldn't see them until they were quiet. Major Dobson, C.O. of the Home Defence, got out the fire hose and began to squirt the strikers, but it burst. Eventually they were tired out and went home, and appeared now to have forgotten all about it.

Gabrielle West put the violence at the door of an influx of girls recruited from elsewhere, many of whom had come because they had 'made things too hot for themselves' at home and were in her view 'the roughest of the rough'. 'A great trial', she called them; 'they steal like magpies, fight, get up scandalous tales about each other, strike, and do their best to paint things red.'

Inevitably the fact that women were fulfilling a crucial national role had both its positive and negative consequences. They were earning more – by the end of the war female munition workers were paid on average over forty shillings a week, whereas before it they might have been fortunate to earn nine. The Chief Factory Inspector's report for 1916 could speak of 'the new self-confidence engendered in women' resulting from the changes recently brought about. But, quite apart from such industrial troubles of the kind described by Gabrielle West, there was another underside to this modest revolution. Laura Verity worked for a firm in Leeds, Bray and Co, which made parts for shells and Rolls Royce engines. There was a substantial rise in illegitimacy during the war and this was reflected among the girls at Bray's:

Girls used to come to me saying 'I'm going to have a baby.' 'What are you going to do about it?' 'Well, I can go to Bradford.' They could get an illegal operation there – well, it was an illegal operation then. I've a few five quids that I've given out to girls. They didn't have it done in Leeds because they were frightened of somebody getting to know; besides the sister of one of my best friends did one in Sackville Street, here in Leeds, and I'll never forget, she got two years.

Did you know of anybody who died of it?
Yes. There used to be often girls die of abortion.

Sometimes, despite best intentions, abortion stories leaked out:

I tell you, one girl – she was a lovely girl – she was having a baby to a mill owner in Leeds. And she went to Bradford and had an abortion. She got over it all right. Now we wouldn't have discussed this with any of the girls there, especially what we called the toffee nosed and the religious maniacs, but one day there was a real hullabaloo in our room at Bray's. I said to this girl 'What's the matter?' She said 'This fellow' – that was the foreman – 'thinks because I've fallen once I'm open to fall for everybody' – and he'd put his hand up her bottom. And she clouted him. I said 'You did right'. She got married, she married a fellow that was in the Army and went to India. For all I know she's still living.

Lady of the Lathe: Miss Joan Williams

Miss Joan Williams at her lathe, 1916 (HU 59113)

The idea of making munitions first came to me in 1915 when a cousin of mine started making shells at Bath, and I should have gone up to join her only I was not able to leave London then. I was very glad, therefore, when I saw a notice in the papers advertising an engineering class for women got up under the auspices of the Women's Suffrage Society, 58 Victoria Street. I applied there at once and began my training early in November 1915, paying, if I remember rightly, a guinea a week and having to buy a few necessary tools and hand book on engineering.

With these words Miss Joan Williams began the illuminating and spirited memoir which she composed at the request of the Women's Work Committee shortly after leaving her wartime employment and to which she gave the title: *A Munition Worker's Career at Messrs Gwynne's, Chiswick – 1915-1919*. At Gwynne's factory – now long vanished from its site by the River Thames – she worked for almost three years in the Air Pump Department, proud to wear her munitions badge and happy in an environment worlds away from her own social background.

I don't think any worker can have enjoyed their work more than I did, even though they attained to a higher degree of skill and did far more important work. When I was on an interesting job it was nothing to leap out of bed at 5.15 on a frosty morning and I almost danced down Queen's Road under the stars, at the prospect of the day's work before me. I don't suppose the air pump itself was a particularly

valuable object and I sometimes used to long to be doing work that was in itself more important to the nation. Still Fate pushed me into the air pump dept. and I did my best there rather than spend time searching for the ideal job.

Her particular expertise was with the lathe:

My own lathe was a 7ft. Drummond, but I also worked at times on the four or five different makes of centre lathes in the shop and on the two little Ames lathes that stood on the bench and from making parts to repair them learnt a bit of the mill-wrights' business.

Gwynne's was an engineering factory converted to war work, not one specially established for the emergency, and still had a majority of men on its books when Joan Williams arrived, 'very nervous', on her first day. The machines had been busy since 7 am; she had been asked to report at 9:

Though I was very glad to be spared the early start that first morning, I found it really more of an ordeal being conducted through the shops after everyone had started and a good deal of whistling and tapping on the benches marked my progress down the long bays of machines.

She was fortunate in her foreman, a Mr Baker, who had come back to the factory after service in the army and who, wittingly or unwittingly, shielded her from discrimination on the grounds of sex:

I believe the men were always very jealous of the women doing the skilled work, but I never had any personal

210

experience of it. Mr Baker of course was only too ready to teach me anything and anyhow it would have been ludicrous for anyone with his degree of skill to be jealous of any of the women and I don't think many men who knew their job and did it well really minded the women. The great grievance of the skilled men was the fact that so many men and women came on to skilled work in a short time owing to the exigencies of the war when they themselves had had to serve a seven years apprenticeship. It certainly was hard, but couldn't be helped any more than the workers in our shop in 1918 starting on 35 shillings a week when I had done a year on 25.

If there was little prejudice on account of sex, there was also little on grounds of class, though she admitted that at times 'the habit of being waited on made you much slower about doing things for yourself'. On the whole people were accepted on their merits and according to their behaviour:

A good many of the workers, whose former work had always been in factories, had never come up against the upper classes at all and had very exaggerated ideas about them, fostered I suppose by labour papers and meetings. Most 'ladies' were to them people who 'drew away their skirts' on encountering any working people, so I was very glad when they found out it was quite possible to make friends with the despised class. However they were very quick to take offence where I daresay none was meant and one once confided to me 'I can't bear Mrs. So and so, she's so sarcastic – much too sarcastic to speak to *me*!' However, in spite of the foreman finding some of the ladies a bother, it was often they who didn't mind having a man of inferior station over them and wouldn't have dreamed of saying as one 'genteel' damsel from the lower middle did to her foreman who had come from the ordinary working class, 'You're the sort I've been brought up to despise'.

Joan never joined a trade union, and plainly had no time for one fellow-worker who had been chosen as a union representative on account of her 'gift of the gab and fine flow of language':

I only came across her in the canteen where she was very free with her 'Damns' and fond of airing explosive views such as not minding about taking German money as long as she got it somehow, with a good deal of explosive stuff to impress the ignorant. She and a few others tried hard to engineer a strike of union women against non-union ones and used to threaten the timid with being turned out of the factory if they didn't join. After some excitement, in the end it all came to nothing.

The announcement of an impending royal visit produced a flurry of unusual activity, with a sudden appearance of geraniums, clean overalls for all and the scrap in their shop tidied away. Work was suspended and the girls spent most of the morning glued to any available chink to see what was going on below. At last they saw the King enter the canteen, from which a staircase led up to their department:

We all flew to our lathes in readiness, but alas, the charms of the canteen were too much for him and he stayed so long tasting the stew and having the canteen helpers introduced to him that in the end he had to hurry off to another factory and never came to see us at all. We were awfully disappointed being a most loyal collection of subjects, though I'm not sure that the unfortunate who had spent the early morning compulsorily clearing up the scrap-heap didn't turn republican on the spot.

We were able to go and see him drive off and let off our loyal steam in joining in the cheers, but the day was decidedly a failure.

However, the lapse was noted and shortly afterwards the Queen came to call:

We had a moment of suspense on seeing her enter the canteen but this time we were not disappointed and very shortly she came in conducted by Mr. Gwynne, the Prince of Wales and Prince Albert following. The Queen was led up to my lathe and I spent a few painful moments replying to one or two 'questions for factories' out of the royal hand-book, but she gave me such a charming smile on passing on I felt sure she sympathised with me as much as I did with her and we mutually wished each other well.

There were very few accidents at Gwynne's and first-aid precautions were excellent; soon after Joan began working there a large ambulance room was opened 'replete with every convenience, including a nurse and a V.A.D.' However, minor problems were almost unavoidable – chips of metal would get into the eyes and once some grit from the grinding machine lodged on one of her pupils:

I didn't take much notice at first but at the end of two days had to go to the hospital and have it scraped. It was quite a simple painless process but by that time both my eyes were so inflamed I could hardly see and I had a weird journey home, running a few steps and then being forced to close my eyes for a bit till they'd recovered enough to run further. I expect the passers-by thought I was a sad case of intoxication.

Joan Williams was discharged from the factory in March 1919, having risen to the 'elevated position' (as the testimonial she received shortly afterwards put it) of tool-room hand; indeed she was the only woman employee so honoured. On her last day she was 'surprised and touched' by being presented with a magnificent inkpot with an inlaid tortoiseshell lid from all the girls and men then working in the shop. She concluded her memoir with the testimonial which she subsequently received from her former Managing Director; it contained this statement:

I can only say that your attention to your work, your energy and perseverance were an example to the girls employed in the factory, and it was due to you, and others like you, that we were able to get such wonderfully satisfactory results from the large number of girls (some 1,000) that we employed at Chiswick, many on really difficult operations.

Wren Telephonist, by G 4955 Wren B.A. Laurenson

The Wrens of Shetland

It was inevitable that once a Women's Army Auxiliary Corps had been established, there would also emerge in due course a Women's Royal Air Force (WRAF) and a Women's Royal Naval Service (WRNS). One area where members of the last named organisation played a small but significant part was Shetland, where in 1919 a remarkable – and by definition unique – hand-made and hand-drawn volume was produced to celebrate the role and achievements of the 'Wrens' who had served there during the war. The Shetland islands boasted the most northerly naval base in Britain, and in due course also housed the northern outpost of the WRNS. As early as 1915 the Navy had begun recruiting women typists in Lerwick and it soon also found work for a number of telephonists and messengers. In 1917 these were absorbed into the WRNS and subsequently other members were recruited until ultimately the complement of the Lerwick Sub-Division consisted of two officers and sixteen ratings, all, apart from one officer, recruited locally. Though a less important station than Orkney's famous Scapa Flow – the northern home of the Grand Fleet – Shetland was much involved in patrol and anti-submarine work, and the recruitment of the Wrens not only provided a valuable contribution *per se* but also released men for sea-going duties.

As the compilers of the book noted, one other result of all this was to put Shetland more firmly on the map:

The War has doubtless been instrumental in disseminating a better knowledge of these comparatively little-known but extremely interesting islands, and the issue of orders from London for a clergyman to take Matins in the Orkneys and Evensong in Shetlands – a distance of 100 miles by sea – is a mistake not likely to be repeated in the future.

THE LIGHT CRUISER.   THE FORTY KNOT-ER.   THE SUPER-DREADNOUGHT.

-TYPES-

Wrens in caricature. Artist unknown.

The Wrens served until well after the Armistice.
To quote the book's last paragraph:

With the close of hostilities work gradually decreased, but
demobilisation kept certain departments busy for some
months, and it was March 15th, 1919, before the first
members of the Lerwick W.R.N.S. returned to civil life.

Though the volume is serious in its chronicling of
events there is a lighter side, too. The arrival of
women into the hitherto exclusively male world of the
Royal Navy was something to be commemorated and
this was done with style, affection and wit. The
senior naval officer in the islands, Rear Admiral C.
Greatorex CB MVO, contributed a fine watercolour
of patrol boats at anchor, but it was one of his
subordinates (male) who produced the cartoons
(unfortunately without signature) which are perhaps
the book's chief glory. These drawings suggest that it
was already evident that whereas some of the new
women sailors might delight the eye (e.g. the 'Light
Cruiser') others could be distinctively formidable
(the 'Super-Dreadnought'), while yet others could
be positively imperial, even magnificent ('The
Nelson Touch'). More sedately, a Wren telephonist
recorded herself or one of her equivalents at work in
a pencil-and-watercolour drawing displaying the new
uniform with its distinctively naval collar. In their
own deft way these sketches mark an important
aspect of the revolution in the feminine role which
was brought about as a result of the war.

THE NELSON TOUCH.

213

PART VII
The Civilians' War

'BUSINESS as usual' was a catch-phrase in the early months of the war, but the air of confident normality it meant to convey was soon to be overtaken by events. That there would be major changes in the civilian way of life was signalled almost at once by the passing of the Defence of the Realm Act – known as DORA – in August 1914; this gave the government extraordinary powers which it used with increasing vigour as the months went by. People soon saw that they could not simply sit back and leave the war to the soldier, a realization underlined by the bombardment in late 1914 of certain East Coast towns and by the beginning of air raids in early 1915. The Zeppelins – and their later counterparts, the Gotha and Giant bomber-aeroplanes – showed that anyone could be at risk, regardless of age, sex or place in society. In keynote speeches in 1915, David Lloyd George – who was to become Prime Minister and virtual war-leader in December 1916 – made a mortal attack on the 'business as usual' concept, also berating 'enjoyment as usual', lock-outs, strikes, sprees. Additionally he denounced drink, and the King was induced to set an example by giving up alcohol for the duration (though he took some in private 'under doctor's orders'), just as later, during the food shortages of 1917, he undertook to abstain from all unnecessary consumption of grain. By 1916 DORA was being used to considerable effect, cancelling Bank Holidays, even Guy Fawkes Night, restricting travel, introducing daylight saving, while 1917 saw the suspension of the Oxford and Cambridge Boat Race, race meetings and the football league. Restaurants almost disappeared and food queues grew to huge proportions.

Meanwhile the populations of all belligerent nations became used to hearing of huge and continuing losses at the battle fronts. Newspapers attempted to make the best of things, but long casualty lists frequently belied their optimistic interpretations. Telegrams or official letters informing relatives of the death, wounding or disappearance of loved ones became a regular and feared aspect of the civilian experience.

This part of the book contains sections on London in time of war (London above all was the place where the civilian and the service world overlapped), on Zeppelin raids, and on the food problem (sometimes looked at askance from the well-supplied dug-outs of the Western Front). A section on casualties is followed by examples of attempts to explain something of what was happening to those least able to understand – young children.

Also reflected here is the enormous growth during the war in the popularity of the cinema. It not only helped often harassed people to relax, it was also seen as an important aid to propaganda. A film of the Battle of the Somme, shown while the battle itself was still in progress, became a huge success at the box office, giving people a sense of involvement in the sacrificial struggle taking place in their name. Film cartoons also had a vogue particularly towards the end of the war, when the need was felt to urge the nation to even greater commitment and to dig into its pockets to raise yet more money for the war effort.

There are also photographs of wartime Berlin, giving an impression of civilian life on the other side of the hill.

Bartholomew Close off Aldersgate in the City of London, on the morning after the Zeppelin raid of 8 September 1915. On the night of 8/9 September there were raids on London, Yorkshire and Norfolk: 22 people were killed and 87 injured (LC 56)

The Civilians' War **Important Dates**

1914

August 8	Defence of the Realm Act (DORA)
November 17	Issue of £350,000,000 War Loan
December 16	German bombardment of north-east coast towns
21	Seaplane air raid on Dover: no casualties
24	Aeroplane air raid on Dover: no casualties
25	Seaplane air raid on Dover: no casualties

1915

January 19	Zeppelin air raids on Yarmouth and King's Lynn: first casualties
May 25	Coalition formed under Prime Minister H. H. Asquith
31	First Zeppelin air raid on London
November	Home Office and Board of Trade founded

1916

May 25	Gotha raid on Folkestone
June 13	Zeppelin SL 11 shot down at Cuffley by Second Lieutenant W. Leefe Robinson
December 7	David Lloyd George becomes Prime Minister
11	Ministry of Labour founded
22	Ministries of Food, Pensions and Shipping founded

1917

March 18	Ramsgate and Broadstairs shelled from sea
April 5	Food strikes in Germany
26	German naval raid on Ramsgate
September 3	German submarines shell Scarborough
17	Ninepenny Loaf Order in force
December 6	Raid by Gothas and Giants on London and Kent

1918

February 25	Rationing of meat, butter and margarine comes into force in London and Home Counties
April 7	Meat-rationing extended throughout Britain

Only a small number of air raids have been included

London in Wartime

In May 1915 the Sussex schoolmaster Robert Saunders paid one of his periodic visits to London and took a Sunday morning walk from Piccadilly to Liverpool Street. He found a city still animated and buoyant under the impact of war. He reported his impressions to his son in Canada:

In the Strand and Fleet Street two recruiting bands passed with soldiers distributing recruiting bills to likely men. In Somerset Yard I watched four lots drilling, recruits without uniforms, with uniforms and no guns, and others complete. On St Paul's steps I watched a recruiting meeting for some time. There was a tremendous crowd round and a soldier who looked like a Colonial was letting forth for all he was worth. He had a number of men in uniform with him and every little while stopped and pointing his finger at some man in the crowd shouted 'Why haven't you joined?' Of course everyone looked at the victim who felt called upon to make an excuse if he could, and one of his assistants pushed through the crowd to tackle the one singled out. One of the funniest things I saw was a big motor transport open truck with some Tommies in, one was playing a mouth organ and four were dancing as though they were in a ballroom though they were rattling on at full speed. Everyone stopped to laugh but the Tommies took no notice and seemed to be thoroughly enjoying themselves. People were remarking 'Isn't that like them, that's just how they go on at the Front. Aren't they wonderful, etc?' This is what I saw in about an hour on Sunday morning when I ought to have been at church.

If London was still full of rousing patriotism it was also still prone to angry outbursts against those in its midst suspected of sympathy with the enemy. A month before Saunders's visit the Kitchener Volunteer Rifleman Bernard Britland had found himself one of an escort of a group of 'aliens' (see page 262) who were to be moved from near Aldershot to a destination in the East End:

The authorities were afraid that if the men got to know they were being shifted some of them would do a bolt. There were two squadrons of Hussars and about forty policemen besides fifty of us so you can see it was quite a fuss. We fetched these men out and they came as quiet as lambs. We then marched them off to the station at Medhurst. The cavalry were patrolling the district all the time to see that none of them escaped. In the train we had to sit all the time with rifles in one hand and sword in the other. We took them to a factory at Stratford in London which the authorities are using as a concentration camp. It was quite exciting marching through London. The crowd were booing and calling the aliens all sorts of names. We were marching up each side of the aliens keeping the crowd back.

The capital was soon to have its first taste of what had already been experienced by communities elsewhere when, on the night of 31 May-1 June that year, 120 bombs were dropped on the East End by German Zeppelins (see page 222). The New Zealand nurse Elsie Grey spent some weeks in London in the autumn of 1916, by which time it had suffered from the attentions not only of airships but of bomber-aircraft. The arrival of the latter, the hated Gothas, had signalled yet another upsurge of anti-Germanism with serious rioting in the East End, but on the whole London was still as lively and volatile as it had seemed to Robert Saunders a year or more earlier. The following extracts from the long letter Elsie Grey wrote to her parents give a vivid picture of the city as it appeared to an observant young stranger in the middle months of the war:

One needs to come to London to realise that a great war is waging. London is dead at night as far as illuminations go – the traffic and bustle still goes on though. We even have to pull our blinds down before we switch on the light ...

We then walked to Holborn – the buildings were beautiful – went into Holborn's Restaurant and it was a wonderful sight. The illuminations inside make up for the darkness of the streets. The band was playing on a platform which resembled a fernery – the bandsmen were all in gaudy admiral costumes, the waiters were all dressed in velvet, the ladies were all dressed in style and we were all laughing and chatting and eating wonderful dishes. There was no semblance of war here. After leaving here we went into another Restaurant – which seemed if possible more wonderful than the first ...

We walked up Regent Street where we gazed spellbound at the shops. The diamonds in the jewellers' shops were worth thousands of pounds, and Liberty's shop was simply magnificent ...

We pass hundreds of soldiers every day, Belgians, French, Canadians, Australians and New Zealanders. It is quite common to see them marching through on their way to and from the trenches. It is wonderful to see how bright and happy they look.

London would be a more subdued city before hostilities ended and the time would come when food shortages would change the 'business as usual' air of the restaurants which so amazed Elsie Grey (see page 225). And she did not report on one aspect of wartime London where scenes of a more sombre kind took place regularly throughout the War. Most soldiers going to or from the Western Front came and went through three of the capital's major rail termini, Waterloo, Charing Cross and Victoria. For those coming home on leave these were gateways to a brief respite from danger. But they were also the points at which, on return, the military machine took them back into its grip and at which they had to relinquish contact with their loved ones. It was almost as though the Western Front had established a salient in the heart of the Empire's capital.

Mrs Elsie Knocker, the future Baroness de T'Serclaes (see pages 185-190), spent Christmas 1915 at home in Wiltshire. She returned to the continent by her usual route, boarding her train to the Channel coast at Victoria. Travelling alone she was able to study what was happening around her and, deeply moved by what she saw, she wrote the following eloquent account as her train headed for Dover:

Victoria Station! well have you been named the 'Palace of Tears'. It is early morning but already at the gates surges a large crowd of heavily laden khaki lads returning from their too brief glimpse of 'other times'. How dismal is the half light of morning – penetrating the smoke grimed glass. Still more khaki lads

Rioting crowds ransack a German-owned shop
(HU 41817)

come to the gates, they are separated from friends and relatives, stern officials examine passes. A stentorian-voiced Military Policeman calls 'this way for you men here, friends pass through on the other side' – symbolic of a more acute parting perhaps in store – 'Dover this way! Folkestone here!' Here and there pathetically grouped yet often grotesque in posture lie weary men who have settled down upon their kit bags, sleep stilling the despondency of their thoughts. My heart always warmed towards the poor 'kilties' who having come from the far north had no friends to cheer the last few moments before departure, no kindly hand to cling to or press.

Here a man reeled as yet unrecovered from the previous night, but pity and sympathy were given him because we understood – that was *his* way of trying to forget – and oh how one longed to forget sometimes. Occasionally a khaki one went out against the incoming stream with a face lit up with smiles – an extra day's leave granted for some reason. A gold coin offered for each minute of that day offered in exchange would have been speedily repudiated!

Friends parted for a moment at the barrier meet again on the platform by the train – hissing insistently, awaiting to ruthlessly tear apart husband and wife, father and child, friend and friend. Such is the ruthlessness of war, individuals cannot be considered.

Small groups stand chatting – just outside my carriage door stand two brawny lads wearing the plaid diamond of the 15th Division on their sleeve. Obviously they had arrived from the north the previous night, for their coquettish over-dressed companions were neither wives nor sweethearts. But even they were helping with their cheery chatter and high laughter – helping those boys to forget, and there were tears in *their* eyes when the train finally moved away.

The crowd at the barrier is thinning – sometimes a solitary figure hurries out – having brought to an abrupt conclusion the intensity of the waiting – for a last farewell. Over there stands a young woman clinging to her husband's arms – gazing fixedly at the big white clock, watching, waiting fascinated as the big black minute hand jerks forward, forward! A taxi has shot into the entrance, out leaps a young officer – pauses as he pays his fare – Yes, he has shaken hands with the driver – but I can see a row of medals on the taxi driver's chest. Those who faced 'South Africa' and are past the age know what it means when they wish 'Good Luck'.

The officer stops at a group of men – they laugh cheerfully at some sally he has made and down he comes – as he approached my carriage door I saw the face of a mere boy.

'Take your seats' comes loudly to one's ear. We are slipping rapidly from the station.

We have been running twenty minutes so my wrist watch tells me and I have filled my thoughts by scribbling this. There are only three officers in my compartment, two are deep in conversation and by their faces I can see that crossing over to France no longer holds for them anything new – they are 'Returns' and have become soaked with that happy Fatalism 'If it's your turn – it is!' But the boy opposite – the boy who has hurriedly arrived by taxi – is trying hard to keep his attention rivetted on *Punch*. We are rattling through the outskirts of London now, already patches of green are becoming more frequent and the houses are thinning. The two veterans are still deep in conversation – one of them is smiling broadly – reminiscences of their leave.

Opposite me the copy of *Punch* lies unnoticed. The young officer is gazing (unseeingly I know) out of the window, his face supported in his palm, his elbow resting on the padded ledge. As I glanced at him tears uncontrolled welled up in his eyes – he bit his underlip and suddenly stooped picking up the discarded copy of *Punch* and held it before his face.

Poor boy – I guessed his thoughts – no difficult task! ...

Menace from the Air:
The Zeppelin Raids

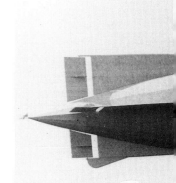

Civilian populations had been merely sideline spectators of previous wars; that they would be more closely involved in this one was clear to many from the outset. The idea of a German invasion of Britain had hitherto provided a stirring theme for fiction and theatre; now it had to be faced as a practical, if perhaps a somewhat remote, possibility. But the most likely source of violence against ordinary citizens was not invasion from the sea but assault from the air.

As it happened the first British civilian lives lost resulted from bombardments from German naval ships off-shore – there was much anger and moralizing when Scarborough and Hartlepool were attacked on 16 December 1914 with a casualty list of over 100. But this method of aggravation was soon abandoned for a newer one with infinitely greater potential and which spread the range of vulnerability far beyond the nearest available coastline. It might be said, indeed, that the realization that the aeroplane and the airship could be used as offensive weapons lit the detonator trail which would eventually lead to Guernica, Hamburg and Hiroshima, though in the event the 1914-18 war would only see the pale shadow of such horrors.

To begin with, people were uncertain how seriously they should take this new threat from the sky. Miss Winifred Tower had spent the last days of peace and the first of the war in the Isle of Wight and had commented in her diary on the marvellous patterns of ships' searchlights at night, aware that they were on the look-out for hostile aircraft. Two months later she found herself in a London subject to strict lighting regulations and obviously bracing itself for attack:

In Princes Gate every other lamp was lighted and in many places only every 3rd or 4th. All illuminated shop-signs were forbidden, also bright head-lights on motor cars etc. Blinds had to be pulled down as soon as the lights were lit and all sky-lights shaded and the penalties for breaking the rules were pretty severe. People began to make preparations for Zeppelin raids: one big wine dealer was reported to have let several of his cellars, and people we knew had furnished theirs and slept with big coats and a handbag for valuables by the bedside. Most people had water or buckets of sand or fire extinguishers on every landing. We rather laughed at this at first but by degrees everyone came round to taking certain precautions.

There were three minor invasions of British air space by German aircraft at Christmas 1914, but the first serious raid, carried out by Zeppelins (ie airships originally developed by the German Count von Zeppelin), took place on 19 January 1915, a date later commemorated by *The Times* as bringing to an end 'the age-long immunity of the heart of the British Empire from the sight of a foe and the sound of an enemy missile.' The event was noted by the diarist F.A. Robinson:

Above: German Military Airship LZ 77. Commissioned August 1915. Carried out raids over Essex, 11 September 1915 (Hauptmann Horn). Brought down by gunfire, Revigny, France, 21 February 1915 (Q 58481, detail) Capacity 1,126,700 cubic ft; length 536.4 ft; 4 × 240hp Maybach engines; mph 61; ceiling 12,800 ft.

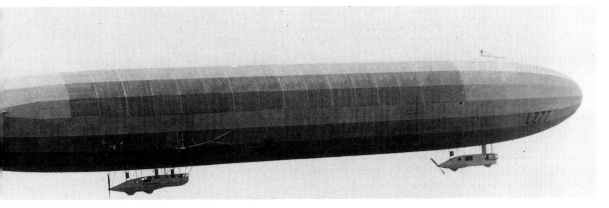

Jan 20. This morning we got rather a shock. The Germans have at last made a raid with their Zeppelins. Three of these craft flew over Yarmouth, Cromer and Sheringham, and dropped about 20 bombs. One of the airships went inland as far as King's Lynn, where it is said they dropped seven bombs. It is thought that they meant to make Sandringham their target. The King, Queen, and Royal Family have been in residence there, and in fact only returned to town yesterday morning, i.e. the same day. The attack which took place late last night was a great failure; they succeeded in killing four inoffensive people, and destroying property to the value of a few thousand pounds.

Jan. 21. The papers are full of the air raid, but there is nothing particularly fresh as regards the facts to record. The Paris *Matin* says it was the act of an assassin to send an airship during the night to bombard the residence of the King, and to attempt to murder the King and Queen and the Royal family at their house, where he (the Kaiser) had been a guest. It suggests that perhaps the next place will be the mausoleum at Frogmore where his Grandmother (Queen Victoria) lies.

Below left: Chief Constable Hunt examining part of a bomb dropped on King's Lynn during the air raid of 19 January 1915 (Q 53584)
Below: Territorial soldiers clearing up after the same raid (Q 53589)

Robinson had merely read about the raid in his newspaper; others who actually witnessed Zeppelin attacks found them so spectacular that they positively enthused about them. Mrs Holcombe Ingleby, the wife of the Conservative MP, described a raid on London in August 1915 in a letter to her son, then an army officer in Cairo:

I was here alone with Mrs Lewis and Skinner the night of the raid. It was a most thrilling and wonderful sight. I was dead tired but hardly had I got to bed when I was roused by the sound of an aircraft and the rushing of motors a few minutes after so I turned out of bed and looking up saw just above us 2 Zepps. The search lights were on them and they looked as if they were among the stars. They were up very high and like cigar shaped constellations they kept pulling away from the search lights only to be found out and caught again. It was lovely and I ran upstairs from where I had a lovely view. Then the Guns began and the whole place was full of smoke but not much where I was. It all made an infernal row and all the time I felt as in a dream. Can this be London? The wonderful part of it was that no one seemed frightened, the omnibuses were going past just as usual only there were quantities of motors rushing about and a great many people in the streets.

A year later, in August 1916, a young Cadet of the Army Service Corps, Archie Steavenson, was a similarly excited spectator on the eastern fringes of London:

The Zepp raid early Friday morning although they did not come very near here was a fine sight and we all much enjoyed it. It was rather cloudy and the search lights showed up magnificently on the masses of vapour – scores of great beams sailing about the sky among the brilliant flashes of bursting shells, to the accompaniment of the sharp boom of the guns and shorter crash of exploding shells, varied occasionally by the tremendous report of the Zep. bombs, which even at this distance of a good many miles made the hut shake. It lasted about an hour, gradually receding.

The results of such raids, however, seen in close-up, produced a different kind of response. The schoolmaster Robert Saunders described in a letter to his son the effects of a raid on London in September 1916:

In an empty building plot what was supposed to be an Aerial Torpedo had made not a hole but a crater, and there was evidence over a large area of its terrible power. One row of unfinished houses looked mixed up like a house of cards, windows everywhere were smashed, tiles and slates blown off and the side of a house facing the crater had a number of holes right through it and looked as if cannon balls had used it as a target. I might go on but I think you will realise something of what these Zep. raids are and you can imagine the language of the East Enders who crowded here to see the damage, some in motors, costers' carts, etc, down to the humble donkey.

'London is angry at last Saturday's air raid', wrote J.L. Beaumont James on 9 July 1917, after a raid which had hit such well-known London sites as Leadenhall Market, the General Post Office and the famous store Swan & Edgar – and had even given rise to a rumour that St Paul's Cathedral was on fire. Robert Saunders recorded a similar reaction many months before, on 24 February 1916:

There is still very great feeling shown over the Air Raids, as most thinking people are beginning to recognize the fact that Air Raids cannot be prevented, and therefore Reprisals are the only means to bring an enemy to reason.

If anything, raids stiffened the nation's sense of resistance, as Captain Oscar Greig RFC, taken prisoner after being shot down in 1917 by the German air ace Baron Manfred von Richthofen, testified in the account he wrote in his diary of an interrogation by a German Intelligence Officer (see page 125): 'He asked me what we thought of the Zeppelin raids. I said they were splendid, the best thing they had ever done, as recruits were now coming in so fast that we hardly knew how to deal with them.'

It was not until 3 September 1916 that a raider was shot down. The sight of the blazing airship SL 11 falling out of the sky provided north London with a thrilling spectacle and the place where it came to ground, Cuffley, drew thousands of eager sightseers. The pilot responsible, Second Lieutenant W. Leefe Robinson, was given an instant Victoria Cross and became a national hero. This act of vengeance against the enemy from the air gave the British public a sense of achievement denied them by the lack of clear Trafalgar-like victory at sea – the hunger for which was not appeased by the ambiguous signals which followed the one great maritime encounter between Britain and Germany at Jutland three months earlier.

However, not all those who witnessed this shooting down watched with undiluted pleasure. For one young woman, Sybil Morrison, the sight was one of pure horror – and for her a personal Damascus Road. Many years later she recorded an account of the event and of her reactions:

To me, well to anyone I would think, it was what I would call an awful sight. It was like a big cigar I suppose and all of the bag part had caught fire – the gas part. I mean – it was roaring flames; blue, red, purple. And it seemed to come floating down slowly instead of falling down with a bang. And we knew that there were about sixty people in it – we'd always been told there was a crew of about sixty – and that they were being roasted to death. Of course you weren't supposed to feel any pity for your enemies, nevertheless I was appalled to see the kind, good-hearted British people dancing about in the streets at the sight of sixty people being burned alive – clapping and singing and cheering. And my own friends – delighted. When I said I was appalled that anyone could be pleased to see such a terrible sight they said 'But they're Germans; they're the enemy' – not human beings. And it was like a flash to me that that was what war did; it created this utter inhumanity in perfectly decent nice, gentle, kindly people. I just turned my back on it then; I suddenly thought it's not right, it is wrong and I can't have any further part in it.

The experience was enough to turn Sybil Morrison into a lifelong pacifist.

In all there were fifty-seven airship raids on Britain. 564 people were killed and 1,370 injured. German aircraft (Gothas and, later, the huge well-named Giants) made twenty-seven attacks, causing 835 deaths and over 1,990 injuries. Some 14,000 bombs were dropped. France too had its Zeppelin attacks: Paris recorded 266 dead and over 603 wounded (see colour section page 148 for a contemporary impression of the first raid on the French capital). All this was deeply shocking at the time, though met with much fortitude and endurance; however, such figures would be multiplied many times a generation later.

By the King
A PROCLAMATION
GEORGE R.I.

WE, BEING PERSUADED that the abstention from all unnecessary consumption of grain will furnish the surest and most effectual means of defeating the devices of Our enemies, and thereby of bringing the War to a speedy and successful termination, and out of Our resolve to leave nothing undone which can contribute to these ends or to the welfare of Our people in these times of grave stress and anxiety, have thought fit, by and with the advice of Our Privy Council, to issue this Our Royal Proclamation, most earnestly exhorting and charging all those of Our loving subjects the men and women of Our realm who have the means of procuring articles of food other than wheaten corn as they tender their own immediate interests, and feel for the wants of others, especially to practise the greatest economy and frugality in the use of every species of grain, and We do for this purpose more particularly exhort and charge all heads of households

TO REDUCE THE CONSUMPTION OF BREAD IN THEIR RESPECTIVE FAMILIES BY AT LEAST ONE-FOURTH OF THE QUANTITY CONSUMED IN ORDINARY TIMES . . . . . .

TO ABSTAIN FROM THE USE OF FLOUR IN PASTRY AND MOREOVER CAREFULLY TO RESTRICT OR WHEREVER POSSIBLE TO ABANDON THE USE THEREOF IN ALL OTHER ARTICLES THAN BREAD . . . .

Given at Our Court at Buckingham Palace this Second day of May in the Year of Our Lord 1917 *in the Seventh Year of Our Reign*

GOD SAVE THE KING

NOW WE THE UNDERSIGNED MEMBERS OF THIS HOUSEHOLD HEREBY PLEDGE OURSELVES ON OUR HONOUR TO RESPOND TO HIS MAJESTY'S APPEAL

Dorothy A. Wright
Bruce S. Wright
Beatrix H. Wright
Arthur S. Wright

Weapons in the food war: typical posters urging restraint

Meat, Potatoes and Other Problems

Opposite left: The King not only dug potatoes in 1917; he also took the step of publicly renouncing 'all unnecessary consumption of grain' as being 'the surest and most effectual means of defeating our enemies'. In this document the royal resolve is endorsed by four members of a patriotic British family (HU 59459)

In September 1916 Second Lieutenant Edward Chapman wrote to his family from France: 'I think constantly of home, and know exactly what everything will be looking like, and the smell of the damp garden. I always wish I could pop in for tea.' When, however, the following May, Chapman learned that it would soon be his turn for leave, he tempered his delight with dismay at what he had heard about conditions in England:

Shall we have *MEATLESS DAYS*? If so I think I will stay out here! Today we have had new potatoes, and fresh cauliflower! And I have drunk red wine of the best. If I come home shall I have to dig potatoes? What a terrible place England is getting. I hope the war will stop soon, to prevent it getting any worse.

Three weeks earlier Colour-Quartermaster-Sergeant R.A. Scott Macfie had written to his father similarly perturbed: 'Have you ploughed up the tennis lawn? If so plant red beet for pickling: I don't like potatoes!' Digging potatoes was a prime national duty that year; even King George and Queen Mary dug them at Windsor, and their example was not lost on such patriots as the Conservative MP Holcombe Ingleby (see page 17), who wrote to his son on 19 August:

A portion of our day is devoted to potato-digging. It's a much more serious matter this year than last. Not only is the area three or four times as large as last year, but the crop is infinitely more bountiful. I weighed the yield of one plant and it topped four and a quarter pounds.

By 12 September, however, Ingleby was complaining of lumbago, and the cause was not far to seek: 'It all comes of an elderly man doing his bit by going potato-digging!'

Meat and potatoes were just two of many items the price of which had risen steadily for many months and which had proved increasingly hard to find. On 16 October 1916 F.A. Robinson typed into his daily diary figures relating to the increased cost of living since the commencement of the war which had been issued that day by the Board of Trade:

The average increase in the retail price of the principal articles of food between July 1914 and September 1916 was 65 per cent.
   Granulated sugar, 166 per cent
   Fish and eggs, over 100 per cent
   Flour, 66 per cent
   Bread, 58 per cent; potatoes, 53 per cent; butter, 54½ per cent;
     cheese, 52 per cent; bacon, 49 per cent; and tea, 50 per cent
   Milk, 39 per cent
   Margarine, 19 per cent

Price rises in certain Dominion countries had been less steep, he noted: in Canada, fourteen per cent; Australia, thirty per cent; New Zealand,

DEFENCE OF THE REALM.

E.P. 6.

MINISTRY OF FOOD.

BREACHES OF THE RATIONING ORDER

The undermentioned convictions have been recently obtained:—

Court	Date	Nature of Offence	Result
HENDON - -	29th Aug., 1918	Unlawfully obtaining and using ration books -	3 Months' Imprisonment
WEST HAM -	29th Aug., 1918	Being a retailer & failing to detach proper number of coupons	Fined £20
SMETHWICK -	22nd July, 1918	Obtaining meat in excess quantities - - -	Fined £50 & £5 5s. costs
OLD STREET -	4th Sept., 1918	Being a retailer selling to unregistered customer	Fined £72 & £5 5s. costs
OLD STREET -	4th Sept., 1918	Not detaching sufficient coupons for meat sold -	Fined £25 & £2 2s. costs
CHESTER-LE-STREET	4th Sept., 1918	Being a retailer returning number of registered customers in excess of counterfoils deposited - - - -	Fined £50 & £3 3s. costs
HIGH WYCOMBE	7th Sept., 1918	Making false statement on application for and using Ration Books unlawfully - - - - - - -	Fined £40 & £6 4s. costs

Enforcement Branch, Local Authorities Division,
MINISTRY OF FOOD.
September, 1918.

Poster *pour décourager les autres,* detailing breaches of the Ministry of Food's rationing scheme (Q 56278)

about nineteen. Overall, however, if one compared the figures with the state of things in Germany and Austria, 'it shews greatly to our advantage. In Berlin, it is stated that the increase in food prices is 116 per cent and in Vienna 178 per cent. In Dresden, owing to the scarcity of food, they have imposed a tax on cats.'

However, comparative statistics mattered little to people who by early 1918 were beginning to find the pressure very great indeed. On Sunday 20 January Robinson commented in his diary:

This week end has been a difficult one for the housewife. There is a great shortage of meat and many families have had to go without. Even in our own quiet village long queues wait outside the shops for hours to get small quantities of margarine, etc. It is the same all over the country and there is little doubt that we shall all be on compulsory rations very shortly. It is reported from Chester-field that horse-flesh is being sold for human food and that it is fetching 1/- per lb, at which price it is said to have found ready purchasers. On the other hand a man was fined yesterday £500, and sentenced to imprisonment for one month as well, for hoarding food. It is true he had laid in a good stock, including 400 lbs of food, 144 lbs of sugar, 14 hams, 37 tins of sardines, and a few other things. It strikes one, however, as being a very arbitrary proceeding.

Food queues were not always quiet and orderly, as a Mrs Mary Graham reported from Newton Abbot on 22 January 1918 in a letter to an officer friend, Lieutenant Archie Steavenson, then serving in the Middle East:

There is only one subject of conversation in this country, and that is the want of food. No one has had any cheese for a long time: butter is very hard to get and even margarine is not to be had. A small grocer's shop here was 'rushed' a few days ago:- I found a huge crowd when I passed – the women and children were packed in a tight mass right out into the road. I made them let me pass through on the path, and I asked a woman what was going on. 'Oh, margarine,' said she.

When I came back about half an hour later, the police were there, they had just finished turning the people out. I heard later that the shop was regularly looted; the boys crammed their pockets with sweets and things; and all his dried fish was stolen, and a quantity of jam and biscuits and other things. He shut his shop up for the rest of the day. It appeared that someone reported that he had margarine, and the whole contents of Newton slums etc ran for supplies. He said he had none, and they would not believe him, and one woman slapped his face!!! at any rate they took all they could before he could get the police up.

All the butchers' shops are shut up two days a week and I should think if things don't improve there will be a general shut up all round. They say London is going to be rationed immediately, but I do not see how that will help us.

Writing on 23 January, F.A. Robinson reported a further development, a 'new and much more drastic order' announced by the Ministry of Food that day regarding public meals, ie meals at hotels, restaurants, clubs etc.

Two meatless days are to be observed. In the London area the days will be Tuesday and Friday, and elsewhere in the United Kingdom, Wednesday and Friday.

No meat may be served with breakfast.

Fats are rationed for the first time.

No milk may be served or consumed as a beverage, except with tea, coffee, cocoa, or chocolate, or by children under 10 years of age.

Guests may provide their own sugar for sweetening beverages. As an exception to this, persons residing in an hotel or club for the major part of any week may be supplied with not more than one ounce of sugar for every complete day, provided that it is reasonably established that no sugar ration has been obtained in respect of such residents.

Not more than 1½ ozs of bread, cake, bun, scone, or biscuit may be served with afternoon teas. The quantity at present is 2 ozs.

Recording all this, Robinson was moved to an unusually outspoken expression of concern. 'We hardly expected to come to such a state of things in England, but it may be that worse things are in store,' he wrote, adding in an even more alarmist tone, 'There may be a siege of these islands, in the same way Paris was besieged.'

In fact this food crisis was one which proved in the end easier to resolve than many. 'On 25 February 1918 the Ministry of Food established a rationing system for meat, butter, and margarine in London and the Home Counties. Once shop-keepers had mastered the novelty of dealing with ration cards, the queues vanished. On 7 April all Britain was required to have meat rationing of some sort, and in mid-July a uniform system was established throughout the country. By this time national rationing also applied to sugar, butter, margarine and lard, while other commodities like tea, jam and cheese might be rationed on the decision of local food committees.'* In this way in 1918 Britain established a system of control over (in the words of Sir William Beveridge) 'nearly everything eaten and drunk by 40,000,000 persons ... The civilian population was catered for like an army; nothing [was] left to chance or private enterprise.' The scheme was not only to prove its worth throughout the remainder of the war, but was also to provide an invaluable blue-print when similar measures became necessary twenty-one years later.

*Quotation from Trevor Wilson, *The Myriad Faces of War: Britain and the Great War, 1914-1918*, Blackwell 1986. Beveridge quotation from same source.

Casualties:'It is My Painful Duty'

Writing to his son in Canada from London on 7 September 1914 Robert Saunders expressed his anger at what he saw as journalistic irresponsibility in the matter of reporting military casualties. He was particularly outraged at certain sensational placards carried by newsboys:

Some of the papers deserve suppression for the alarmist headings they put. For instance last night one had a placard with '15,000 British losses'. Seeing such news thoroughly upsets people with relatives at the front and they naturally thought 15,000 had been lost in a big battle instead of being the total during the campaign.

Later references to casualty figures were less strident in tone as the reality of what was taking place struck home. On 11 February 1915 he wrote: 'Have you noticed our losses so far are 104,000, nearly half of what we used to consider our whole standing army?' And on 14 June: 'Every day brings the terrible nature of the war home to us by the people we know who are killed or wounded and by the reports brought home from the front.' His letter of 17 October included this passage (Newick was the next village to Saunders's Fletching):

Jack Brook's body was found long after he was reported missing and was identified by a letter to his father found on him. His brother Aubrey was reported missing, then three weeks afterwards his name was among the killed. Two other Newick boys aged 19, named Smith, and who were cousins, were killed and last week three more Newick boys were made prisoners. Both Paine and Wadey are missing and after writing to their officer, all they could find out was that when last seen they were cut off and being bombed by the Germans. Poor Carrie Paine's letter to Ma about it was heartbreaking.

For F.A. Robinson the shock of the death of a close acquaintance had come almost a year earlier. On 3 November 1914 he noted:

Today we get news of the first tragedy (so far as our circle of friends is concerned); it is recorded in the following cutting from the *Western Morning News* of this date:-
'Holman. – On the 30th October, in the Base Hospital, Boulogne, from wounds received in battle October 29th, John Holman, Lieut. 4th Royal Irish Dragoon Guards, second and dearly-loved son of the late John H. Holman and Mrs Holman, of Tregenna, Camborne, aged 20.' As fine a young fellow as ever gave his life for his country, and one whom we have known since he was born. Although a Cavalry officer, he was fighting in the trenches, and was shot through the spine. It seems hard that a young life like this should be sacrificed on its very threshold, but alas he is only one out of many thousands of similar cases.
Never could Macaulay's words be more appropriate and true, 'How can man die better, than facing fearful odds.' The odds are certainly 'fearful', and the sacrifice of the flower of English lives is awful – and we are certainly not within

Consolation for a bereaved wife: His Majesty the King presenting war widows with their husbands' medals (Q 56741)

sight of the end of it yet; in fact, many authorities think we are only at the beginning, and that the war will last two or three years.

'It is my painful duty to inform you that a report has been received from the War Office notifying the death of ... ' – throughout the war the form bearing these dreaded words was sent out by the local military record offices by the thousand. Bad enough in the first two years of the war, the casualty figures rose dramatically after the opening of the Battle of the Somme in 1916, and from August that year until Armistice Day 1918 F.A. Robinson took to recording the numbers as given in *The Times* virtually every day – except on Sundays when *The Times* did not appear. His figures make grim reading.*

Aug. 9   In *The Times* to-day the list of casualties includes 5,000 names, and so it goes on day after day and yet no Official statement is issued as to what our total casualties have been during the recent 'push'.

Aug. 10 The casualty list in *The Times* today contains 4,300 names.

Aug. 11 The casualty list today numbers 4,220.

Aug. 12 The official casualty list today contains 4,000 names.

Aug. 14 The list of casualties today comprises 6,299 men and 195 officers.

Aug. 15 We are not having it all our own way it seems. Today's casualty list comprises 5,661 names.

On 19 August the reports of a speech by Mr Lloyd George, formerly Minister of Munitions and now Secretary of State for War, at the Welsh National Eisteddfod, in which he had urged people to continue to sing despite the nation's state of crisis, moved Robinson to anger. He described the speech as 'ridiculous' and added: 'Today's casualty list numbers 4,674 names – not much cause for "singing" with a list such as this appearing every day'. And so on. On 2 September 1916 he noted the significant role being played by the Anzac forces now heavily engaged on the Western Front. 'The casualty list today comprises 2,750 names but in addition there is a list of 3,228 Australians.'

His last entry, on 11 November 1918, provides a salutary reminder as to the high price being paid right to the end of the war:

November 11, 1918. The casualties quoted today are 182 officers and 4,440 men. Thank God this dreadful daily list will soon be ended.

*Casualty figures included wounded and missing as well as known fatalities.

Second Lieutenant Percy Boswell,
8th Battalion King's Own Yorkshire Light Infantry
Died 1 July 1916, aged 22
Commemorated on the Memorial to the Missing
of the Somme, Thiepval, France
(HU 35941)

The King commands me to assure you of the true sympathy of His Majesty and The Queen in your sorrow.

He whose loss you mourn died in the noblest of causes. His Country will be ever grateful to him for the sacrifice he has made for Freedom and Justice.

Milner

Secretary of State for War.

Royal sympathy: From the documents of Private Reginald Read, 2/8th Battalion the Worcester Regiment, missing/killed in action 3 December 1917
(HU 59428)

Notification of Death Much has been written about the shock of receiving War Office telegrams bearing news of a relative's death. Robert Saunders, whose son Ron was at the front during the Somme battle, wrote in mid-July 1916 that 'we are dreading the telegram that so many have received lately'. But it was also common for the fateful information to arrive by the ordinary post. Writing in May 1917 Saunders described how the news of a family fatality was received at Fletching by the village butcher, Mr Grover. The latter assumed that the official envelope delivered one morning in May 1917 by the local postman was to do with sheep and cattle; only at dinner time did he open it to read that his son had been killed in France twelve days previously. Grover would have received Army Form B. 104-82B and with it a formal message of sympathy from the King and Queen (see above and right). Other such forms being sent in thousands throughout the war were B 104-83 – 'I regret to have to inform you that a report has been received from the War Office to the effect that [such and such a serviceman] was posted as missing' [on such and such a date] – to be all too frequently followed, normally after a delay of many months, by form 82A – 'It is my painful duty to inform you that no further news having been received relative to [the serviceman in question] the Army Council have been regretfully constrained to conclude that he is dead'. (HU 59457)

Last letter of a fallen officer The following letter, typical of many, was written on 30 June 1916, on the eve of the Battle of the Somme, by a young subaltern of Kitchener's Army. Second Lieutenant Percy Boswell's battalion, the 8th King's Own Yorkshire Light Infantry, 8th Division, was in the first wave attack launched at 7.30 am on 1 July. The normal strength of a battalion going into action was, on average, 800, of whom 26 would be officers; the 8th KOYLI's casualty list that day was 21 officers and 518 men. Boswell was killed in the first few minutes of the attack. (HU 59456)

> 30.6.16.
> B.E.F.
>
> Dear Father,
>
> I am just writing you a short note which you will receive only if anything has happened to me during the next few days.
>
> The Hun is going to get consummate hell just in this quarter & we are going over the parapet tomorrow when I hope to spend a few merry hours in chasing the Boche all over the place. I am absolutely certain that I shall get through all right, but in case the unexpected does happen I shall rest content with the knowledge that I have done my duty — and one can't do more.
>
> Good Bye & with the Best of love to all from
>
> Percy.

Germany in Wartime

From a series on the German Home Front 1914-1918, with verbatim captions

Left: 'Feeding Berlin's Poor in War-Time, Serving Soup from a "Goulash Gun", the portable field kitchen seen in the poorer districts of Germany's Capital.' An indication of the fact that Germany also suffered hardship and shortages, increasingly so as the Allied blockade was tightened later in the war (Q 88190)

Right: 'German War Disabled on the Home Front, 1914-1918. An exhibition of artificial limbs and aids for wounded German servicemen, displayed in Berlin. Specimens of the work of the firm Berthold Maag of Dortmund.' (Q 88185)

Below: 'Trenches near Berlin. A Charlottenburg citizen has given 1,000 marks for the construction of a trench which is made with every modern appliance, to illustrate to Berliners how German troops live while on active service.' (Q 88169)

Explaining to the Children

Among the numerous recipients of the letters of Robert Scott Macfie were some of his young relations. Soon after arriving in France he sent to a nephew this brief child's guide to entrenchment:

Every day we go out and practise what we should do if the Germans come. Today we dig big holes in the ground in which we would stand, with a little slit at the top to shoot through. It took a long time, but it would have been very difficult to hit us when we were in the holes, and at the same time we could easily shoot the Germans if they come near enough.

Another nephew had evidently asked him where he was, inspiring a reply which showed that Scott Macfie had no great respect for the more absurd aspects of censorship:

I am not allowed to tell you where I am, because the General is afraid you might tell someone at school, and he might tell the German master, and the German master might telegraph to the Kaiser and tell him. And then, of course, the Kaiser would send an aeroplane to drop bombs on us.

Captain J.I. (Jack) Cohen, writing in May 1915 to his sister, a schoolgirl in England, after more than a year in France, concentrated on the lighter aspects of Western Front life:

You have been back at school two days now. I hope you have settled down nicely, and have a good term.

I am wearing your socks now, you will be pleased to know that they are really comfortable.

The weather is very hot and sultry, quite like July. We play football in the evenings though – and when the light is too bad for that, I take a ripping little brown dog (partly Irish, partly pug) out ratting. He has a splendid scent for rats, and is a good sportsman. I caught four this morning just after breakfast on my way out to work. The rats are prolific here, and often their nests are made under a tree or piece of timber lying by the roadside. As the dog passes by, he scents the rats, squeaks, and starts scratching away with his forepaws – head well down and working like a nigger.

Very often the rat gets away to another hiding place too quickly for the dog to catch him, but where he has a clear run the chances are always with the dog.

We have a YMCA marquee outside our camp, and the men got up a sing-song. We officers were asked to go. When I found there was no piano or other instrument to accompany the singers with, I felt a bit bored when I found I had to go. But when some of the performers didn't turn up, and I found I had to fill the breach – you may imagine my state of mind! However 'Tavistock Foozey Fair' and 'Pack Up Your Troubles' went down very well – but it's awful work singing in front of your own men.

I hope you are quite well.

Much love from your affectionate brother

Jack

My dog is called Jim.

According to its caption, this photograph shows a child recognizing a relative in a picture in the windows of the Ministry of Information Photographic Bureau at 12 Coventry Street, London, opened to the public for the sale of official photographs in October 1918 (Q 31176)

Below: The picture she was looking at, taken over two years earlier; its caption reads: 'An artilleryman with the post for his battery, near Aveluy September 1916' (Q 1152)

Private George Rowson, of the 10th Battalion the Lincolnshire Regiment, when writing to his niece Annie in October 1916 had a more difficult task – to explain why he was now in England:

You don't know how pleased your Uncle George was to have a letter from you one morning when I was in the muddy dykes that khaki boys have to call trenches. I wondered whose writing this can be as I never thought of Annie writing to me but Oh I was delighted. Since I got your letter I have let those nasty German fellows hit me with a piece of shell so I have had to come to England and I have got a real nice bed in a real nice hospital with some nice ladies to look after me. I am getting better quickly so I shall soon be coming to see you all and Annie you must tell your mother that I want to see her walking about so tell her to hurry up and get well. I hope you have enjoyed your long holiday, but I am afraid some of the days have been wet ones and you would not like those. I hope your father is real well and tell him I shall be pleased to come and help him again soon.

With love from your
Uncle George

George Rowson was killed in April 1917 during an action near Arras in which his unit suffered exceptionally heavy losses. Six months later in September 1917 Gunner Harry Ferris, of the Royal Garrison Artillery, was also killed near Arras. He left a wife and four sons, the eldest of whom, Allan, then aged twelve, shortly afterwards received a letter from his father's officer, a letter he was to treasure all his life:

My dear Laddie,
I do not know your name or I would have started 'My dear John' or 'My dear William'. However you won't mind that will you? Although I do not know your name and perhaps shall never see you, I felt I should like to send you a letter – which I am writing in my dugout by candle light. It is a cold wet night, so I am having to sit with my topcoat on. When I was as old as you I used to play at soldiers with a broom handle for a gun and thought it was fine fun. I've changed my mind since I've had the real thing!

However that isn't what I want to talk about. In fact I find it hard to begin. You see I'm a Gunner Officer – a soldier – not a parson or I might find it easier.

Well, now for it! I want you now, my laddie, to make up your mind, once and for all, that you will never do anything or say anything that your father would not like. I've been a boy and I still love boys, and I know how easy it is to slip into more and more careless ways and how hard to set your teeth and do what you think is right when other boys laugh at you. Still it is worth doing.

I knew your father well, and have seen him doing his work, not just as little as he could do, but willingly doing all there was, as hard as he could – leaving shirkers to shirk. And it is hard to work sometimes when wretched bits of iron are singing around. But he did it, bravely and steadily – anything he had to do, he did well. Now you model your life on that, for you are getting halfway to manhood now – and he will be pleased too.

And there's those brothers of yours. You are their 'Big Brother' and they will do and say what their 'Big Brother' says and does. So see what a grand chance you have of helping them to grow up straight, strong and clean-minded Britishers. And there's your mother. You are her eldest son. Don't be ashamed of giving her a bit of 'fuss' now and again – and a bit of that time you now give to Billy and James and other playmates. It's worth it.

So now good-bye, my laddie, and try your best.

'My Dear Billie': A Father's Letters to His Son

From 1917 to early 1919 W.L. Britton was based in Salonika. A former regular, he had served in India in the 13th Hussars, had been discharged in 1913 and had re-enlisted on the outbreak of war. He became a Private in the Army Service Corps. Now married and a proud father, he was keenly anxious on being sent overseas not to lose contact with his young son Billie, so to compensate for being unable to offer the day-by-day guidance and affection he would have given him in more normal times, he sent him a stream of breezy, encouraging letters, lavishly illustrated with pen and watercolour sketches. Only occasionally were his drawings of martial subjects and his letters always made light of the strains and problems of his life as a soldier. (Nor did he tell his son when he was mentioned in despatches for his

outstanding work as a Fire Engine driver during the great Salonika fire of August 1917.) His main purpose was to keep his son cheerful and happy and to exhort him to be well behaved and to be kind and good to his mother. Sometimes he adapted the drawings of other artists – Bruce Bairnsfather was obviously a favourite in Salonika as well as on the Western Front and sometimes the influence of contemporary children's comics can be detected – but generally his sketches are entirely his own. Witty, well-drawn and full of invention, they are a remarkable tribute to their creator's fatherly concern in a war which subjected countless families to long periods of separation, and from which many fathers would return as virtual strangers to their children.

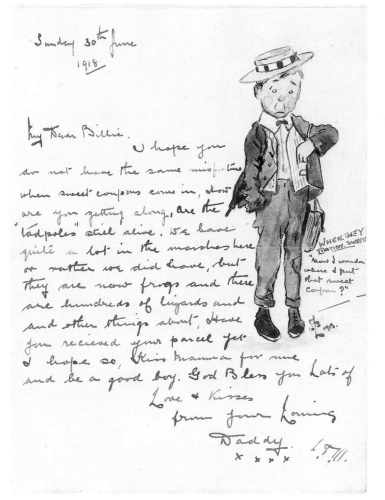

A typical letter to Billie (see also colour section, p 149)

The Cinema Goes to War
1: Film Documentary

The Battle of the Somme began on 1 July 1916. It lasted until November. Yet, remarkably, a film entitled *The Battle of the Somme* was running on cinema screens in Britain by the second half of August – weeks before the outcome of the battle was known – and by early September was even being shown to troops fighting the actual battle in France. Since the beginning of that year, the objections of Lord Kitchener having at last been overcome, a trickle of newsreel stories had emerged from the Western Front, but there had been nothing so long (1 hour 12 minutes), so dramatic or so compelling as this. It drew superlatives from the newspapers and it won huge audiences. It is not incorrect to say that it was a sensation, if not at the front – where they had the real thing to contend with – certainly at home.

Two film-cameramen were at work on the Somme front in late June and early July 1916 (Geoffrey Malins and J.B. McDowell, wearing officers' uniforms but with no badge or rank) but it was not their brief to produce a feature-length documentary. Only when their 'rushes' were seen in London was it realized that there was enough material to produce something much more ambitious than was first intended, and something worthier of what was already developing into an epic and sacrificial struggle. A two-day delay in the opening of the offensive – it had originally been planned for 29 June – allowed much more filming of the preparatory bombardment and of the march of the battalions to the front-line trenches than would otherwise have been the case. Moreover, and crucially, other graphic sequences were available to help tell the story, including scenes which showed men apparently in the act of going 'over the top' at the actual moment of the attack.

It is now believed that these scenes were almost certainly filmed away from the battle front, possibly at a trench mortar training school (they would now be described as 'reconstruction'). If this is so it was not disclosed and it is not known whether there was any discussion among those who put the film together for the British Topical Committee for War Films – William F. Jury as producer, Charles Urban and the cameraman Geoffrey Malins as editors – as to whether they should declare their hand. Since their aim was not to assemble evidence for analysis by future historians but to produce a vivid and potent boost to national morale at a time of crisis, they can scarcely be blamed for including what was to prove, for many in the audience, a winning card.

The novelist H. Rider Haggard, for example, found these scenes particularly impressive, especially one in which a soldier falls back apparently shot dead. 'There is something appalling about the instantaneous change from fierce activity to supine death,' he wrote in his diary. 'War has always been dreadful, but never, I suppose, more dreadful than today.' Equally impressed, one provincial newspaper, whose local 'Pals' battalion, the Grimsby Chums, had suffered nearly 500 casualties on 1 July, saw these scenes as proof of the authenticity of the whole film:

No picture of this war would be at all complete if we did not see a representation of 'Over the top, boys.' And here we see what this sentence really means. There is the hurried scramble up the trench side, the rush over the top, the negotiations of the wire entanglements and the disappearance of the troops into No Man's Land, where the hand to hand fighting is obscured from the view of the camera.

That the picture is real, taken in the face of German bullets, is proved by the fact that all the boys do not get 'over the top.' One is hit just as his head appears over the parapet and he slides back with outstretched arms, his rifle lying in front. After the battle one sees the sad scenes on the field. There are killed and there are wounded.

There were those, however, who were deeply shocked by the film, opening a debate about the morality of showing scenes of suffering or death on public screens which has gone on ever since. 'I beg leave to enter a protest', wrote the Dean of Durham, the Reverend Henley Henson, 'against an entertainment which wounds the heart and violates the very sanctity of bereavement.' It appalled him that someone should see a relative alive and well in the film who was 'now dead in the fields of Flanders'. Others complained that the film was sometimes shown with trivial fictional dramas or even comedies as supporting programme. But the general verdict was highly favourable, indeed laudatory, so that, for example, the managers of the Royalty Kinema of Richmond, Surrey could quote six rave press notices in the advertisement which they inserted in their local paper, including this from the *Evening News:* 'THE BATTLE OF THE SOMME ... IS THE GREATEST MOVING PICTURE IN THE WORLD – THE GREATEST THAT HAS EVER BEEN PRODUCED'.

It was shown to a specially invited audience at the Scala Theatre on 10

Invitation to the first special showing of *The Battle of the Somme*, 10 August 1916 (HU 59419)

SCALA THEATRE,
CHARLOTTE STREET, FITZROY SQUARE, W.
Proprietor : Dr. E. Distin Maddick.

THE BRITISH TOPICAL COMMITTEE FOR WAR FILMS
request the pleasure of the company of Bearer and Friend on
THURSDAY NEXT, AUGUST 10th, at 11.30 a m. prompt,
when they will present
OFFICIAL PICTURES
of the

"BATTLE of the SOMME,"
Taken by Special Arrangement with the
WAR OFFICE
and under their direction.

¶ No "Exclusive Rights" of this film will be granted.
Schedule of prices can be obtained from the sole booking director, W. F. JURY.

August 1916, and it opened on 21 August at thirty-four cinemas in the London area, to appear in the major provincial cities a week later. According to *The Times* it was seen by 'hundreds of thousands' of people in its first week, with more being turned away at the doors. In September it was shown privately to the Royal Family at Windsor. The film was still being booked by cinemas months after it was first shown. It was also shown overseas in eighteen countries.

On 11 August 1916 *The Times* wrote as follows:

In years to come, when historians want to know the conditions under which the great offensive was launched, they will only have to send for these films and a complete idea of the situation will be revealed before their eyes – for we take it as a matter of course that a number of copies of them will be carefully preserved in the national archives.

With the advantage of hindsight one can see how limited was the representation of the actuality of battle. There is no enemy, and no real action. Yet much the same could be said of the coverage decades later of the Falklands War (also subject to severe restrictions), and it has been well said of Malins and McDowell that 'by luck, skill or accident [the] two men had produced a haunting masterpiece'.* It is an essential document for the understanding of the First World War, not only for what it was but in terms of how it was perceived at the time and how it has been perceived ever since.

By way of postscript it should be added that whereas there is ample evidence of the film's enormous impact at home, comments of soldiers who saw it in France are hard to find. However, Lieutenant-Colonel Rowland Feilding, Commanding Officer of the 6th Connaught Rangers, saw it on 5 September 1916 'on a screen erected in a muddy field under the open sky' at Morlancourt, just behind the Somme front, and wrote at length about the experience to his wife:

Presumably by way of contrast Charlie Chaplin was also to have appeared, and I confess it was chiefly him I went to see. However, I came too late and saw only the more harrowing part of the entertainment.

This battle film is really a wonderful and most realistic production, but must of necessity be wanting in that the battle is fought in silence, and moreover, that the most unpleasant part – the machine-gun and rifle fire – is entirely eliminated. Of the actual 'frightfulness' of war all that one sees is the bursting of shells; and perhaps it is as well. I have said that the battle is fought in silence; but no, on this occasion the roar of the real battle was loudly audible in the distance.

I must say that at first the wisdom of showing such a film to soldiers on the brink of battle in which they are to play the part of attackers struck me as questionable. However, on my way home, my mind was set at rest upon this point by a conversation I overheard between two recruits who were walking behind me.

Said one, 'As to reality, now you knows what you've got to fice. If it was left to the imagination you might think all sorts of silly b----- things.'

I wonder where his imagination would have led him had he not seen the Cinema. Would it, do you think, have gone beyond the reality? Hell itself could hardly do so. I think sometimes that people who have not seen must find it difficult to comprehend how undisturbed life in the trenches can be on occasion: equally, how terrible can be the battle.**

The Authentic and the Inauthentic in *The Battle of the Somme*
Top left: Authentic – the blowing of the mine on the Hawthorn Ridge near Beaumont Hamel, 7.20 am on 1 July 1916
Top right: Almost certainly inauthentic – still-frame from the controversial attack sequence probably filmed some days earlier
Lower sequence: Some of the scenes that disturbed those concerned about the film
Top: From a sequence captioned: 'British Tommies rescuing a comrade under shell fire. (This man died 30 minutes after reaching the trenches)'
Middle: From a sequence captioned: 'Activity at Minden Post, while the battle raged furiously. Arrival of wounded Tommies etc.' Filmed on 2 July
Bottom: 'A dead British Bomber in a trench'

*S.D. Badsey, *Battle of the Somme: British War-propaganda*, Historical Journal of Film, Radio and Television, vol 3 no 2, 1983.
**War Letters to a Wife: France and Flanders, 1915-1919*, by Rowland Feilding, London, 1929.

The Cinema Goes to War
2: Political Cartoons

1918 saw a spate of propagandist cartoons on the cinema screens. The aim was partly to raise money for the war effort, as in the films represented on these two pages, partly to inspire the nation to greater efforts by mocking and guying the enemy.

Below: Four key frames from *There Was A Little Man and He Had a Little Gun*

Above: Two key frames from *Stand By the Men Who Have Stood By You*. The film ended with the appeal:

'British Parents
Encourage your Children to Save
Every Penny Saved is a Good Work Begun
Each Six Pence Will
Help to Blot out
THE HUN'

From *Britain's Effort*

(1) Britannia wakes up John Bull who is sleeping by the white cliffs of Dover and tells him that there is trouble across the Channel.

(2) Civilians respond to John Bull's call to arms: from left to right, a fisherman, a farmworker, a sportsman, a city gent, a labourer, a transport worker.

From *The U-Tube*

(1) The Kaiser and Crown Prince Wilhelm (generally known as 'Little Willy') play with a toy U-Boat.

(2) The Kaiser then has a bright idea; why not devise an under*ground* weapon by which they could go, say, from Berlin to Birmingham? Not a U-Boat, a U-Tube! Subsequently a prize is offered for the 'Best Tube Boring Invention'; an inventor produces a winning design, aptly called 'The Bore'. The Kaiser and the Crown Prince set off in it for Birmingham.

(3) The six civilians are transformed into six soldiers in uniform.

(4) Women do their bit. A munitions worker checks shells while her boss beams benignly.

(5) Prime Minister Lloyd George pats John Bull on the back for getting all those shells to the continent for the soldiers to use to beat the Germans.

However, a carelessly placed Iron Cross upsets the magnetic compass and unknown to its crew the U-Tube goes wildly off course.

(3) Instead of Birmingham they end up at the North Pole, though it takes some time for the dunderhead Crown Prince to realize this fact.

(4) Their unexpected and unhappy situation allows the obvious pay-off. Laughter and applause in the cinema – one more nail in the enemy's coffin.

PART VIII

The War Experience

THE war was not merely a matter of politics and fighting; it had its moral and psychological dimensions, too, and it inevitably strained accepted assumptions and beliefs. In the firing line in this context were the chaplains, who often had to cope with circumstances as shocking to themselves as to the soldiers they were sent out to serve. Two Western Front chaplains are featured here, together with the post-war reflections of a third; also included (slightly abridged) is the text of a sermon delivered immediately after a major action. By definition a chaplain, if not condoning war, at least accepted its legitimacy, but there were other people who did not, and to whom the arrival of conscription presented a profound moral dilemma. The stories of two such Conscientious Objectors are told here, of whom one was actually sentenced to death but reprieved, and the other spent many months in prison. Imprisonment of a different kind is the subject of another major section – on internees and prisoners of war.

One important weapon against wartime strains was humour, and the wit of the fighting man – sometimes light-hearted, sometimes heavily sarcastic – is represented in a section on service magazines, which sprang up in almost every war theatre. Far from being outdated, much of what made their first readers laugh remains highly palatable today.

Later sections bring the story of the war to an end, though not before demonstrating the depths of despair to which it was possible to sink as the conflict appeared to drag on interminably. By contrast the Armistice of 1918 was greeted with a prodigious outburst of rejoicing – in which, however, not everybody felt able to join.

Finally there is a brief coda focusing on commemoration and remembrance.

A patrol of the Loyal North Lancashire Regiment entering Cambrai, 9 October 1918 (Q 11363)

The War Experience   Important Dates

1916

January 25   First Military Service Bill passed in Britain, introducing conscription for single men

May 16   Second Military Service Bill passed in Britain, extending conscription to married men

1917

March 15   Tsar Nicholas II of Russia abdicates

April 6   United States of America declares war on Germany

November 6   Bolshevik coup in Petrograd

December 2   Suspension of hostilities between Russian and German armies

1918

March 18   Germans repulsed on Belgian front

21   German offensive in Picardy begins

23   Paris shelled from Western Front

April 9   German offensive on the Lys in Flanders begins

12   'Backs to the Wall' Order of the Day issued by Field Marshal Sir Douglas Haig

14   Marshal Foch appointed as General-in-Chief of the Allied Armies in France

May 27   German offensive on the Aisne begins

July 15   Start of German Champagne-Marne offensive

18   Allied counter-offensive on the Marne

August 8   Battle of Amiens begins: the 'black day' of the German Army

15   British troops cross the Ancre

30   British troops cross the Somme

September 26   Start of Franco-American offensive in the Meuse-Argonne sector

28   Allied advance in Flanders begins

29   British and Dominion forces begin main attack on the Hindenburg Line

November 3   Austria-Hungary signs armistice with the Allies

9   Kaiser Wilhelm II of Germany abdicates

11   Armistice between the Allies and Germany ends hostilities on the Western Front

Chaplains

Church parades in the First World War were, by definition, compulsory. They are often referred to in contemporary letters or diaries. The following extracts represent a wide range of reactions.

In June 1915 Rifleman Bernard Britland attended a church parade in France and reported to his family that he had found it 'very impressive':

We sang some good old hymns, three of which I knew but the other I did not know. They were:- *Fight the Good Fight, Lead Kindly Light* and *All People that On Earth do Dwell*. It seemed to make it more impressive because we could hear big guns going off during the service. The Chaplain took for his subject that story from the New Testament about the ten lepers which our Lord cured and then told them to show themselves to the High Priest. Out of ten only one came back to thank Him. The Chaplain compared this with the case of men coming back safe out of the trenches, and he wondered how many of us thought of thanking the Lord for being brought back unhurt. He preached a very good sermon on it, and it seemed to make a deep impression on most of us. I know it did on me.

Private William Knott, who served as a stretcher-bearer at Gallipoli and Salonika, was a keen evangelical Christian much given to meeting with kindred spirits for prayer and Bible reading. He had, however, no love for worship by order. He noted in his diary:

Some of these Church Parades are the great hypocrisies of the British nation and I trust we shall soon be privileged to gather again with people who congregate to receive blessing and help not because they are driven to it like slaves.

Lieutenant Holroyd Birkett Barker, at a church parade on his first Sunday at Salonika, found the sermon so meaningless and irrelevant that he decided he could 'switch off without imperilling my prospects of finding the road to salvation, and was at the 17th hole before a shuffling of feet restored me to the matter in hand'. His diary entry continues:

There is much to be said for this open air hymn singing by large bodies of men and its obvious sincerity nearly always impresses me to the point of tears, but one wonders if the interposition of a sermon to men whose main mission is to kill their fellow men is of any material advantage.

Not dissimilar, if more vehemently expressed, was the reaction of Lieutenant Thomas Hughes, after being 'herded' into a service held in the basement of a French lunatic asylum; the chaplain, he commented in his diary, 'preached a damnable sermon on the "purging power of suffering".'

For their part, chaplains also had their difficulties. Canon E.C. Crosse DSO MC, formerly Senior Chaplain to the 7th Division in France, defined some of them in a post-war essay intended as a preface to a history of chaplaincy in the 1914-18 war which was never published. Chaplains were given little or no training, their pay never rose above that of a Second Lieutenant – which meant that many married clergy or ministers could not afford to apply – and temporary (ie hostilities only) chaplains were taken on for only one year at a time. Whereas in the idealistic days of 1914 clergy were welcomed, eighteen months later the problem in trying to billet a new padre was not 'where was it most desirable for the padre to live, but rather which of the many messes in the padre's care was willing to have a padre billeted on them at all'. They were often seen as 'rather a nuisance'; in their presence 'people felt they had to mind their p's and q's' – laying upon the chaplain the burden, in Crosse's view, to show 'they couldn't shock him if they tried'.

Church parades were often a trial for chaplains as well as their enforced congregations:

There was usually nowhere to hold them but in the open air – and it happened not infrequently that no account was taken of the direction of the wind in forming it up. In winter it was often so cold that the most inspired padre could not hope to make the service more than a ceremony.

Crosse was fully and sympathetically aware of the genuine doctrinal difficulties posed by the war, as the following quotations from various sections of his essay make clear:

It was useless to go to France with a cut and dried gospel because it was unintelligible to men placed in such abnormal conditions.
Before a padre could be of much use he had to throw overboard his natural temptation to be a spiritual profiteer.
A chaplain who knew his duty could accomplish much not in the way of teaching the mysteries of religion but in improving the general morale.

Chaplains also had to be aware of the firmly set attitudes of many of the men:

Scarcely any soldier thought of Christianity as offering any sort of philosophy of life.
There was more peace talk to be heard in the line itself than anywhere and it would have been foolish to try and stop it.
It just did seem a fact that on the whole it was the best not the worst who got killed.

This last was a widely held assumption that somewhat devalued the doctrine – as preached to Rifleman Britland's battalion – that survivors should thank God that they had been spared. If God was meant to be just, then justice was not always seen to be done. Things were simply not fair. Crosse quoted the example of a private twice court-martialled for desertion who everybody knew would get through whatever happened. Writing in his hospital bed in London about his battalion's attack on the Somme in which so many had died and which he had barely survived, Second Lieutenant Norton Hughes-Hallett commented bitterly on one incompetent officer who had failed to transmit vital orders before the action: 'He, like all undeserving people, got a "cushy" wound in the arm, which I hear is quite cured, and nothing worse, tho' his mistake might have cost many lives.'

Chaplains could find themselves in unenviable positions in other respects, too. 'I can quite well remember,' wrote Crosse, 'being asked to spin the coin between company officers as to which should go into a

given battle. The men were spinning for their lives, and they knew it.' Chaplains themselves, of course, could also be at risk, particularly those who felt it their duty to go as far forward as they possibly could to identify with their men and share their dangers and privations. Crosse's essay cites the fact that during the war 100 Church of England chaplains were killed.

Notwithstanding such hazards, chaplains could be both effective and popular, particularly if they used their freedom to move between the ranks with diplomacy and understanding, and – crucially – if they showed that they were prepared to suffer with the soldier and not merely sermonize him. If they did the former, they would be listened to with greater respect when they attempted the latter. The Reverend Victor Tanner had been at the battalion aid post when his 2nd Worcesters were engaged in what became known as the Menin Road Action during the Third Battle of Ypres and had done sterling work in helping to carry out casualties (see page 66). He was to be awarded the Military Cross for his gallantry. He had plainly put himself where his faith took him and he saw no problem in immediately preparing a sermon (he called it a 'talk') which, unambiguously, he entitled 'Thanksgiving After Action', and which he delivered to the remnants of the battalion as they recuperated

Church parade of the 1st Battalion, the North Staffordshire Regiment (Prince of Wales's) in a field at Cassel, 8 September 1917 (Q 3055)

in their billet village behind the lines. Most sermons of those distant church parades have been lost to the winds, but Tanner retained his script among his papers. The following are its key paragraphs:

We are only too conscious that our thankfulness is tinged with very real sorrow for there are big gaps in our ranks today. Comrades with whom we have stood shoulder to shoulder in billets on the march and in the front line trench are absent now. Some are in hospital, and we shall look forward to seeing them again, but many have passed through the veil which hides us from the great spiritual world. Bravely they fought and nobly they died in the greatest and most sacred cause in which men have ever taken up arms, and humanity will for ever bless their memory. For them we need not mourn. Death is like the drawing aside of a veil and passing from one room into another. A nobler activity is theirs today, greater opportunities for the development of character and a sphere of wider usefulness, as we Christians firmly believe, but when we think of some of them, lads of scarce 20 years and of the majority of young men in the prime of life and full of the vigour of manhood, there cannot but come before our mind's eye a picture of the promising future which, humanly speaking, lay before them. Why does God allow them to be cut off in the prime of life? Prematurely cut off, did I say? Jesus died at 33 years just when his manhood's powers were at their height. No, his was no untimely end. 'I have finished the work that thou gavest me to do' were almost his last words as he entered the final struggle. And, as for him, so for us. God has an appointed task for each man's life and if that man is called upon to lay down his life in the fulfilment of his duty we may be sure that his work on earth is finished. 'Are there not twelve hours in the day' said Jesus on one occasion when he had announced his intention of going into a place where his enemies were known to be lying in wait to kill him 'if any man walk in the day he stumbleth not'. 'I must work the works of him that sent me while it is day'. No, for our fallen comrades we need not grieve. God has other work for them to do. But for the heartbroken mothers and wives whom they have left behind and for the little ones who have been looking forward so eagerly to Daddy's return from the war, for them our hearts bleed and we pray that they may be given grace to bear their sorrow with Christian courage and holy hope, remembering that their loved ones are for ever in the safe keeping of the Good Shepherd.

But there is one thing more that I want to say. What effect should the death of our comrades have upon us? Surely in the first place:

1. It should strengthen our resolve to carry on without faltering till the object for which they died has been attained – England's honour vindicated, liberty established and a common brotherhood. When a feeling of war weariness comes over us, as it does from time to time, let us pray for the spirit of dogged perseverance and endurance.

2. If God spares us to return home it must be our resolve to build a new England on the principles of righteousness, justice and brotherhood. Here unity is strength. Let those who love righteousness and want to see those things removed from our national life which have in the past brought dishonour on the fair name of England – social injustice, luxury on the one hand and grinding poverty on the other, bad housing, immorality, class hatred and the like – band themselves together and say 'These things need not be. These things shall not be'.

If, then, God spares you to come through this World War, will you not pledge yourself to fight against sin, the world and the devil and become a member of Christ's Society and so help to make its witness an effective force in solving the great problems of reconstruction which will have to be faced in the days to come?

How Tanner's sermon was received is not known but two days after it was preached he wrote the following in his diary:

This afternoon as I was walking through the village two of our fellows came up and asked if they might be prepared for confirmation. They said the Ypres-Menin battle had made them think very seriously. One of them added: 'I must tell you, sir, how much I admire the way you went about during the battle. I only wish I could do the same.'

Equally courageous and forthright was Father J. Bernard Marshall, who went to France in 1915 as a Roman Catholic chaplain, attached to the 62nd Infantry Brigade, 21st Division. He wrote a detailed account of his experiences in a series of school exercise books. Month after month his close acute-angled handwriting travelled across the pages, as he served through some of the great battles of the war – Loos in 1915, the Somme in 1916, Passchendaele in 1917. Throughout he laboured with one over-riding purpose in view – to save the souls of his 'parishioners', in this context the Catholic soldiers of the British Army whenever and wherever he might find them. His zeal was at its greatest in circumstances where men were especially at risk. If soldiers were going into any kind of action, from minor raid to set-piece attack, it was, literally, vital that they should be right with God. A typical entry is the following, from his account of what he called 'My First Battle' – Loos, in September 1915. At one point during the fighting he took cover with a group of Tommies in the remains of a farm:

I made use of the time by finding out the Catholics amongst the men there, and heard a few confessions standing where we were amongst all the noise and din of battle – great aids to contrition.

He was much concerned with the problem presented by men who could not be reached by a priest at times of danger, though he was less than satisfied by the solution adopted by a senior colleague:

He told me that when action was on he told men to make an act of contrition at any time, and they could know that he was absolving them, because he kept pronouncing a general absolution over the whole battlefield. This struck me as going a bit far even for the theology of the front.

He was well aware, however, that some changes in practice were inevitable. Under 1 June 1916 he described a visit to the line where he had been introduced to a Catholic sergeant:

He took me right along the fire trench, fetching the Catholics out of dug-outs and so forth. All seemed glad to see me. I chatted with them, heard a few confessions and scattered absolutions in the free and easy way we do out here.

Some of those he met were about to take part in a trench raid. He found his encounter with them an uplifting experience:

None of the men seemed the least embarrassed before their comrades by the visit of a priest. They bared their heads and made the sign of the cross openly. Some of them knelt down in the trench, two remained kneeling together after I passed on from them. There was cheerfulness and badinage everywhere, although it was quite certain that death would visit those trenches that night.

He spent the night at the dressing station in anticipation of any dangerously wounded Catholic coming in: 'In the early morning one of the

**Rev Victor Tanner, MC
and Bar, at home on leave**
(HU 59421)

men I had seen in the trenches was brought in badly wounded and I gave him the last sacrament.'

Marshall had several rows with his military superiors. A decision by 'our authorities' to ignore Whit Sunday 1916 during the build-up for the Somme offensive provoked the following, not untypical, outburst:

What a pity that they could not recognize the military value of an appeal to the Holy Ghost – even at the expense of a slight delay in preparation for the coming battle. But my greatest fear for us in the whole of this struggle is the neglect of God by officialdom. The Sunday previous to this the 10th Yorks were unable to come to Mass because the Brigadier was inspecting them. An inspection in place of a service of God! I protested to the Brigade Major – always most friendly, a perfect gentleman, a fine type of Englishman – and with just the ordinary Englishman's dearth of religion. I said it was wicked to hold an inspection on a Sunday morning. He took up the word 'wicked'. 'Wicked, my dear padre, you seem to forget that we are here to beat the Bosch.' I told him I forgot nothing of the sort and that we should have a better chance if we didn't forget God. Instead of laughing so freely at the Kaiser's protestations to Heaven it would be well if we remembered God ourselves. But it was a point of view that meant little to him.

Marshall had scant respect for other denominations. He would not allow Catholics to attend a Church of England service. 'War or no war, principles admitted no compromise', he wrote. 'Our position was that we were members of Christ's Church and we could not have any part in a formal gathering of heretics.' When a re-organization of chaplains was put into effect, he commented, 'I do not see we are much better off by our alliance with Methodists, Baptists and all manner of Non-Conformists. The only thing was that in the old scheme all points of honour and promotion were held by C. of E.' But he wanted no promotion himself: 'I am a priest and that is my rank – to call me Captain, Colonel or General does nothing to that.' However, his staunch Catholicism did not prevent him caring for men outside his faith, as the following entry makes clear:

Yesterday we had a suicide in the 12th. A man who had rejoined three days after being wounded shot himself with his rifle early in the morning. He was taken to the ambulance and did not die for some hours. In case he was a Catholic I went to see him. He was not, but as he was conscious and able to talk I stayed with him a bit. I could not find much religion in him, but I tried to put the essentials of faith before him and work him up to contrition. He at least repeated the words of an act of contrition. God grant they were sincerely spoken.

Marshall's diary contains many vivid, often harrowing descriptions. One such is his account of his visits, following the start of the Somme offensive in July 1916, to a 'moribund tent' – set aside for cases 'marked out by the doctor as too far gone to be able to spare a place for on an ambulance at the expense of others in better condition.' He was plainly much moved by the experience:

The moribund tent – sometimes there was more than one – was a tragic place. A bell tent with one, two or three men on stretchers on the ground at close quarters with death – and none with time to stay by them and help them and watch them. Now and again one of the doctors would look in to see developments – and the padres did their best to ease and spiritualize those deathbeds.

But they mostly lay alone and died alone – for how could doctor or chaplain spend long hours by their side with the constant stream of war's victims arriving at the station?

There were several Catholics who found their way to the moribund tent – and what a blessed thing the faith was there – such light in the gloom for the sufferer – such definite spiritual business for the priest. One boy who died there – he looked very young – was a Scotch lad in the Black Watch. His was a perforating wound in the abdomen and he suffered terrible agony. When I warned him to prepare for death his first thought was 'It will kill my poor mother'. I stayed as long and visited him as often as I could. I raised him in my arms from time to time because it eased the awful pain. He made his confession, received extreme unction and prayed with me as well as the torture would allow. It was an edifying death.

Like Tanner, Marshall was awarded the Military Cross, and for not dissimilar reasons – 'giving help to wounded men in a shelled area', which he dismissed as 'much less than the ordinary stretcher bearer is continually doing'. The real motive, he noted, for his being in the trenches on the night in question was the one which always took him to points of high danger during action: 'the wish to annoint any dying Catholic who could not be got back alive'.

Marshall's diaries cease abruptly in November 1917, after running to some 630 pages and 130,000 words. It is presumed a further volume or volumes must have been lost. Little is known about the subsequent career of their author.

Incident at an advanced dressing station during the advance of September 1918. A British padre saying a prayer over a dying German (Q 11336)

Conscription and Conscience

When hostilities began in 1914 Britain, unlike the other belligerent powers, put her reliance firmly on the volunteer principle in raising the forces necessary to propagate her cause. Kitchener's campaign was one of moral persuasion only; it was backed by no legal sanctions. But as the months went by it became clear that Britain would not be able to supply the military machine with enough men by simply sitting back and waiting for them to enlist. A half-way house scheme was established under Lord Derby's name in 1915, whereby men were encouraged to attest their willingness to join up when the appropriate time came. This persuaded more men to come forward, but by no means enough.

The next, inevitable step was conscription. The Military Service Bill of January 1916 imposed the obligation to serve on all single men aged between eighteen and forty-one in the home countries, apart from Ireland, from March of that year; later statutes included married men and extended the age range. Among the small list of categories who might claim exemption – such as men who were medically unfit or in essential occupations – were 'those who could show a conscientious objection'. The tribunals set up under the 'Derby Scheme' now turned their hands to the task of assessing the claims of COs – 'Conscientious Objectors', often known as 'conchies', a term almost always used in derision and contempt.

Robert Saunders, Sussex schoolmaster, expressed the widely held attitude to the CO in a letter of 21 March 1916 – a timely month for such views:

The appeals for exemption to the different Tribunals have disclosed the existence of a class of men having no trace of patriotism, courage or self-respect, though the conscientious objector claims both the latter, and quotes his moral courage in refusing to fight as proof. I think myself the Government should bring in a Bill for general conscription and organize the whole population for whatever service is necessary for the country's good.

But for many men conscription posed a profound dilemma. There were those for whom, for religious, philosophical or humanistic reasons, the concept of bearing arms was anathema. Altogether about 16,000 became COs, of whom 1500 took the extreme 'absolutist' step of refusing to partake in any service at all with the result that they were sent to prison until the end of the war.

Howard Marten, a Londoner, applied to become a conscientious objector on religious grounds but was turned down. Deemed therefore to have enlisted, he was committed by a magistrates' court to a military escort and taken to Mill Hill Barracks. As he stated in his recorded interview about his experiences, he felt he had two choices: to lie on the floor and kick, or accept that he should be kitted out as a soldier. He decided against the undignified course, telling the NCOs in charge, 'I've no objection to put on uniform, but it won't change my attitude.'

Marten was to suffer arguably the conscientious objectors' ultimate trauma. He was one of the thirty-four men sentenced to death by court martial on whose behalf the journal of the No-Conscription Fellowship *The Tribunal* campaigned in mid-1916 (see page 255).

After imprisonment at Harwich for refusing to obey military orders he and some other COs were taken to France, where disobedience in the field was legally a capital offence. When passing through London one of their number threw a note from the train which not only alerted the NCF but also helped to fuel, as he put it, the 'tremendous fight going on in Parliament' about the treatment of conscientious objectors.

In France the unwilling conscripts continued their policy of declining to co-operate:

We never saluted anybody; we never stood to attention. Well, that was a frightful crime in the eyes of the military authorities.
Interviewing an officer I'd think nothing of putting a hand on his desk in a very friendly, casual sort of way, and of course that was disgraceful. It didn't even occur to me. I treated them as I'd treat any normal person.

Marten soon found himself one of four brought before a court martial in Boulogne, where, surprisingly, the attitude of their assessors was 'fairly sympathetic'. However, they were told some days later that there would be a second court martial – they presumed because the first one had not proposed a sufficiently stiff sentence. A few days later they were conducted to a parade ground to hear their fate:

There was a big concourse of men, mostly of the Non-Combatant Corps and the labour battalions, lined up in an immense square. We were taken to one side of it, and then under escort taken out one by one to the middle of the square. I was the first of them, and until my verdict was known, nobody knew exactly what was going to happen. An officer in charge of the proceedings read out the various crimes and misdemeanours; refusing to obey a lawful command, disobedience at Boulogne and so on, and then:
'The sentence of the court is to suffer death by being shot.' Then there was a suitable pause. And one thought, 'Well, that's that.' And then: 'Confirmed by the Commander-in-Chief.' 'That's double-sealed it now', I thought. Then another long pause: 'But subsequently commuted to penal servitude for ten years.' And that was that. And the thing that interested me and the others particularly was that penal servitude meant your return to England and would get us into the hands of the civil authorities at a civil prison. So long as we were in the hands of the military authorities we were subject to military punishments – we could only go on offending.

What did it feel like to have a death sentence read out against you?

You had a sort of feeling of being outside yourself. A sort of impersonal feeling; something that wasn't affecting you personally; that you were almost looking on at the proceedings. Very strange.

Back in prison in England Marten eventually took advantage of what became known as the Home Office scheme, whereby the conscientious objector could undertake 'work of national importance', which usually turned out to be manual labour or work in agriculture or forestry.

Pro- and Anti-CO: A page
from the pacifist journal
The Tribunal (HU 59112)
and one of a series of
postcards printed in 1917
(Q 102926)

Commenting on his decision Marten stated, 'I never felt that you were compromising by accepting the Home Office scheme', adding, significantly: 'Not that I felt we were doing a lot of good by it'.

'You are fine after six months' imprisonment, not a word of regret and a resolute determination to face the possibility of a longer period. Who says that the only heroism is found in khaki?'

Thus a fellow-Socialist and friend writing in April 1918 to Percy Wall, who had just been released from Wormwood Scrubs and would shortly be returned to gaol in Liverpool, where he would remain behind bars until well into 1919. When finally freed Wall would have served seventeen months in prison and would have behind him three appearances before tribunals, two before courts martial and one in a police court. As a conscientious objector Wall was an absolutist; he would not consent to perform any service which might assist the war effort in any way – and, unlike Marten, refused outright to collaborate with the Home Office scheme.

When conscription became legal in 1916 Wall applied for exemption. By profession a 'grocer's manager' living in South Wales, he was summoned to state his case before a tribunal at Aberdare on 24 March 1916. He was given exemption from combatant service only, and was subsequently enrolled as 4490 Private Wall, 5th Western Company, Non-Combatant Corps. He appealed against the tribunal's decision and was summoned to appear on 15 April at the Police Court at Pontypridd, where his appeal was dismissed. He attempted to take his case to the Central Tribunal in London, a process only available to him if his local tribunal agreed. The appeal tribunal for Glamorgan refused to sanction his request.

He was subsequently sent formal instructions to enlist on four occasions; he ignored them all. He was finally arrested at his home on 30 October 1917 and taken to Cardiff barracks, the depot of the Welch Regiment, where, being officially a serving soldier, he was brought before a court martial. In his account of his experiences, written shortly after his release in 1919, he described how – after creating consternation at the Pay Office by refusing to accept the shilling a day due to him by virtue of his forcible enlistment – he was escorted to the room where the court martial was to be held:

I almost began to think I was really dangerous, as I had a Military Policeman in front, another behind, a Provost-Sergeant at my elbow, and a Sergeant-Major hovering near by.

According to the 'Summary of Evidence in the case of No 4490 Pte Percy Wall' dated 3 November 1917 and signed by Major James P. McGaul, Adjutant of the Depot, the first witness was a Lieutenant H.C. Bailey, of the Glamorgan and Monmouth Recruiting Staff, who stated:

On the 31st October at the Headquarters Recruiting Cardiff I personally ordered the accused Percy Wall to sign his documents. He persistently refused to obey. I produced Army Form B 2513 which he refused to sign and the Certificate of Civil Conviction. These have been read and explained to the accused and he has been warned that they will be used in evidence against him.

34 DEATH SENTENCES IN FRANCE

COMMUTED TO TEN YEARS' PENAL SERVITUDE

MR. TENNANT STILL HELPLESS

HAS "NO INFORMATION."

In spite of the repeated assurances of Mr. Tennant as to the impossibility of the death sentence being inflicted on conscientious objectors in France, we received on Thursday, June 22, news that on the previous Thursday, at Boulogne, four conscientious objectors, who had been court-martialled for refusing to obey military orders, were sentenced to be shot.

The four men were Messrs. Marten, Scullard, Foister, and Ring. On the date mentioned above, the regiment was drawn up and the men paraded for their sentence to be pronounced, the court-martial having been held some days previously. It is said to have been an impressive and solemn function.

The court-martial sentence of death was pronounced by an officer; after which there was a pause, and then came the announcement of the subsequent commutation of the sentence to

TEN YEARS' PENAL SERVITUDE

These men were members of the first party of conscientious objectors sent on May 8 to France, where the Non-Combatant Corps is stationed, and employed on such duties as qua___ road-making. Before going to France they had first ser___ of imprisonment in Harwich Redoubt. They have ___ refused to obey all military orders on the ground ___ against their conscience.

It is understood that sentence of death was co___ General Sir Douglas Haig. The prisoners have been ___ to Rouen, and it is expected that they will be retur___ land.

SENSATION IN THE HOUSE

Immediately the news came to hand on Thursday, ___ to the House and caused a sensation among the me___ Barnes, who does not agree with the conscientiou___ such, raised the matter on the motion for the adjou___ said : I desire to ask the Under-Secretary a questio___ have given him notice. It is in reference to a repo___ the Lobbies to-night that four men in France ha___ tenced to death. These men are stated to be consc___ tors, and there is a very general feeling of resent___ that after the many statements which have been ___ Front Bench in regard to the treatment of these ___ promises which have been made about them bei___ to the civil power by the military, and the assura___ men would not be sent to France at all—it is som___ that a report of this sort should be current. I ca___ is true, and I merely raise the question now to giv___ gentleman an opportunity of assuring the House ___ ular report is not true. I hope he will also gi___ that something will be done by which public ___ llayed in regard to this matter.

MR. TENNANT'S IGNORANCE

Mr. Tennant said the great majority of rumo___ ___ent of conscientious objectors were untrue, and ___ ___as one of them. He had no information on th___ ___elieved it to be wholly untrue. He would be ___ ___ouse full information when he had investig___ ___hese men were soldiers and must be treated ___ ___uite true promises had been given in relatio___ ___nd it was quite impossible that desertion in the face of the enemy ___ould occur in regard to non-combatants. "There is no intention ___ of dealing with them in any way harshly, and there will be no ___ ___ their being sentenced to death."

when and where I shall be removed. Through all I have ___ supported by a sense of the deepest peace, and humbly cons___ of my own unworthiness to bear my small share of testimo___ the teachings of our dear Lord, and thankful for the blessi___ His Holy Spirit. Naturally I think long and often of all the ___ ones, and sincerely hope that before being confined to pr___ may be given the opportunity of seeing one or more of yo___ as yet I know nothing of the future."

Mr. H. Scullard writes from Boulogne on June 17, conf___ his sentence, and informing us that he and his three comra___ being removed to Rouen en route for England.

Extract from a letter sent to Mr. Frederick Bonner, o___ Street W., Luton, by his son, Bernard Bonner (one ___ prisoners in France) :—" We twelve have been court-ma___ and four are on their way back to the homeland. Th___ received a very heavy sentence, as we also expect to. Th___ read out on the 15th inst., and the sentence was death, b___ muted to ten years' penal servitude. They have started ___ way back the same way as we came, and we may be f___ very shortly. The other 23 have also been court-martia___ are waiting to be read out.

We have also received a letter from Mr. Fred Murfin ___ ___tenham, who was one of the batch of conscientious ___ court-martialled in France on June 12. He says he ha___ ___ is expecting the same as his f___ ___ very fai___

___d Punishr___ ___ions the f___ ___court-mart___

___E HOU___

___ATION.

___. Morrell ___ectors now ___al to be s___ ___muted.

___ the case ___onscientiou___

___en commu___ ___e impriso___

___ he could ___as to the ___n was dro___

___could no___

___had been ___nant could ___ennant sai___ ___face of th___

___derstand t___ ___mbatant co___

___fferent me___ ___gested by ___operation. ___statement

___RIFTING

___day nigh___ "___ When questioned on Thursday nigh___ of the sentence of death passed on four Conscie___ in France, Mr. Tennant said he had heard ___ declared that he believed it to be wholly un___ ___ ___s the men were not in the face of the ___ Yesterday Mr.

WHAT A C.O. FEELS LIKE.

WHEN HANDED OVER TO THE MILITARY BY CIVIL AUTHORITY

ON SEEING THE PRISON WALL

WHEN ADDRESSING HIS COURT-MARTIAL

WHEN BEING EXAMINED BY THE PRISON DOCTOR

IN PRISON CLOTHING

WHAT A C.O. WILL FEEL LIKE WHEN HE GETS HIS FINAL DISCHARGE

WHEN HE ARRIVES ON THE HOME OFFICE SCHEME

Other witnesses followed who made similar statements, Wall's only significant contribution being to reply when asked if he had anything to say, 'As a conscientious objector I consider myself exempt from Military Service under the Military Service Act 1916.' His own account continues:

The court martial found me guilty of course and sentenced us to six months hard labour. Four days later, we left for Wormwood Scrubs, after going through the day before the ceremony called 'being read out'. This ceremony took place before a parade of troops when the court martial papers are read out, with the sentence attached; when each prisoner is mentioned he has to step forward and take his hat off. As we declined to do this, the Sgt. behind gently took off our hats and pushed us forward so that the tradition was complied with. He was evidently much used to the job.

Wall was put to sewing mail-bags, then after the first month he was attached to the more congenial work of the chapel cleaning party:

The first month was the real time of trial, and once having passed through this period I felt that I had seen and gone through the worst they could do, and thus should thence journey on with confidence and as cheerfully as possible.

COs were not allowed to write any letters for eight weeks, then six, then they could write monthly for twelve months, at which point the letters were cut down to half size and allowed fortnightly. When with other COs a silence rule was officially enforced, but Wall was told by one warder:

'When talking do not turn towards the person you are addressing, nor move your lips.' This is the proper way to talk in prison.
  On the whole the officers were very decent. I found that humanity could enter into an iron-barred institution and a blue uniform.

Under the provisions of the Conscription Act, when a CO completed his sentence he was still liable to service with the colours and if he continued to refuse to enlist he would again be court-martialled. When Wall was released from Wormwood Scrubs he was sent to Oswestry, where, awaiting his inevitable second sentence, he found himself in a large military camp where he had the opportunity to talk to some of his comrades in khaki:

The attitude of the soldiers to us during the time we were at camp fell roughly in three divisions. There were those – a very small minority – who told us they would like to see us shot; those who wished to know exactly what we were standing for – these expressing more or less sympathy and some of them told us they would be COs next time; and another section who seemed to think we wanted to get out of going to the trenches (as they admitted they did) and this was our way of doing it. These latter seemed unable to understand a matter of principle at all, their philosophy comprising only likes and dislikes.

Wall was duly brought before a court martial at Oswestry. This time he was sentenced to two years' hard labour – a sentence ultimately abbreviated by the end of the war. However, the release of Conscientious Objectors was deliberately held back until about six months after the cessation of hostilities, so that returning soldiers should be given the better chance to find peace-time employment. COs were also disenfranchised until 1926.

Internees and Prisoners

The first prisoners of the war were civilians rather than soldiers – aliens marshalled into places of internment. Thus any Briton aged between seventeen and forty-five who happened to be in Germany in August 1914 was liable to be detained for the duration of hostilities. One so held was George Packe, who had been on a fishing holiday in the Black Forest and subsequently spent most of the next four years at an internment camp at Ruhleben in Berlin. These comments from his 1916 diary give some indication of his mood after many months as an internee:

15 May: Realize that we shall be here for at least another year, which means a third winter with accompanying misery from cold, and feeling pretty hipped in consequence.

20 September: One's life here consists of having too much time to do nothing and yet not enough time to do anything.

11 October: Life must be somewhat like that in a monastery except that here bad language and tobacco take the place of prayers and incense.

Also liable to internment were merchant seamen who found themselves in German ports when war began. Captain Stephen Gulston was one of these; he was first confined to his ship in Hamburg, then kept in a derelict hulk, and finally transferred to Ruhleben. His frustration shows through constantly in his diary, with such comments as 'Feeling very evil today and cross with everyone. Isn't it horrible but we all seem to get like that now and again'; or 'Up 6 am and as miserable as ever outside and in.'

There were, however, occasional moments of light relief:

28 January 1915: As before, nothing of much importance to write about. But wait a bit. I quite forgot about the Kaiser's birthday of the 27th Jan. Someone before breakfast made an attempt to destroy the flag halyard on the staff in the middle of the camp. He succeeded in cutting one part and that was flying in the wind when they went there to hoist the Prussian Standard. Eventually they got it up and a very pretty flag it is too. After soup orders came round, no one is allowed to leave their barracks until it had been found out who had cut the said halyard. Great sport watching people crossing the compound with soldiers round them with their rifles. Thought there was going to be some bad trouble once or twice. In the evening the Captains of the barracks interviewed the Commander and patched things up somehow and we were freed next morning. Rather great, eh!

The civilian internee was a hostage, an innocent victim. For the soldier, becoming a prisoner of war was one of the many possible consequences of enlistment. It was part of the job-description. Yet, however honourably acquired, the POW label was inevitably a pejorative one.

Returning POWs received documents from the War Office and the King and Queen relieving them of blame, but few were happy with such formal consolation. They had not taken up arms to end up behind bars. As POWs they had to suffer the humiliation of being entirely at the enemy's mercy and they could have no idea when their freedom would be restored. POWs also bore the extra burden of knowing that while they were militarily ineffective, others had to shoulder the task of confronting the enemy. They were on the sidelines – dependent on events over which they had no control. There was perhaps one compensation, as expressed in the thoughts of the first POW quoted below, Eugene Cruft. He hoped his wife would be feeling much happier after hearing that he had been taken prisoner 'as it's just a matter of waiting now to the end of the war, whereas before, there was always that fearful possibility, each time I had to go to the line.'

Some POWs were treated well, others badly. There was generally a marked contrast between the conditions in which officers were held as opposed to their men. In a highly class-conscious world, 'other ranks' had much less chance of an easy life than their social superiors.

The following extracts are from the accounts – one written, two verbal – of three British prisoners of war who found themselves in German hands.

Eugene Cruft was a rising young musician – a distinguished double-bass player – who already had an orchestral tour to the United States and a six-week orchestral season in Berlin behind him when war came. Married with one small child, a man whose instincts were entirely artistic and peaceable, he became a soldier following the introduction of conscription. He served with the 2nd Battalion, the Rifle Brigade, at Passchendaele in 1917 and on the Somme Front in 1918. On 24 April that year, by which time he was a Lance-Corporal, he was taken prisoner at Villers-Brettoneux. He at once started keeping a diary in a tiny notebook which he had managed to secrete in his uniform. The diary rapidly mutated into a day-by-day love-letter to his wife Winnie, but the small size of the book meant he could write to her during the first few weeks only. On 17 May he wrote:

Kiddie, two months ago by the date I was rushing home to you. Oh what glorious thoughts dear heart and what a still more glorious time you gave me, during those two little days and three nights. We *were* happy sweetheart, but what a difference now, my only happiness at present darling, is writing these few thoughts to you, and I'm afraid I must end, as the book is nearly full, and there's no chance of getting another. It was my intention when I started to keep a diary, but dear wife my thoughts during whatever happened, were of you, so instead of calling it a diary Winne, I called it 'Thoughts', and shall keep it sweetheart for you, until I come home, so that you will know, although I couldn't write, it was, and is, ever of you dear wife I'm thinking. Have been working on the Aerodrome today, digging dug-outs. I find it so hard, my hands not being hard enough for that kind of thing, but they soon will be, it breaks my heart, when I think how I've practised and worked to get my fingers right for my instrument, and now they are ruined, all my ability is going and I shall be such a dud by the time this war is over.

Cruft was deeply distressed at his loss of freedom and at the humiliating conditions in which he was held, as is clear from the following entries

Studies of Prisoners of War
Left and bottom (British):
Two photographs from a
series entitled 'Tommy
POWs' faces' (Q 23840,
Q 23838)
Below (German): Soldier
aged sixteen captured near
Potijze, Ypres Salient,
September 1916 (Q 2862)

Above: Drawing of
Ruhleben Internment
Camp, Berlin, 1914–15:
from the papers of the
British internee, Arthur
Claypole

from the last pages of his book, written as he and his fellow-POWs were being moved from France to a camp in Germany:

Sunday 2 June: [At Cambrai] Breakfast 7.30 am. What a fine town; many French civilians here, the sight of women and children brings one back to earth and reminds one that the world does not only consist of men, thirsting for each other's blood.

Thursday 6 June: Oh! for a cigarette, or something solid to eat, something to read or write a letter to you, but no, nothing now but distracted thoughts, prowling round the cage, just waiting for meal times. Filthy from lying on the dirty yard, overrun with lice, grimy through want of soap, unshaven and, I feel now, one of God's lowest of creatures. May God bring Peace to the world soon.

Happily, Cruft and his hands survived the war and he was able to resume what was to become a highly successful musical career; not only was he recognized as an outstanding double-bass player, he was also awarded the MVO and the OBE for his work in organising the orchestra for the 1937 and 1953 coronations. He died in 1976.

Sub-Lieutenant Thomas Mitchell-Fox RNVR saw service at Gallipoli and in France, where he was captured. He was a POW in Germany at a time when the Allied blockade was at its most effective – most of the time at a camp in the Citadel of the Rhineland city of Mainz. His impressions are from a recorded interview:

The quality of the food was extremely poor and very meagre inasmuch as the Germans, at that period of the war, had very little of their own. The good food of course went up the line to the soldiers and what we had, particularly in the towns where I was prisoner, was minimal. It was about one meal a day, which consisted of a piece of black bread about half the size of the palm of your hand, which was the whole day's ration of bread; the main course would be a plate of sauerkraut or another day it might be a sort of liquid cheese. And there was a cup of so called coffee. Malnutrition and so on meant a considerable loss of body weight in the majority – in all I should say – of the prisoners. To give an indication of how weak one became; there was a flight of stairs – not very steep stairs – up to my particular bedroom and after a while I could negotiate the first two steps standing upright. The remainder of the steps I had to do on my hands and knees.

After a period of time the Germans decided everybody must be vaccinated. Now in the majority of cases these officers and men were in a very weak state, physically, they were very low in the matter of nutrition. And the result was that among those who were vaccinated there was a tremendous sickness and a number of deaths which some people attributed to the vaccine itself.

There was one particular fellow – Captain Gribble. He was a man about six foot four – an awfully nice man – and he'd gone straight from Eton into the services and become a captain. The morning he was vaccinated news came through that he had been awarded the Victoria Cross. We had a celebration that evening and of course the only way we could celebrate was with some Rhine wines – some hock. That was the sort of thing we could get at the canteen and it cost a lot of money. However, we had a little party and congratulated him. The following day he was dead – after his vaccination.

Sergeant Thomas Painting, 1st Battalion, King's Royal Rifle Corps, was a regular infantryman who took part in the retreat from Mons and the First Battle of Ypres and then was captured during a minor action in the early days of trench warfare. It was the last thing he expected, as he recalled in a recorded interview:

I thought I might be killed or wounded. But I never thought of being taken prisoner. And it broke my heart. I thought I was a better man than Gerry, man for man. But there it is. It broke my heart.

Painting didn't take kindly to his new situation. He got into trouble with the authorities, and even had a spell of solitary confinement. His thoughts were always of escape. After a failed attempt to cut his way through the barbed wire surrounding the camp with a file, a better idea was proposed – that he and the other would-be escapers should mingle with the men who went out regularly to work in the guards' cookhouse, which they did so frequently the guards took little notice. On the appointed day, wearing khaki over civilian clothes, he and another man succeeded in reaching the cookhouse carrying a sack of potatoes. A general rendezvous had been selected – a little fir copse about 400 yards from camp – and the way each man was to go had been carefully worked out:

From the cookhouse I had to nip into an outbuilding. And the route I took went past the German latrines across a flat field about two hundred yards long and into a little stream or ditch. Well, I crawled there like a serpent flat as a pancake all the way into this water and then made my way to the rendezvous and found the others there.

We then set off across country. After we'd gone some miles we discarded our khaki uniforms. It was very frosty, ice on the water, ice on the ground we were walking on. But it wasn't thick enough to carry you. Every time you put your foot in the ice cracked. You wet yourself through.

When we'd gone about seven miles we went up a ridge, a little bit of high ground and turned round and had a look at the camp, to see it all illuminated. The other side of the ridge there was a river. We had to wade through the river up to our neck. Well, we carried on then following the North Star, just keeping the North Star a tiny bit right-handed. We kept going till dawn came. Then we lay in a wood all day.

We lived off my little bit of concentrated food, Horlicks and that. And the Oxo made us a little dry so we sucked ice so that you got something in your throat.

Their destination was the Danish frontier. They reached it at night and walked slap into a German sentry:

He said '*Gute nacht*' to us. And we said '*Gute nacht*' in our best guttural German. Well, he went on. That gave us a warning, they'll have other sentries about here somewhere. So we lay in a ditch. We could see the sentries walking about in the moonlight. One sentry, when he got to the end of his beat, stopped and had a chat with the other fellow. That made a gap of about two hundred metres. So we said, 'That's the place for us'. And when he did the next journey, up through there we went, through the wire. It was only a thin belt of barbed wire like you might see in a field, nothing really.

We lay in the long grass until the sentry went back to his chum. And then we got up and went. After we'd been going some distance we came to a main road. And there was a road sign there and it wasn't in German. And then we examined the telegraph poles along the road. And the notices on them were not in German. So we said 'Well, we're not in Germany now, we're in Denmark'.

Painting and his comrades were well treated in Denmark and were able to return home. He eventually rejoined his battalion. Before that – having arrived in Britain in civilian clothes – he had the curious experience of being presented with a white feather.

An Alien in Britain

Richard Noschke was a German who had lived in Britain for twenty-five years when the war began. He had married an English wife and was a respected member of the London company for which he had worked exclusively since his arrival. Following the sinking of the *Lusitania* there was a huge upsurge of anti-German feeling and in July 1915 Noschke was sent to a civilian internment camp at Stratford, East London, where he was appalled at the bad treatment meted out to all so-called 'aliens' and the level of animosity directed against them. Conditions improved to some extent for him when he became camp gardener, except that working outside the barbed wire had one major disadvantage – as he explained in the memoir which he wrote (in English) after being repatriated to Germany in 1918:

'The railway was running alongside the piece of garden with constant trains passing by, filled with soldiers who on every occasion used the most fearful language, drawing their swords [ie bayonets] and threatening us in the most frightful manner, and if they could have got out of their train, I am sure they would have murdered every one of us, even so-called Gentlemen in their first class compartments shook their fists at us when the trains passed by.'

Being inside the compound, however, did not mean that the inmates were safe from abuse:

'Carmen sitting high on their seats could see quite clearly inside the yard, but on nearly every occasion they spat at us and used every swearing language which was horrifying. All this constant insult from the trains and from the public could not escape the notice of the commanding officer and his staff, but no notice was taken to put a stop to it, they rather seemed to enjoy it.'

Noschke found the attitude of his former colleagues and of his British relatives even more mystifying than that of his guards:

'I had made many friends, as I had spent the best part of my life over there, but I am sorry to say that nearly all, with very few exceptions, have turned against me, even my own direct family relations never sent me as much as a postcard all the time I was interned. Also my employer for whom I had worked for over twenty years and we were on the best of friendship, he made me many promises before I was interned, but never kept one of them.'

At Christmas 1917 Noschke wrote a 'piece of poetry' to his erstwhile employer on the theme of his continuing grief and amazement at what was happening to him, of which the following are key stanzas:

I wish you all a happy Christmas
As happy as can be
I hope the time will not be long
Before I shall be free

What crime have I committed
That I deserve this fate?
This is what makes me bitter
But never shall I hate

But bitter memories I shall carry
Until my life departs from me
As the people whom I loved once
Treated me so shabbily.

O What a Jolly Old War:
Service Newspapers

Doubtless the Roman Legions cracked jokes as they marched, and certainly the fighting men of 1914-18 had their ways of lightening the grimness of war. Permanent proof of their genius for 'making the best of it' is to be found in service newspapers and magazines, the product of a rich sub-culture of wry humour and forthright comment which developed its own codes and distinctive style with increasing sophistication as the years went by. *The Wipers Times* is perhaps the most famous of these publications, but virtually every theatre of war produced its examples. *Dug-Out Gossip* appeared in the Dardanelles from the Royal Naval Division, which when sent to fight on land in Flanders incorporated that title with its new improved version, which they aptly named *The Mudhook*. *Barrak* (from the throaty expression 'BRRRRK' used to make camels kneel) came from the Imperial Camel Corps in the Middle East; it was revived by enthusiastic survivors fifty years later, only ceasing publication in 1989. *The Moonraker* was devised by a Wiltshire battalion in Macedonia, which also had for wider consumption a daily army journal *The Balkan News*. *Te Awapo* ('The Dark Stream') was the official organ of a New Zealand troopship; *Aussie* was (to quote its sub-title) 'The Australian Soldiers' Magazine'; *Action Front* was produced by a Canadian Artillery Battery; *Clickety Click* was a late arrival on the scene from the RAF. Standards of production varied widely. *Clickety Click* was typed, while the anti-aircraft magazine *The Bird* was hand-drawn; by contrast *The Mudhook* or *The Dump*, the latter published annually by the 23rd Division in France, were superbly printed to a high professional standard.*

Soldierly humour is by tradition oral, colourful, not for the squeamish; the essential point about what appeared in these magazines is that, being printed, it had to be printable. Although they were chiefly targeted at a small precise readership, they might, and sometimes did, end up being read beside home fires. For some indeed the distant reader was virtually as important as the near-at-hand-one. The New Zealand troopship magazine, *Te Awapo*, wrote, somewhat decorously, of its first number:

If in its perusal it brings a smile to the face of the reader, and particularly if it brings a ray of sunshine into the hearts of those who wait for news so many miles away in our Homeland, then we shall know its first purpose is achieved.

The devisers of *Barrak* also expected that their magazine would be seen by family and friends, but expressed themselves with rather more gusto – and with a justifiable pride that their effort was being written and edited in the field on territory won from the enemy, even though the actual printing was almost certainly done in Cairo:

*Some service magazines were actually printed in London.

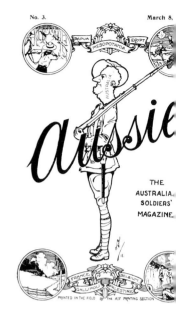

> Shelterless under a Turkish sun
>   We yet contrive to obtain some fun –
> Witness the doughty deed we've done,
>   This Magazine, what ho!
> Produced on a foeman's conquered soil,
>   See the result of our sweatsome toil,
> Though the pen may melt and the ink may boil,
>   Are we downhearted? No!

For a bluff, straightforward statement as to the scope and purpose of most service magazines, there could be no better or pithier one than that to be found in the first 'editorial' of *The Moonraker*, brought out by the 7th Battalion of the Wiltshire Regiment in March 1917, as already stated, in Macedonia. This makes clear that the basic intended audience, was, as one would expect, the servicemen themselves:

Everything and (we suppose) everybody has some difficulty in managing to get born. A Battalion Magazine is no exception, least of all a magazine written in Macedonian trenches and published on a Balkan Hill. There is the difficulty of the Coy Contributor, the difficulty of having to Meet the Censor's Eye, to say nothing of the Difficulty of Getting the Thing Produced.

We make no pretensions. If you want literary excellence, go to your *Spectator*, your *News of the World*, your *Comic Cuts*. We are written for Soldiers by Soldiers; that is to say by people who haven't much time to write for people who haven't much time to read.... If we have beguiled an hour for anyone between work and sleep, we have done our job. If you think us worth keeping as a relic of the war, that will be better still.

Covers of typical service magazines and (far right) cartoon from *The Dump* Christmas 1918

In a sense these are school magazines with the extra edge given by three special circumstances; the 'schools' were far removed from any way of life that could be called normal, nobody knew when term would end, and the games played on their playing fields were lethal ones. It is therefore not surprising that those who belonged to these curious private societies could feel very much aware of the contrast of commitment and sacrifice as between themselves and the world of the distant, uninvolved civilian. If there is any animus in their publications it is against him. The following 'advertisement' from *The Mudhook*, emanating from the vicinity of Ypres in November 1917, expresses a widely held attitude:

Holiday Exchange – Resident in pretty trench, south-east aspect with good views of Boche front line. Would exchange for holiday season with any armchair critic or over-age fight-to-the-finish hero with comfortable home in England.

The same magazine was also less than amused by the posturings of journalists such as the outrageous Horatio Bottomley, editor of the popular weekly *John Bull*. When Bottomley made a swift dash to the front and subsequently described in graphic hair-raising terms his visit to the 'Jaws of Hell', *The Mudhook* commented derisively:

Your articles were edifying to us: what can they have been to their civilian readers? During the recent heavy fighting, we chanced upon Major X (we dare not breathe his name) crouched in a shell-hole, shaking with fright, his shrapnel helmet rising and falling with his emotion – It was not the Hun Barrage, Horatio, nor yet the devilish chattering of their Machine Guns, – No, he was but reading the account of your thrilling adventures and beginning to realise the sickly horrors of war.

Civilian incomprehension of the realities of war also produced such typical minor items as the following. From *Behind the Lines*, sub-titled as 'The (Unofficial) Magazine of No 10 Stationary Hospital, B.E.F.':

A dear old lady met a wounded warrior who had been mixed up in a shell explosion. 'Did it burst?' she said. 'No, mum,' he answered. 'it just crept up quietly behind and bit me.'

From *The Mudhook* again, under the title 'Striking Impressions':

'And what struck you most about the Ypres battle?' asked the dear old lady at the hospital bedside.
'Shrapnel, lady,' was the enthusiastic reply.

The word 'striking' also appeared in a different context in *The Dump*, admittedly in its Christmas 1918 number, when the war was over, but it reflected a view long held at the front. The civilian tendency in some industries to down tools even though the nation was at war enraged uniformed men who had no such option and who were putting their lives at risk in fighting for their country's cause. Hence the cartoon below: 'A STRIKING CONTRAST'.

A STRIKING CONTRAST.

'The RND Tank of the Future': *The Mudhook*'s vision of the appropriate future weapon of the Royal Naval Division after four years of fighting on land. From the edition of October 1918

But there was much honest-to-goodness cheerful humour in these magazines – indeed the urge 'to obtain some fun', as the laureate of *Barrak* put it, was the most powerful motive of all. A particularly popular form was the limerick. The Christmas 1917 edition of *The Mudhook* offered the following gem:

> Said a man to his wife down in Sydenham
> 'My best trousers – where have you hydenham?
>   It's perfectly true
>   They weren't very new
> But I foolishly left half a quydenham.

Unusually, this limerick had no military reference. More typical are the following, from *The Dump*:

> I once asked a Choleric Colonel
> To write something short for this jolonel
>   But I'm sorry to tell
>   He replied 'Go to ----' well,
> He consigned me to regions infolonel.

> There once was a man in a trench
> Whose dug-out was 'bon' (which is French),
>   Till a Minnie one day
>   Blew the whole thing away
> But all that he said was 'Don't mensh.'

A 'minnie' was a *Minenwerfer*, a mine (i.e. bomb) thrower, a particularly unpleasant German weapon.

One of the joys of the limerick is to find rhymes for some exotic place-name; the more ludicrous the rhyme, the greater the fun. In its Christmas 1916 edition *The Dump* had several of these, the first of course being dependent on a pronunciation of the town in question *à la Française*, not as in the famous song.

> There was a young man at Armentières
> Who went to his work with a jaunty air.
>   'For', he said, 'it is clear
>   That the atmosphere here
> Is healthier than the Laventie air.

There was an old dame at La Bassée
Who was quite undeniably passée
 When they said 'Mad'moiselle
 'Vous êtes encore très belle,'
She replied 'Je suis très embarrassée.'

There was a young Boche at Bazentin
Who liked the first trench that he went in
 But a 15-inch 'dud'
 Sent him flat in the mud.
And he found that his helmet was bent in.

The Moonraker, defeated by the challenge of certain Grecian names, nevertheless turned its bafflement to advantage. The following appeared in its Christmas 1916 number under the heading 'Competition Corner':

There was a young fellow of Samothrace
Who put half a crown on a Mammoth Race
 At the end of the day
 He found with dismay
(Finish it Steve and the money's yours.)

There is little 'naughty' humour in these magazines; when it was attempted the limerick was a favourite vehicle. These are again from *The Moonraker*:

I know a blithe blossom in Blighty
Whom you (I'm afraid) would call flighty
 For when Zepps are about
 She always trips out
In a little black crêpe de chine nighty.

A damsel who dwelt on La Tortue
Said 'George dear, do you think we ortue?'
 George replied, 'My dear girl
 My head's in a whirl
Ought or oughtn't be hanged, pull the dortue.

Sixth-form humour of a slightly different kind can be detected, surely, in the news item in *The Balkan News* (not entirely incredible in an area where digging trenches often brought up archaeological remains) to the effect that a large vessel had recently been unearthed bearing the legend:

ITIS APIS POTANDA BIGONE*

Inevitably, service magazines were also a natural outlet for quips or jokes about the army; this was an opportunity for the safe, though sometimes sharp, expression of soldierly cynicism. *The Moonraker*, for example, printed this barbed one-liner:

Strategist: a person who doesn't care how many lives he risks as long as he doesn't risk his own.

Aiming at an easier target, *The Mudhook* had this item, along with a number of other 'Jottings by the Way':

The driver who has been punished for giving his bread ration to his horse certainly deserved it. *Mudhook* will always discourage cruelty to animals.

*Quoted in the memoir of an officer who served at Salonika, Captain Ifor Powell of the Leinster Regiment.

The Canadian *Action Front* printed the following, the butt here being that ubiquitous Aunt Sally, the senior NCO:

Sergeant-Major: 'Anybody here know anything about drawing?'
Dave (with a vision of a soft job): 'Yes; I was a fashion artist before I enlisted.'
Sergeant-Major: 'Well-a-hum double down and draw a bucket of coal from the orderly officer.'

Parody was a favourite device, the Field Service Card being particularly vulnerable to attack (see opposite). A more elitist parody appeared in the *Fifth Glo'ster Magazine* of February 1917, entitled 'After W.B. Y--TS':

> I will arise and go now and go to Picardy
>   And a new trench line hold there, of clay and shell holes made
> No dug-outs shall I have there, nor a hive for the Lewis G.
>   But live on top in the b. loud glade.
>
> And I may cease to be there, for peace comes dropping slow
>   Dropping from the mouth of the Minnie to where the sentry sings,
> There noon is high explosive, and night a gun-fire glow
>   And evening full of torpedoes' wings ...

All these magazines, however, had their serious side; there was after all a war in progress. Honours and Awards were often listed. The *Fifth Glo'ster Magazine* printed Rolls of Honour, with photographs of those who had fallen. *The Moonraker* published this ode to 'The Glorious Dead' after an action in which lives had been lost in April 1917:

> Bravest of the Brave
> Britannia in her final hour of triumph
> Proud, Victorious and Defiant,
> Mourns you, her soldier sons at rest.

Most movingly of all, perhaps, *Aussie* included this poem in an edition of March 1918, entitled 'The Last Barrage':

> When the last barrage has lifted,
> And the dawn of Right breaks thro'
> And back we trail to the Bushland
> We will drink, dear friends, to you
>
> We will drink a toast to our comrades
> Who fought with us side by side,
> And fell as the barrage lifted
> And the dust of battle died.

Always present was the hope, the longing indeed, that it would soon all be over and that everybody could go home. At Christmas 1917 *The Moonraker* stated:

> To all our readers we wish a cheery Christmas and a Happy New Year – and many of them. But not, oh not, in Macedonia.

A month later, in January 1918, *The Mudhook*, on the front which had just witnessed the long struggle of the Passchendaele battle and the false dawn of Cambrai, attempted to comfort its readers with the following:

> It's a long road that has no turning
> It's never 'too late' to mend:
> The darkest hour is before the dawn
> And *even this* war must end.

The British Field Service
Postcard (below) with
humorous variations from
The Dump, Christmas
1916 (right) and *The
Mudhook*, October 1918
(below right)

NOTHING is to be written on this side except the date and signature of the sender. Sentences not required may be erased. If anything else is added the post card will be destroyed.

[Postage must be prepaid on any letter or post card addressed to the sender of this card.]

I am quite well.

I have been admitted into hospital
{ *sick* } *and am going on well.*
{ *wounded* } *and hope to be discharged soon.*

I am being sent down to the base.

I have received your { *letter dated* _____
{ *telegram „* _____
{ *parcel „* _____

Letter follows at first opportunity.

I have received no letter from you
{ *lately*
{ *for a long time.*

Signature }
only }

Date _____

Wt. W65—P.P.948. 8000m. 5-18. C. & Co., Grange Mills, S.W.

Xmas, 1916.   THE

A LONG-FELT WANT.

We have often felt that the Field Service Post Card, excellent though it be, does not offer sufficient scope for the expression of the different circumstances in which the British Soldier may find himself. We therefore beg to offer the following suggestions to those whose business it is :—

I am in { the trenches.
{ the pink.
{ hospital.
{ the soup.
{ the guard room.

We have not been paid for { a week.
{ a fortnight.
{ a month.

I hope to get leave { this year.
{ next year.
{ sometime.
{ never.

We are living on { bully and biscuits.
{ biscuits and bully.
{ bully.
{ biscuits.

Gott strafe the War.

From your loving { son.
{ husband.
{ sweetheart.
{ brother.
{ father.
{ grandfather.
{ great-grandfather.

Signature only

For The People At Home.

Owing to the popularity of the Field Service Post-card, the "Mudhook" offers the suggestion of a similar card for use of the people at home.

Service Post Card.

Cross out the words not required and add nothing but a halfpenny stamp.

I am well.

I am suffering from... ... ...

I have received your { Field card
{ O.A.S.
{ Request for money.

I have (need) a new hat (or and) costume.

The chickens and rabbits are ... ...

The children are   (1) ... ...
                    (2) ... ...
                    (3) ... ...
                    (4) ... ...

(For families of more than four, a second card should be used.)

With love from.

Signature)
only.)

TO LET.

PALATIAL PILL BOX.

Every Inconvenience. Water, Gas and Telephone laid on.

Fine Uninterrupted View of Surrounding Country.

Lighting Arrangements supplied by the well-known Flare Experts, FRITZ AND Co.

Splendid Shooting to be had on the Estate throughout the year.

Previous owner was reluctantly forced to give up this fine Estate after a lengthy residence. In fact, great difficulty was experienced in forcing the late tenants to vacate this valuable site, by whom it was elaborately fitted up at great expense.

AUSTRALIAN BEER FOR SALE

The AUSSIE BREWERY COMPANY is pleased to be able to announce to all members of the A.I.F. in France that the

Best Brands of Australian Beer

may be obtained at all Hotels in N.S.W., Victoria, Queensland, S.A., W.A. and Tasmania.

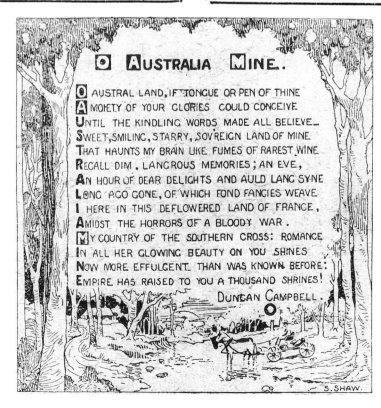

O AUSTRALIA MINE.

O AUSTRAL LAND, IF TONGUE OR PEN OF THINE
A MOIETY OF YOUR GLORIES COULD CONCEIVE
UNTIL THE KINDLING WORDS MADE ALL BELIEVE—
SWEET, SMILING, STARRY, SOVREIGN LAND OF MINE.
THAT HAUNTS MY BRAIN LIKE FUMES OF RAREST WINE.
RECALL DIM, LANGROUS MEMORIES; AN EVE,
AN HOUR OF DEAR DELIGHTS AND AULD LANG SYNE
LONG AGO GONE, OF WHICH FOND FANCIES WEAVE
I HERE IN THIS DEFLOWERED LAND OF FRANCE,
AMIDST THE HORRORS OF A BLOODY WAR.
MY COUNTRY OF THE SOUTHERN CROSS: ROMANCE
IN ALL HER GLOWING BEAUTY ON YOU SHINES
NOW MORE EFFULGENT THAN WAS KNOWN BEFORE:
EMPIRE HAS RAISED TO YOU A THOUSAND SHRINES!

DUNCAN CAMPBELL.

S. SHAW.

From *Aussie*:
Above: Australian wit: back-page advertisements, March 1918
Below: Australian nostalgia, October 1918
Opposite: *The Dump* reflects on four years of war. From its final edition, Christmas 1918

THINGS I HAVE NEVER SEEN AT THE FRONT.

A Kirchener Girl tripping through Ypres.

A Transport Officer and a Quartermaster taking unnecessary exercise before breakfast.

An Army Commander lunching off bully beef and biscuits.

An Officer of G.H.Q. choosing and matching ribands.

Volunteers for a working party.

Specially drawn for THE DUMP by H. L. Oakley.

The End at Last

As the months and then the years went by, the realization that the war would be a long hard struggle gave way to the fear that it might go on indefinitely. Optimism had been high at the beginning and, under the impact of an ever-buoyant press, had lingered in the civilian world longer than in the military one. But as the names of new battles and new campaigns filled the headlines, to the accompaniment of ever-growing lists of dead and wounded, optimism itself became a casualty. In May 1917 a student nurse in London, Joan Hardy, wrote to Captain Oscar Greig in his German prisoner of war camp:

> Dear Oscar
>
> I hope you are getting on all right. I somehow feel you will never get this letter and I don't expect you got the other one I sent but I will write it any way as I expect any letters are welcome to you and in that case if it's only one chance in a hundred that you will get it it's worth writing.
>
> We are trying not to get down-hearted. It seems as if the war will *never* end, though. One of the soldiers at the hospital says it is good for another two years but of course he doesn't know.

There were yet darker days to come. In November that year Russia, following the Bolshevik Revolution, left the war, releasing vast numbers of German troops to fight in the west at a time when the British were recovering from the blood-letting of Passchendaele and the dashed hopes of Cambrai and the French from mutinies in the wake of the failed offensive under Nivelle earlier in the year. Desmond Allhusen, who had served in Salonika and was now with the 8th Kings Royal Rifle Corps in the front line near Ypres, wrote of this time in a post-war memoir:

The whole outlook had become unutterably black. All the battles of the spring and summer seemed to have been in vain. Arras and Messines had been so bright with promise, and even this awful show [Passchendaele] had raised our wildest hopes. But it had all ended in this, with fresh German troops streaming across from their long holiday on the Eastern Front, to face our worn out divisions and start it all over again.

The future seemed to be an endless vista of battles, each one worse than the last. We still felt that one day we would win, but had stopped saying so. The war was the only real and permanent thing, thriving and increasing in a world that was going to ruin. All our discussions ended by complete agreement on one point: that whatever might be the end for the nations, our destinies were clear enough. We would all be hit, and if we recovered we would return and be hit again, and so on till we were either dead or permanently disabled. The ideal was to lose a leg as soon as possible.

Perhaps we were unduly pessimistic, as two or three out of the twenty-five officers did survive uninjured to the end of the war. At that time it seemed impossible to believe that anybody could survive long. It seemed to be courting disaster to entertain any hope of anything. The morale of the army had settled onto a rock-bottom of fatalistic despair, in which the majority carried on mechanically, waiting for their next wound, while the weaker members went under, either to lunacy, desertion, or self-inflicted wounds.

Allhusen was not one of those to emerge unscathed; he was badly wounded soon afterwards and was to remain partly disabled.

Allhusen had been educated at Eton; not far away from Allhusen at this time was his fellow-Old Etonian, Lieutenant Thomas Hughes, RFC, who was to lose his life a few weeks later in February 1918 (see page 134). The arrival of 1918 produced a bitter attack on the conduct of the war in Hughes's diary. For him any idealism had long since vanished and the conflict had resolved itself into the mindless determination of one imperialism to extinguish another:

Tues 1 Jan 1918. The fifth year of the Great War has begun. What a moment for improving reflections. Let us look back on the achievements of the past three and a half years which have justified the slight sacrifice which we have all so gladly made. What are these achievements? Well, we have – er – er – we have – er held our own against the – er – numerically and morally inferior hordes of our assailants. We have – er – shown the whole world that Britain is fighting as she has always fought – in India, Ireland, South Africa and elsewhere – to uphold the rights of the smaller nationalities to determine their own destinies and forms of Government, and to redress the wrongs of the weak. We have from time to time set before ourselves many noble aims, modified from time to time by our inability to carry them out or by our realization of their unprofitable nature.

We will never sheath the sword until we have finally crushed Prussian militarism and even then we won't sheath it much, as we intend to starve the German nation, men, women and children, by an economic boycott for ever and ever and ever, as a means of removing the causes of the war and of paving the way to a lasting peace.

Germany will presumably sit contrite and humbled in sackcloth and ashes, joyfully expiating the sins of her rulers; without thought of revenge, without hope of prosperity; just as we should, of course, do if we were so humbled.

The only hope seems to be that someone might realize that we have in a manner of speaking already beaten Prussian militarism – at his own game – by swallowing it whole.

Yet 1918 was to be the year when, at last, on the eleventh day of the eleventh month, the war came to an end – though not until after the shock, for the Allies, of Germany's breakthrough on the Western Front in the spring and, from August, the final forcing-back of the German Army virtually to her frontiers. This would mean more massive casualty lists – in respect of which, of all the five years over which the war extended, 1918 was to win the palm. Britain lost more men in 1918 alone than she did in the whole of the Second World War. Yet this was a year of enormous achievement and, indeed, military brilliance on the Allied side, with the British and Dominion force under Haig proving particularly, and increasingly, effective. It is perhaps unfortunate that the outstanding successes of 1918 have always been overshadowed in the popular memory by the grim years of deadlock which preceded it.

Characteristically, the end of the long period of static fighting could produce wry reactions in those who had lived through it. 'Can it be,' wrote Major P.H. Pilditch in his diary, 'that we are really at last on the eve of that much-talked-of but seldom seen phenomenon, Moving Warfare?' And again: 'This morning we were informed that the Bosch had really begun to withdraw and that we were to send out mounted patrols and begin to advance. I must say, I think this is very inconsiderate of them, after remaining more or less stationary for four years.'

Inevitably, the Army which played so large a part in the final victory was a very different one from that which had fought at Mons or on the Somme. Its core of regulars had almost all disappeared, as had many of the eager volunteers who had responded to Kitchener's summons. For over two years now its recruits had been conscripts, many of whom had been mere lads in 1914. The following account of the last days of the war is from a letter to his mother by a typical Tommy of 1918, James Bird, a sapper in a signals company attached to a Canadian division. As Germany sued for terms and her armies fell back, the advance took him steadily eastwards: Valenciennes, Onnaing (just inside France), Brisieux (just inside Belgium), Boussu, Mons:

My two days at Onnaing I spent watching the constant stream of troops and artillery going forward. I never thought for a minute that we had so many men in the Army. All the bands were playing and everyone seemed happy, as we had just heard the news of the German delegates crossing the line.*

We left Onnaing on the Friday as it was possible to get along the road, as the troops were not so plentiful. The weather improved at this point but not the roads which were *mud* to the knees.

The Huns had made an awful mess of the roads and railways, blowing up all the crossroads with mines, and every joint in the rails of the railway being blown up. We reached Brisieux, which was in the German hands the day previous.

Saturday we left for Boussu where I got a fine billet. The gentleman of the house was head professor of the school and could speak good English. When my wireless mate and I asked if we could have a room, he said, You are most welcome, and showed us upstairs to a lovely room with a double bed. It was a beautiful house, electric light and all modern conveniences.

The Saturday afternoon was very exciting, the band of the Canadians played in the square, and during the afternoon two of our planes did all sorts of tricks and stunts, flying very low, this simply made the inhabitants go mad with delight.

The troops simply poured through the town, infantry and artillery, each unit being greeted with great cheers, especially the 'Jocks'.

That night we had coffee before we went to bed, and more coffee when we got up in the morning.

This was Sunday, and the town band, which had not played for four years, turned out, with every one in their Sunday best to greet them. As usual, great enthusiasm. Another band of the Canadians played in the afternoon. I may say all we did was listen to the bands, as we were really out of action.

We were expecting to go into Mons, but fighting was still going on there, but on the Monday we left Boussu, and our host was so disappointed.

This was the day of the finish of the war. I walked into Mons in the afternoon, we were mobbed and nearly lost all our buttons. It was indeed a great day for Britain, as well as France. It made one feel glad to be alive, and to think that after four years hard fighting we had at last reached the place where our troops were in 1914, and also to think the war finished the same day.

The Armistice came into effect at 11 am on 11 November. The suddenness of the end produced a wide range of reactions; profound thankfulness, mass euphoria (as in the great celebrations in London and

*To meet the delegates of the Allies at Compiègne, where the Armistice was signed.

Paris), grief at the thought of loved ones lost, numbed indifference. The following quotations give some indication of the attitudes of the time:

The reaction of an officer at the front: Lieutenant A.S. Gregory RFA:

B.E.F. November 11th 1918
10.45 a.m.

My dear Mother

A quarter of an hour more War! Cumulative rumours have been crowned by an official intimation. This is my last letter ON ACTIVE SERVICE. Never again, I hope, shall I wear tin hat and box respirator.

We were expecting to go up into action early this morning, but – didn't.

I am 6 miles S. of MONS.

Well that's enough for one letter.

The church bells are ringing now.

TE DEUM LAUDAMUS

Arthur

THE WAR EXPERIENCE

A remarkable scene from the last phase of the war. Massed men of the 137th Brigade, 46th Division, being congratulated by their divisional commander at Riqueval Bridge on the St Quentin Canal, part of the German Hindenburg Line, broken on 19 September 1918 (Q 9535)

DEAR TOMMY,

    THANKS FOR THE LOAN OF THIS
GROUND, IT SERVED ITS PURPOSE.
NOW YOU ARE WELCOME TO HAVE IT
BACK.

                              FRITZ

The reaction of a soldier in hospital in England: Rifleman Harold Clegg, King's Liverpool Regiment:

Above: Notice left in a dug-out near Bailleul, France, October 1918 (HU 59492)
Below: Unidentified official British cameraman filming 'the last shot before the Armistice, Western Front, 11am, 11 November 1918' (Q 3353)

We were all sitting at our mid-day meal on November 11th, when the Matron entered with a telegram in her hand; in our isolation we had not seen the newspapers for some days. It was a complete surprise to us to hear that the armistice had been signed. Somehow the news did not convey very much to us; the fact that the war had ended was news that had come too late; it mattered little to most of those seated in the dining hall at Elswick whether the war finished or whether it continued for years. We had nothing to gain by its coming to an end; we were out of it for ever. Had the news come two years earlier it might have been of interest to us.

However, there were present those who are always ready to celebrate anything, no matter what it is, so we broke all bounds in the afternoon and visited the local hostelry in the neighbouring village of Great Eccleston. The host opened his back door despite strict regulations and in the bar parlour we found the local policeman.

On Armistice night, we had a Whist Drive.

A civilian comment in a letter to a soldier: F.W. Graham writing from Newton Abbot, Devon, to Lieutenant A.G. Steavenson:

18 November 1918

The celebration of signing the armistice was duly observed here. Those who had flags, no matter what nationality, hung them out most of them upside down; and those who had none put their coloured petticoats and combinations out to air: so it made a motley scene. The excitement was at its height when some boys came out with an air gun and a New Zealander fired off his revolver. (The N.Z. discharge depot is at Torquay and we are inundated with them especially on market days when they carry off all our butter, eggs and fowls.) We have now settled down again but the influenza or plague is very bad here, and the weather is mild and dull, we hope for frosts but they don't come.

A comment by the father of a conscientious objector to his imprisoned son, Percy Wall:

Abergavenny 18 November 1918

There was not any great excitement in any place where I go on account of the war finishing. They got bands out and organized marches but the people generally while they seem glad that the end is arriving don't have the heart to demonstrate much.

The Chaplain of the 2nd Worcesters, Reverend Victor Tanner, was in hospital in France recovering from Spanish 'flu. A walk after lunch allowed him to witness some French and German reactions:

On the way we passed a group of Boche prisoners. 'Boche finis' they said as we passed and they seemed more pleased than otherwise. When we got to the bottom of the hill we passed the village school. On seeing us and some Tommies behind they broke loose, climbed the school railings and waved to us shouting 'Guerre feeneesh! guerre feeneesh!' We then continued our walk in the direction of the village church, and as we approached the main door three old Frenchmen came running breathlessly up the path to ring the bells. On seeing us they waved their arms and gesticulating wildly shouted 'Guerre fini. Très bon, très bon!' Then, unlocking the door they got hold of the bell ropes and pulled for all they were worth, entirely regardless of rhythm. It was wonderful to see such an unrestrained and spontaneous expression of joy.

Last Act at Sea

On 21 November 1918 the German High Seas Fleet met its British counterpart at the entrance to the Firth of Forth. They had not come to fight, however, but to surrender, in accordance with the terms of the Armistice agreed ten days earlier. Two hundred and forty British ships, under the command of Admiral Sir David Beatty, escorted them in.

Later the same day in a letter to his mother Sub-Lieutenant Hyde C. Burton RN, whose ship was the Grand Fleet battleship HMS *Neptune*, of the 4th Battle Squadron, described the day's events and his own mixed reactions:

At 9.30 the enemy battle fleet was reported in sight at a range of about 7,000 yards and in about ten minutes time I went up on deck to have a look. I couldn't see very much owing to the haze but on our port beam was a long line of ships almost hidden in the mist with the sun just catching their sides. In the meantime our fleet had deployed into two lines of battle each line steaming on either side of the German ships. All our ships had their ensigns at the masthead (only flown in that position in sight of the enemy), guns trained fore and aft ready for training on to the enemy if necessary. When our leading ship reached the last ship of the German line she turned sixteen points i.e. a half circle and returned on the same course as and parallel to the Germans with other ships following in her wake. It was now easy to distinguish the German ships, *Bayern, Moltke, Koenig* and four Kaisers led by the battle cruisers *Hindenburg, Derfflinger, Seydlitz, Von der Tann*. Mighty ships they were as they steamed between our lines, but with the

exception of the Admiral's flag not a single flag adorned their halliards.

The humiliation caused by handing over such a magnificent lot of ships must have been appalling. I cannot understand how they could possibly have surrendered so ignominiously without making some sort of show. Somehow I think we were all too sorry for their utter defeat to be cheerful and I know that I would have given anything if even at the last minute before they met us they had shown fight. I don't mean that I wanted them to suddenly turn on us but if they had only sent a wireless signal saying that they were going to fight to the last ship. I suppose this sounds very bloodthirsty but the disappointment of being done out of our scrap is awfully keen. I can't imagine for a moment if we were in their position of handing over ten of our finest ships to the enemy. I don't believe there is anyone who wouldn't fight till he went down or else blow up the ships rather than hand them over wholesale. I can't express just what I mean but to see this great fleet silently follow ours into harbour with never a sound or signal was really very sad. This doesn't sound a very thankful letter for such a great victory, though of course everyone realizes that thousands of lives have been saved by their surrender, but we are needless to say glad beyond words that the slaughter and bloodshed are all over.

Ernest Fox was a Chief Steward in HMS *Ramillies*, but because she was in dry dock he was allowed to go out in another ship and so, as he put it in a recorded interview, 'saw the whole thing from the bridge of the *Royal Oak*'. If he had been in his own ship he would have seen nothing because he

would have been down below at his action station. His sentiments coincided with those of Sub-Lieutenant Burton:

To see such magnificent ships surrender to another fleet was pitiful really. You know, I could have cried, honestly I could, to see those ships surrender. And it crossed your mind: what would have happened had Britain been in the same position. Would we have surrendered? I don't think so. It was not that I felt sympathy for the Germans but I felt the depression of such magnificent ships being surrendered. It wasn't for the human side of it – it was more a professional attitude I suppose you could say.

Three days later, on board his former flagship HMS *Lion*, Admiral Beatty spoke to the officers and men of the 1st Battle Cruiser Squadron, as they prepared to escort the German warships to Scapa Flow, the Grand Fleet's base for much of the war – much admired for its natural beauty but disliked by many sailors for its often bleak and inhospitable climate. Beatty, too, had found something 'pitiable' about the surrender, but his general attitude was one of bluff contempt, as is clear from the following extract:*

I have always said in the past that the High Seas Fleet would have to come out and meet the Grand Fleet. I was not a false prophet; they are out (laughter), and they are now in. (Loud laughter) They are in our pockets, and the 1st Battle Cruiser Squadron is going to look after them.

*From a copy preserved in the papers of Captain E.R. Jones RN

Above left: The German flagship SMS *Friedrich der Grosse* leading *Koenig Albert* and *Kaiserin*, three battleships of the *Kaiser* class, 21 November 1918 (Q 20615A)
Above: Seamen on board HMS *Barham* await the surrender of the German fleet, 21 November 1918 (Q 19679)

We never expected that the last time we should see them as a great force would be when they were being shepherded, like a flock of sheep, by the Grand Fleet. It was a pitiable sight, in fact I should say it was a horrible sight, to see these great ships that we have been looking forward so long to seeing, expecting them to have the same courage that we expect from men whose work lies upon great waters – we did expect them to do something for the honour of their country – and I think it was a pitiable sight to see them come in, led by a British light cruiser, with their old antagonists, the battle cruisers, gazing at them.

They are now going to be taken away and placed under the guardianship of the Grand Fleet at Scapa, where they will enjoy (laughter), as we have enjoyed, the pleasures of Scapa. (Laughter) But they have nothing to look forward to as we had. That which kept our spirits up kept up our efficiency. They have nothing to look forward to except degradation ...

In fact, they did have one another option, hinted at by Sub-Lieutenant Burton when he wondered why they did not blow up their ships rather than let them fall into enemy hands. The German Fleet would scuttle itself in Scapa Flow on midsummer day 1919.

National commemoration: Germany celebrates a fallen warrior.

Vize-Feldwebel is the German equivalent of Staff-Sergeant. Notably, Hans Werner lost his life on one of the most famous dates of the war, 21 March 1918, the first day of the great German attack known to its instigators as the *Kaiserschlacht* – the 'Kaiser's Battle' – and to the British who fell back before it as the 'March Retreat'. The biblical text, from the First Epistle to John (chapter 3, verse 16), reads in the English Authorized Version, 'We ought to lay down our lives for the brethren'. The parallel text favoured by the British – much quoted on gravestones in Commonwealth war cemeteries – is from St John's Gospel (chapter 15, verse 13); 'Greater love hath no man than this, that a man lay down his life for his friends'.

This scroll pre-dates the end of the war; the signature is that of Kaiser Wilhelm, who abdicated on 9 November 1918.

Commemoration and Remembrance

Personal commemoration: A British family mourns its lost son. Double page card, with message on front and photograph inside.

Corporal Thomas George Victor Fardo, originally 10th King's Liverpool Regiment (Liverpool Scottish), later 6/7th Gordon Highlanders, was killed on 12 October 1918; he is buried at Avesnes-le-Sec Communal Cemetery Extension, near Cambrai, France, where his gravestone bears the message ''Tis as a soldier he will stand before the great white throne'.

Post-war commemoration: Britain honours a fallen warrior.

Known as the 'Next of Kin Memorial Scroll'. The form of words was largely devised by M.R. James, Provost of King's College, Cambridge and noted writer of ghost stories, though the reference to the King was added at the request of the monarch himself. The final sentence was by the historian and novelist Charles P. Keary. The 'print-run' is believed to have been about 970,000; manufacture began in January 1919. Next of kin also received a memorial plaque.

Second Lieutenant William Edgington, 62nd Battery, Royal Field Artillery, was killed in action at Ypres on 8 May 1915. Aged 36, he was the son of Mr and Mrs G. Edgington of Southwark, London. He has no known grave, and is commemorated on the Menin Gate at Ypres, one of 54,896 names inscribed on that famous memorial.

Envoi

In the early days of May 1919 I returned home; the War of Nations was finished; the battle for existence had begun.

I found I belonged to that generation of men who, even if they had escaped its shells, were destroyed by the War. The youths of 18-20 who were thrown back into civilisation whose only training had been that of musketry, bombing, killing and bloodshed; those who regarded carnage with complacency; whose conversation during the most impressionable period of their lives had been War, Women and Food.

While men were being churned up by shell fire until there was nothing left of them but pieces of flesh adhering to the revetting on the trench, Army Contractors and Munition Makers at home had been waxing fat and greeted those returned from the Wars with a gross display of opulence.

During our absence the old order had changed; the genteel of 1914 were gone; blatant riches reigned in their stead; money was the power in the land; money that had been reaped from the bodies of the dead.

This was the Victory. The War to end War.

Harold Clegg, former Rifleman, Liverpool Rifles

Since last I wrote, Norman 'like many other good fellows' has been killed and the war has been won. However, he died thinking that it had been lost. He was hit at four o'clock on the morning of 24 March 1918. They were being pushed back and back. For two days he was splendid and early that morning was sent out to High Wood on some important job. When he was hit he told the men to leave him but they carried him back in a blanket and put him into the hospital train. He died either in the train or at Étaples where he is buried. Five foot ten of a beautiful young Englishman under French soil. Never a joke, never a look, never a word more to add to my store of memories. The book is shut up for ever and as the years pass I shall remember less and less, till he becomes a vague personality; a stereotyped photograph. I was dancing at four o'clock on the morning of the 24th. My partner said to me 'whereabouts is your brother now?' I told him and he said, 'Good God, aren't you anxious?' Now I had been anxious to the verge of frenzy for four years and I believed in the goodness of God; but nevertheless I felt that icy hand on my heart which I shall never now feel again.

From a letter dated 16 April 1919 by Joyce Taylor, formerly Women's Legion, sister of Captain Norman Austin Taylor, 1/21st Battalion, London Regiment, who died of wounds during the German offensive on the Somme in March 1918

IMPERIAL WAR MUSEUM

None of us can forget and this Museum will ever preserve the memory in future ages, that we owe our success under God not to the armed forces alone, but to the labours and sacrifices of soldiers and civilians, of men and women alike. It was a democratic victory, the work of a nation in arms, organised as never before for a great national struggle. We cannot say with what eyes posterity will regard this Museum, nor what ideas it will arouse in their minds. We hope and pray that as the result of what we have done and suffered they may be able to look back upon War, its instruments and its organisation, as belonging to a dead past. But to us it stands, not for a group of trophies won from a beaten enemy, not for a symbol of the pride of victory, but as an embodiment and a lasting memorial of common effort and common sacrifice through which, under the Guidance of Divine Providence, Liberty and Right were preserved for mankind."

George R.I.

Written by E.S. Sutton A.R.C.A. in the Year of Our Lord. MCMXXIV.
Ex. Gunner R.G.A. served in France and Flanders 1915–1918.

**Extract from the speech of King George V, at the
official opening of the Imperial War Museum**

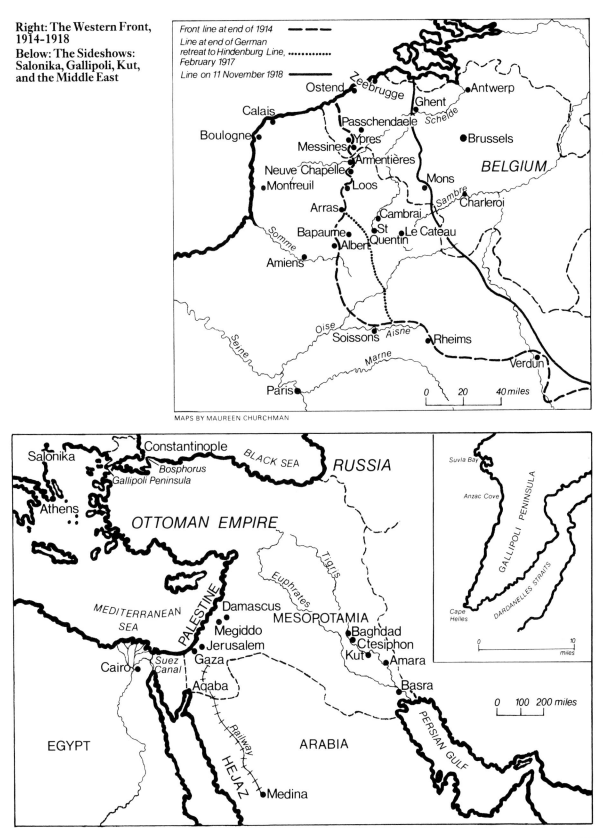

Right: The Western Front, 1914-1918

Below: The Sideshows: Salonika, Gallipoli, Kut, and the Middle East

Front line at end of 1914 – – – –

Line at end of German retreat to Hindenburg Line, ············· February 1917

Line on 11 November 1918 ———

MAPS BY MAUREEN CHURCHMAN

Index of Contributors

This index is intended to serve two purposes: to list those whose writings or reminiscences are here quoted and to give due acknowledgement to the copyright owners who have kindly allowed the publication of material held in the Museum's collections. Their names appear in brackets after those of the contributors with whom they are associated. Every effort has been made to trace such copyright owners; the Museum would be grateful for any information which might help to trace those whose identities or addresses are not known. The letters SR indicate that the quotations used are from tapes collected by the Department of Sound Records. Ranks and units are as they were at the time of the experiences described. Figures in italics refer to illustrations.

General Index

Figures in italics refer to illustrations